Perspectives on a Young Woman's Suicide

Perspectives on a Young Woman's Suicide is a unique and updated analysis of a diary left behind by "Katie," a young woman who took her own life.

By drawing on clinicians, researchers, survivors of suicide loss and those closest to Katie, this book delves into common beliefs about why people die by suicide and into the internal worlds of those who do, as well as ethical and moral questions surrounding those deaths. Several contributors discuss Katie's suicide from the perspective of recent theories of suicide, including Joiner's interpersonal theory and Klonsky's three-step theory. Two contributors who have lost a child to suicide look at Katie's diary from their perspective, one of whom discusses whether it is truly possible to prevent suicide. Finally, Katie's sister reveals her reactions to this project and Katie's ex-boyfriend shares his account of her death.

This book is a vital addition to the library of any researcher, academic or professional interested in suicide and suicide prevention.

John F. Gunn III, is Assistant Professor of psychology at Gwynedd Mercy University, and has examined suicide in a number of contexts, most notably examining theories of suicide across different populations.

David Lester, is Emeritus Professor of psychology at Stockton University, and has published extensively on suicide, murder and other issues in thanatology, with over 50 books in the fields of suicide and thanatology.

Perspectives on a Young Woman's Suicide
A Study of a Diary

Edited by John F. Gunn III
and David Lester

NEW YORK AND LONDON

Cover image: © Getty Images

First published 2022
by Routledge
605 Third Avenue, New York, NY 10158

and by Routledge
2 Park Square, Milton Park, Abingdon, Oxon, OX14 4RN

Routledge is an imprint of the Taylor & Francis Group, an informa business

© 2022 selection and editorial matter, John F. Gunn III and David Lester; individual chapters, the contributors

The right of John F. Gunn III and David Lester to be identified as the authors of the editorial material, and of the authors for their individual chapters, has been asserted in accordance with sections 77 and 78 of the Copyright, Designs and Patents Act 1988.

All rights reserved. No part of this book may be reprinted or reproduced or utilised in any form or by any electronic, mechanical, or other means, now known or hereafter invented, including photocopying and recording, or in any information storage or retrieval system, without permission in writing from the publishers.

Trademark notice: Product or corporate names may be trademarks or registered trademarks, and are used only for identification and explanation without intent to infringe.

Library of Congress Cataloging-in-Publication Data
Names: Gunn, John F., editor. | Lester, David, 1942– editor.
Title: Perspectives on a young woman's suicide : a study of a diary / edited by John F. Gunn III and David Lester.
Description: New York, NY : Routledge, 2022. | Includes bibliographical references.
Identifiers: LCCN 2021032979 (print) | LCCN 2021032980 (ebook) | ISBN 9780367636203 (hardback) | ISBN 9780367636180 (paperback) | ISBN 9781003125655 (ebook)
Subjects: LCSH: Suicide victims—Case studies. | Suicide victims—Diaries. | Suicidal behavior—Case studies. | Suicide—Case studies.
Classification: LCC HV6545 .P469 2022 (print) | LCC HV6545 (ebook) | DDC 362.28—dc23
LC record available at https://lccn.loc.gov/2021032979
LC ebook record available at https://lccn.loc.gov/2021032980

ISBN: 978-0-367-63620-3 (hbk)
ISBN: 978-0-367-63618-0 (pbk)
ISBN: 978-1-003-12565-5 (ebk)

DOI: 10.4324/9781003125655

Typeset in Times New Roman
by Apex CoVantage, LLC

Contents

List of Contributors vii
List of Figures ix
List of Tables x

1 Introduction 1
DAVID LESTER AND JOHN F. GUNN III

2 Who Is Katie? 7
DAVID LESTER

3 Katie's Diary: The First Month 10
KATIE

Commentaries 33

4 The Complexity of Suicide: Exploring Katie's Diary
Through a Bioecological Lens 35
JOHN F. GUNN III

5 Katie From the Perspective of the Interpersonal Theory
of Suicide 43
DAVID LESTER

6 Using the Three-Step Theory to Understand Katie's Desire
for Suicide 51
E. DAVID KLONSKY AND OSCAR F. CETNAROWSKI

7 Understanding Katie's Experiences From the Perspective of the Integrated Motivation Volitional Model of Suicidal Behavior   57
TIAGO C. ZORTEA AND RORY C. O'CONNOR

8 Katie's Implicit Life Plan for the End of Summer: How Implicit Prospection May Influence the Course of Events   73
DMITRI I. SHUSTOV, OLGA D. TUCHINA AND ANASTASIA U. BORODKINA

9 What Is the Meaning, Katie? Katie's Diaries Read Through a Meaning-Making Lens   93
BIRTHE LOA KNIZEK AND HEIDI HJELMELAND

10 A Safe Place for Katie: A Gestalt Therapy Perspective on Her Suicidal Experience   109
KAROLINA KRYSINSKA, JAN ROUBAL AND DAVE MANN

11 Writing to Remain: Two Diaries From Young Women Who Wrote to Survive   124
LINDA COLLINS

12 Why Are We so Bad at Preventing Suicide?   141
DONNA HOLLAND BARNES

Conclusions   151

13 From the Ashes of Suicide: A Life Repurposed   153
KATIE'S SISTER

14 What Happened During Katie's Last Few Days: Mark's Account   161

15 Why Did Katie Die by Suicide?   167
DAVID LESTER AND JOHN F. GUNN III

Name Index   174
Subject Index   179

Contributors

Donna Holland Barnes, Ph.D.

Howard University, Department of Psychiatry & Behavioral Health, Washington DC

Anastasia U. Borodkina

Clinical Psychologist, V.M. Buyanov Moscow City Clinical Hospital, Moscow, Russia

Oscar F. Cetnarowski

University of British Columbia, Canada

Linda Collins, M.A.

writer and poet, New Zealand

Heidi Hjelmeland, Ph.D.

Department of Mental Health, NTNU, Norwegian University of Science and Technology, Trondheim, Norway

E. David Klonsky, Ph.D.

University of British Columbia, Canada

Birthe Loa Knizek, Ph.D.

Department of Mental Health, NTNU, Norwegian University of Science and Technology, Trondheim, Norway

Karolina Krysinska, M.A., Ph.D.

Gestalt psychotherapist, Melbourne School of Population and Global Health, Australia

Dave Mann, MSc

UKCP Registered Gestalt Psychotherapist, Gestalt Psychotherapy Training Institute, Matlock, England, UK

Rory C. O'Connor, PhD

Suicidal Behaviour Research Laboratory, Institute of Health and Wellbeing, University of Glasgow, Scotland

Jan Roubal, M.D, Ph.D.

Masaryk University Brno, Czech Republic

Dmitri I. Shustov, M.D., Ph.D.

Department of Psychiatry, I. P. Pavlov Ryazan State Medical University, Ryazan, Russia

Olga D. Tuchina

Psychologist, Research & Clinical Department, Moscow Research and Practical Centre for Narcology of the Department of Public Health, Moscow, Russia

Tiago C. Zortea, PhD

Suicidal Behaviour Research Laboratory, Institute of Health and Wellbeing, University of Glasgow, Scotland

Figures

4.1	Outline of Bronfenbrenner's bioecological model	36
4.2	Themes from Katie's diary	41
7.1	The integrated motivational-volitional model of suicidal behavior	59
7.2	Volitional moderators that may increase the likelihood of suicidal thoughts being translated into a self-harm (including suicide attempt)	68
8.1	Katie's future-oriented statements, % of all the other statements in Books 1–5	80
8.2	Forms of explicit future thinking in neutral (Type 1) and implicit suicidal (Type 2) future-oriented statements in Books 3 and 5	82

Tables

8.1 Distribution of future-oriented statements by types
     in Katie's diary, N (%)   80
8.2 Katie's future thinking in Books 3 and 5   81

1 Introduction

David Lester and John F. Gunn III

Almost all articles and books on suicide begin with data on how serious a problem suicidal behavior is. Worldwide, the World Health Organization reports close to 800,000 suicides each year and, in addition, it is estimated that about 8 million people make attempts to die by suicide each year but survive the attempt. Each suicide leaves family members and close friends mourning the person, with underestimates in the range of 5 million and more liberal estimates exceeding 10 million people. Though in recent years suicide rates have been declining in many countries, they have been on the rise in other countries such as the United States. For example, the suicide rate in the United States has risen from 10.5 per 100,000 per year in 1999 to 13.9 in 2019 (wonder.cdc.gov). For men during this period, the suicide rate rose from 17.8 to 22.4 (an increase of 25.8%) and for women from 4.0 to 6.0 (an increase of 50%). Clearly, suicidal behavior is a major public health problem that, at least in some countries, has been resistant to prevention efforts.

Research into suicide has continued to appear in scholarly journals. Although scholars have written about suicide for centuries, modern suicidology (as we call our discipline) dates back to a book written by Émile Durkheim in 1897. One of the editors of this book, David, tried to read every scholarly paper on suicide, in all disciplines, from 1897 to 1997 and published his reviews in four editions of *Why People Kill Themselves* (Lester, 1972/1983/1992/2000). He stopped in 1997, not only because 100 years seemed like a good time period, but also because the number of scholarly papers appearing each year was growing so fast that reading them and writing them up interfered with his job (professor of psychology at a university). Consider the number of articles on suicide listed in PsycInfo (a database of scholarly psychology publications) each decade from 1970 to 2020.

1970	118 articles
1980	116 articles
1990	497 articles
2000	579 articles
2010	1,168 articles
2020	1,156 articles

DOI: 10.4324/9781003125655-1

These numbers, already daunting, include only research in psychology and miss many journal articles published in criminal justice, sociology, public health, social work and various other disciplines.

It would seem that we know so much about suicide, and yet neither editor of this book is willing to say we know why people kill themselves. Indeed, Herbert Hendin, a leading authority on suicide and past medical director of the American Foundation for Suicide Prevention, in reviewing one of the volumes of *Why People Kill Themselves* noted that the book did not provide an explanation of why people do kill themselves.

As a result, David decided that he could continue his research and publishing scholarly articles if he could understand just one suicidal person. He started by reading biographies of Ernest Hemingway and Marilyn Monroe, and he felt that he could see how their life pathways did seem to lead inexorably to their deaths by suicide. But, as is his obsessive style, David continued and read biographies of almost 100 suicides, writing essays on each which you can read at www.drdavidlester.net. Indeed, these essays are so useful that they have been used now for research into understanding suicide (Lester & Gunn, 2020; Zhang et al., 2013).

Suicide is very difficult to study because, obviously, the subjects of any study of suicide are dead. As a result, suicidologists have often turned to the study of persons who have attempted suicide or who have thought about suicide and who are available for interviews and to fill out psychological inventories and tests. But critics often point out that these individuals are *not* suicides. They do not have the same suicidal intent as suicides, and they may not have the same psychodynamics leading to their suicidal behavior.

How can we study suicides? There is, of course, simple epidemiological research. We can calculate suicide rates over time and over regions, and by age, sex and ethnic group. We can conduct psychological autopsy studies, which involve interviewing family members, friends and co-workers of suicides, often using a standardized interviewing protocol. About a quarter of suicides leave suicide notes, and we can study these, although we wonder how those who leave suicide notes differ from those who do not leave suicide notes. We have conducted studies on posts on Twitter (Gunn & Lester, 2012), poems and blogs (Lester, 2014a), letters (Barnes et al., 2007) and a tape left by a young man just hours before his suicide (Lester, 2010).

But let us be honest. We can certainly study suicide notes and glean a little information about the individual suicide and about suicides in general, and we can certainly add to our scholarly productivity. Can we really understand suicide from these suicide notes? Yang and Lester (2011) argued that, when writing a suicide note, the person is making a decision on how to present himself or herself to significant others. Does the person want the survivors to feel guilty over the suicide, or does the person want them to feel that they were not to blame? Does the person want to leave instructions as to the disposition of his or her assets? Here are the first three notes from a series of 33 suicide notes presented by Shneidman and Farberow (1957).

To the Police. No note-one was written before this. Los Angeles Police already have a record of one attempt. Notify-Anne M. Jones, 100 Main St., Los Angeles, telephone BA 00000. I live at 100 Spring St., Los Angeles. I work at Ford, 100 Broadway. That is all. I can't find my place in life. J. William Smith

I hope this is what you wanted.

Dearest Mary. This is to say goodbye. I have not told you because I did not want you to worry, but I have been feeling bad for two years, with my heart. I knew that if I went to a doctor I would lose my job. I think this is best for all concerned. I am in the car in the garage. Call the police but please don't' come out there. I love you very much darling. Goodbye, Bill

From the first two notes, we learn very little. From the third note, we learn about the precipitating cause. That is not much. Shneidman and Farberow matched each of the 33 genuine suicide notes with a simulated suicide note written by a non-suicidal person, and these 33 pairs have generated dozens of studies. (For a review, see Lester, 2014a.) This indicates great scholarly productivity indeed, but not a great contribution to understanding of suicide.

Recently, a few suicides have left diaries. Lester (2014a) has published chapters on seven diaries written by those who have died by suicide. Four are published diaries and three were given to Lester by survivors who knew of his interest in suicide. Katie's diary is one of these seven diaries—provided to David by Katie's sister after her death.[1] In a diary, the writers are most likely writing truthfully about themselves. Of course, they may not have complete insight into the biopsychosocial processes behind their decision to die by suicide, but they are describing their thoughts and emotions as they write. Diaries may provide more information about suicides than any other source of information. However, the use of materials like suicide notes and diaries may also raise a number of ethical issues. We do not have the permission of those who wrote them to use these materials, but we are given them, most often by the surviving family or friends.

This is the second book on Katie's diary. Why do we need a second book and what does this book tell us that is new about Katie? The first book appeared in 2004 (Lester, 2004), and several major theories of suicide have appeared since that date. For example, Thomas Joiner (Joiner, 2005) published his Interpersonal-Psychological Theory of Suicide (IPTS), which has dominated the field of suicidology for the last 15 years (see Chapter 6). In addition, those who have attempted suicide and the survivors of those who die by suicide have become more active in the field of suicidology and have begun to attend suicide research and prevention conferences (such as the American Association of Suicidology annual conference). The previous book on Katie's diary focused on scholarly interpretations of the diary. Though we still incorporate a number of scholarly perspectives, this work includes invited writers with lived experience of suicide and survivorship to contribute to this new book to write from their perspective. We have also obtained a contribution from Katie's sister who started this project, and indeed this whole field of study, by giving Katie's diary to David Lester.

In this first chapter, we would like to review what we learned about Katie from the first book on her diary. But before doing that, we would like to address the issue of whether this book is useful. Why not publish the whole diary and let readers think about Katie's life and death without the guidance from suicidologists? As one commentator said in an Amazon review of the first book:

> It was, I felt, a really self-centered and self aggrandizing thing to have the psychologists writing their 'personal feelings,' fill the majority of the book, and then include only the smallest, tiniest and measliest excerpts from "Katie" and her Diary. All I wanted to read was more from the girl's personal diary. I wanted to read the real thing. I wanted to read it all.
>
> If you want absurd speculations and high falootin' psycho-babble from ivory tower 'intellectuals' about a girl who committed suicide-then you'll probably love the book?

In fact, David did want to include the whole diary into the first book (and this book too), but the diary was too long to include in the book. To compromise, David put the final month in the first book, and here we have included the first month of the diary (June, year 1)

Were the contributors to the first book (and are the contributors to this book) self-centered and self-aggrandizing? Perhaps to some extent, our disappointed reviewer is correct. Perhaps some chapters focused less on Katie than was ideal and too much on theory and personal perspectives on suicide. Is it psycho-babble? We think not. The layperson (a nice way of saying non-expert) may have their own thoughts about suicide in general or a particular suicide, but they are often, we think, wrong. Lay people often have prejudices. We have had people say to us that suicide is a selfish act because the suicides give no thought to the survivors who suffer. We have replied that we think it is selfish to ask or require someone who is in tremendous psychological pain (psychache, as we call it) to continue to live so that we do not have to mourn them and grieve. This is not to say that the scholars who contributed to the previous book and this one do not carry their own prejudices—however, we do our best to check them when possible or to allow for the possibility that they are influencing our perspectives. Whether or not we live up to this hope is for you, the reader, to decide. However, there are a number of myths and cultural stereotypes surrounding suicide that often bleed into layperson interpretations of suicide.

There are laypersons who think that suicidal people are crazy or thinking irrationally (and, we might add, a few psychiatrists also think this). Again, we disagree. One of us has argued forcefully that suicides do not necessarily have a major psychiatric disorder, and he attacked the whole discipline of psychiatry for being unscientific (Lester, 2014b). He has also argued that suicidal people are not necessarily irrational. There is, after all, the classic joke about psychiatric patients that makes this point.

> A man is driving in the rain along a country road and gets a flat tire. He gets out in order to change the tire, and he notices that he is parked outside a psychiatric hospital, and there are patients strolling around (with umbrellas, of course). Some come to the fence to watch him. He jacks the car up, takes the nuts off the wheel, put them in the hubcap and, as he goes to the trunk to get the spare tire, he accidentally kicks the hubcap, and the four nuts disappear into a muddy ditch, lost forever. He is stunned. How can he attach the spare tire to the axle? One of the psychiatric patients says, "Hey Buddy, just take one nut from each of the other three wheels and use those to attach your spare wheel." "That's brilliant," the man said. "I would never have thought of that. But how did you think of it? You're a psychiatric patient." The patient replied, "I'm here because I'm crazy, not because I'm stupid.
>
> (Lester, 2014b)

Putting aside use of terms like "crazy"—this joke illustrates that just because psychiatrists would assign you a psychiatric diagnostic label does not mean that you are incapably of rational thought in some areas of your life. The desire to escape from pain is a perfectly natural human response—and certainly not one that should be dismissed lightly. So lay interpretations of suicide are often wrong about suicides, but you are welcome to read the part of the diary printed in this book (in Chapter 3) and form your own opinion.

In the next chapter, we will briefly review the details of Katie's life, and then we have included the first month of her diary for you, the reader, to read in her own words. Throughout the remainder of the manuscript, you will be exposed to different ideas surrounding suicide—and different interpretations based on readings of the diary. These perspectives are varied, with perspectives drawn from the leading theories of suicide [such as the IPTS and the three-step theory (3ST)], from different forms of psychotherapy (such as Gestalt), from the perspectives of those who have survived the loss of a loved one to suicide, from those who have lived experience with their own suicidal thoughts and behaviors and even from the sister of Katie—who made this work possible by providing David with the diary in the past. Topics will include themes found within the diary, comparisons between Katie's diary and another's, discussions of why we are so bad at preventing suicide and even a discussion of whether works such as this (i.e., that use diaries and suicide notes) are even ethical endeavors. We have done our best to cast a wide net in collaborators to this work, and we are very pleased to present their interpretations and perspectives.

Note

1 Katie is a pseudonym, and all names are changed throughout the diary.

References

Barnes, D. H., Lawal-Solarin, F. W., & Lester, D. (2007). Letters from a suicide. *Death Studies, 31*, 671–678.

Durkheim, E. (1897). *Le suicide*. Paris, France: Felix Alcan.

Gunn, J. F., & Lester, D. (2012). Twitter postings and suicide. *Suicidologi, 17*(3), 28–30.

Joiner, T. E. (2005). *Why people die by suicide*. Cambridge, MA: Harvard University Press.

Lester, D. (Ed.). (2004). *Katie's diary: Unlocking the mystery of a suicide*. New York: Brunner-Routledge.

Lester, D., & Gunn, J. F. III. (2020). Is perceived burdensomeness present in the lives of famous suicides? A lack of support for the interpersonal theory of suicide. *Death Studies*, early online. https://doi.org/10.1080/07481187.2020.1863521

Lester, D. (1972/1983/1992/2000). *Why people kill themselves*. Springfield, IL: Charles Thomas.

Lester, D. (2010). The final hours. *Psychological Reports, 106*, 791–797.

Lester, D. (2014a). *The "I" of the storm*. Berlin, Germany: De Gruyter.

Lester, D. (2014b). *Rational suicide: Is it possible?* Hauppauge, NY: Nova Science.

Shneidman, E. S., & Farberow, N. L. (1957). *Clues to suicide*. New York: McGraw-Hill.

Yang, B., & Lester, D. (2011). The presentation of the self. *Suicidology Online, 2*, 75–79.

Zhang, J., Tan, J., & Lester, D. (2013). Psychological strains found in the suicides of 72 celebrities. *Journal of Affective Disorders, 149*, 230–234.

2 Who Is Katie?

David Lester

Katie's parents had emigrated from Europe to the United States. Her father was German and her mother Hungarian. The father, a carpenter, was a domineering and violent husband, preventing his wife from learning English and from driving a car, for example. He was an alcoholic and abusive to his wife and children. Katie was the first-born child, followed just over a year later by a sister, Laura.

Katie's father sexually abused her. In her diaries, Katie refers to this abuse but does not give explicit details. It is possible that she does not remember the incidents clearly, but she may also be reluctant to describe the incidents in detail in her diaries. I do not know whether Laura, Katie's younger sister, was also sexually abused by her father.

Katie's mother threw her husband out of the house when Katie was nine years old. He sometimes returned to the house while the mother was out working (at a factory), and his daughters would have to call the police to have him removed. Two years later, when the mother was filing for a divorce, he died, possibly of a heart attack. Soon thereafter, the mother was diagnosed with schizophrenia. The state authorities decided that she was not competent to raise her two daughters who were then placed in foster homes.

Katie's mother received inpatient care and was released but, after living in the community for eight years in squalid conditions,[1] she was institutionalized in a state psychiatric hospital with her younger daughter named as her legal guardian.

The two daughters were placed in several foster homes during the next few years, only occasionally placed together. They went to different colleges in the state, Katie two years ahead of Laura. They kept in touch and were quite close. Laura felt that Katie was somewhat immature, and she became protective of Katie as the years passed.

Katie developed an eating disorder at the time that she was taken away from her mother and placed in foster homes. Her anorexia was severe enough that she was hospitalized on several occasions, often around Christmas. She was

DOI: 10.4324/9781003125655-2

also frequently depressed. There is no indication that Katie had attempted suicide in the past. The daughters had been raised as Catholics, but Katie developed eccentric religious ideas to the extent that Laura worried that Katie suffered from hallucinations.

Katie blamed her mother for all of the trauma that she had experienced, and she saw her mother as having been purposely vindictive to her children. She preferred to tell others that her mother was dead. Laura, on the other hand, loves her mother and does not hold her responsible for the trauma she suffered at the hands of her father.

From the diary, we learn that Katie has a boyfriend whom she loves, Mark. Their relationship is troubled. Mark seems to have had sexual intercourse with an ex-girlfriend while he was seeing Katie, and this causes anguish for Katie and friction between her and Mark. Katie has trouble getting good grades in her college courses, and she sometimes withdraws from courses before the semester ends. She has financial problems paying for her college education and in getting a job to help with the finances.

For the period covered by the diaries, Katie perceives herself as overweight, and she is discouraged about this, continually trying to lose weight, but without success. She refers to attending group meetings for those who are overweight and for those who were victims of incest. She also mentions drinking and using recreational drugs, including marijuana.

On June 29, Katie's boyfriend Mark went to her college dormitory room (a single-story dormitory for disabled students[2]), but Katie did not respond. The light was on in the room, and Mark could see under the door that Katie was lying there. Mark went outside and broke the window so that he could enter the room, and he found that Katie had hung herself.

Others in the dormitory called campus security who in turn called the local police department. There was no disorder in the room, except for the broken window, and there were no signs of foul play. No suicide note was found.

Mark reported that he had last seen Katie on June 16 and that she had recently been depressed. No one in the dormitory had seen Katie for the last few days. However, an employee of the bookstore had seen Katie on the day before her body was found.

The autopsy report indicated that Katie was 20 years old and 65 inches tall and weighed 143 pounds.[3] There were no signs of any illness, disease or trauma apart from the hanging. Toxicological analyses revealed no alcohol or drugs. The medical examiner did not report examining Katie's reproductive system, and so it may be assumed that she was not pregnant.

Five volumes of a diary were found, together with a book of poems and a scrapbook of magazine clippings. Laura took possession of these. As mentioned in the Preface, Laura entrusted the volumes to David.

The first volume of Katie's diary is reproduced in the next chapter to provide an example of the material that the contributors to this book used in order to write their commentaries.

Notes

1. She failed to pay her real estate taxes and utility bills, so that she lived without heat and water, and she was unable to hold a job.
2. Katie had moved to this dormitory after having disagreements with her roommate.
3. Katie's weight was within the range for a woman of her height with a large frame. It was outside the range for women with small or medium frames.

3 Katie's Diary

The First Month

Katie

June 8

Dear Journal:

I am so depressed and suicidal. My body feels restless and tired. I don't know who to turn to for help. I don't want to bother anyone with my battle. I've been acting out in all sorts of ways. I just feel like crying. I presume that all has to do with the fact that I love Mark so deeply. I think he cares for me but, however, I don't know if it's true love for him. It definitely is for me. I really want to marry him so badly. I don't care if he reads my journal at all. I am just so stressed out. I haven't done any of my work. I have a hard time getting along with people. I really hate my body. I really hate my life where it is, with everything I am. I decided to start exercising today. I need to do it every day. I leave all my life's frustrations there out on the track.

God give me strength. Help me today. I feel so unbelievably lonely and battered.

June 8

Dear Journal:

I lied to both of my professors today. I had to. It was wrong, I know, but what makes me feel better is that Mrs W told me to do what I had to.

I'm going to OA tomorrow night. I'm glad. I hope the support group works well. I'll make it work well. I have to get myself together. I have things to hold on to here, people who love me. I suppose a big part of the upset lies in the past. I wonder if Mark really loves me. Does he? I feel that this relationship is stuck. Because of my own periodic emotional (more positive) state, I'll get myself out. I never want to get to this out-of-control place again.

All I know is that I love Mark with all my heart and soul. It gets deeper all the time.

But I am responsible to him to take care of myself. I love him. I really want to make him happy. I know what he wants in a girlfriend, and I am all that.

DOI: 10.4324/9781003125655-3

Well, inside I am. I want him to feel safe with me, but how can he, right now, if I don't even trust myself.

I really owe this realistic approach to myself also.

It sucks to let, for me to allow, to waste my life away. It's absolutely horrible. There is such a desolate feeling with this relapse. It sickens me. My hand needs to be tired at times for me to prevent, forcing, hurting myself in these ways. It kills me inside the way I've acted on and off. It really kills me. My heart knows better. I used to have my actions smooth with people, but now I've gotten so fucking sloppy, because I used to care too much, but I don't care about my life that much anymore.

June 8

I really want to make these meetings religiously. This is where I must draw strength from, or until something more secure comes along. HOP

I'll let it go. I have really forgiven him a lot with Claudia, but I just will let the, our past go. It was whatever it was, and now we need, it's time to move on to a different plane with him. It feels good. We should've been there a while ago. I know helping myself will help him. MARK CHEATED

I also have had such a problem with sex. People did such bad things to me when I had no clothes on. I just feel so unable to express myself right now because I always compare myself to Claudia physically. ABUSE?

June 14

I really hate people. All they are are problems, conflicts, a pain in the ass.

I don't need my mother in my life anymore. I never needed someone who was so sick and raped me—my mind, heart, soul. But why do I love and miss her so much? Boohoo. Boohoo. LESTER RESENTMENT STUDY

I feel so uncomfortable with my body. I really hate it. The only way I feel connected is when I exercise. It's my meditation. It would be so nice if I lost 2–3 lbs. I would be so excited. OVERWEIGHT?

Sometimes I think romantic "attracted" love is so damn shallow. Where am I now? I really want Mark to call me. I wonder if I lost any weight? I have to weigh myself every Friday. I miss my sister. When I was a little girl, I acted out a lot on my sister. I feel really bad. I hope she forgives me. She did it back too.

God save my mother! I can't do it. I could never do it.

I see that best friend of Vicki's in my class. She's a bitch the way she looks at me. Same with Fran's and Stacy's friends. They are always staring at me. I hate it. I miss my freshman year at college. Why am I trying to go back? I really miss those people and things. Why does Scott keep calling me?

Fuck you all! I'm going to kill myself! Fuck you all! Kurt Cobain

I don't feel I have any friends. I feel so alone, almost paranoid.

I feel so abandoned and unconnected with everyone, everyone. I feel like I'm going to die . . . Let everyone get a mass suicide.

I'm just angry, just angry. I'm angry at all I've taken so far from people and life and fate. No more. Fuck you all! Who tries to hurt me, control me, fuck with me? Fuck you all! ANGER GOOD

June 15

Today Vicki's friend told me how they used to flirt . . . He cheated on me—it hurts so bad. Does it have to so with me? I realize not. I didn't make him do it—he did it all alone. I really love him. I love my dreams with him, but I don't feel like I have a friend in the world now—nobody. I feel no connection with anyone, and it scares me so much. The world seems so cold, dark and scary. I'm alone, alone and left to myself. He flirted while he was dating me with a number of girls. I never flirted with anyone. He is unloyal. I'm so hurt over Vicki . . . I don't want to eat anymore. I'm sick of numbing out my feelings. I'm in such pain and disarray. I feel so unhappy. MARK'S FLIRTING & CHEATING LEADS TO HER FEELING DISCONNECTED LEADS TO NOT EATING.

I suppose it's good Mark's not coming back next semester. It's too good a feeling to last. How stupid! I started getting myself and life together for him, so he could be with me in my dream life. It was all a lie anyway. It all hurts me so much—it all hurts. I know Mark's having a hard time now. I wish him the best. I thought he was my hero. Oh well, here I sit again, just where I started, shattered and broken-hearted. I can't believe I tried trusting him and anybody else.

I want to kill myself. Bullet though my heart—the only way I'll ever stop caring about people.

I wish I was rich! Please God, help me become a millionaire. I've never asked for this before. So I can afford to be on my own and never lean on anyone else again. I don't feel like a nice and caring, go-lucky kind of person anymore. I don't feel free to be happy—only to be sick. UNREALISTIC HOPE

I did try reaching out again for the last time. People are so mean and selfish. I want to kill myself on my birthday. I have to. RE MARK

I suppose all death is to me is a hug, or a place where I can be tortured and close to my parents.

Tomorrow night I am going to Mark's. I am glad, but I think I will look really fat. I don't know what to wear. Joyce is really getting on my nerves. I don't want to and can't deal with her. I hope she doesn't come tomorrow night. I read two chapters today. I can't read anymore. It makes my mind fry. I feel so damn. . . . I think I'd better start exercising on something, so I can go to bed.

I feel so alone and scared. I don't know what I would do without Mark. I can't afford the phone bill anymore. I won't use the phone anymore. Mr. W acted so weird on the phone today. Jane's answering machine is off. Phone! Please let it be for me. I guess Mark wouldn't call. I don't trust Hilda with my messages. I hate this. I am obsessing so much. I think Mark works till 11:00 PM. I really need to hear his voice. I'd rather write Mark than talk on the

telephone. I always want to be with him. My world looks so dark and grim.
CONFLICT & AMBIVALENCE WITH FRIENDS.

June 17

I still get half grossed out about sex. I get scared. I wish my Mom never said and did certain things to me. Maybe I'm just too sensitive.

I miss my Mom. I really wish she was better. Oh, how I wish she was my Mom. I need her to love me—so deeply. I don't feel anyone will ever love me so deeply. The only person who has given me this kind of depth is Mark, and I love him so much for this.

June 22

Maury always spent hours telling me how much he liked me. God! He is another story—all shallow, pretty much, difficult and dry to connect with. I felt he was a desolate, cold, dry, dead person. I do miss him in some strange way though. AMBIVALENCE

But anyway, these people really hurt me. Maybe I'm just oversensitive. But these guys, they only want one thing from me, most likely more. I really resent them.

I miss Mark around campus. When I look at certain buildings and places, I can't help but think of him. I remember how much I liked him from the very first time I saw him. I remember seeing him the beginning of my second session here (freshman year). I thought he was absolutely beautiful, but I figured he only thought that really skinny girls were beautiful. I didn't even think he noticed me. I remember walking by his classroom a few times my freshman year and seeing him. I still get that excited feeling. It's really nice. I remember when I first spoke to him after Lori's party. I was walking Julia home—she was drunk—so funny, so funny—but anyway, I really wanted to go over and talk to them (Josh and Mark). Julia was the perfect excuse to do so. By the way, I love you journal. I felt mellow. I don't know, but I remember feeling nervous. I miss Brooke and Tracy. Brooke and Tracy did like Mark a lot. I remember how much I liked him. I didn't like anyone like this in over a year or so. It felt wonderful. I always thought he was sweet and caring. I felt like I could share things with him (not all from this one conversation—through a few). I remember something he said. He said, "I'm addicted to love." My heart just melted. Only a truly caring and strong human being would say such a thing. I felt at that moment that I had found someone, finally, who I wanted and could be in a relationship with. His instinctive maturity showed this to me. He was like the sun who found its way into a dying domain, like the first or only blossom on a once dead rose bush. At the same level he seemed too good to be true. I so badly wanted him to be my hero, my knight in shining armor. I felt as if I was locked away in a tower dungeon, intangible, left to exist alone, unloved, only abandoned and mistreated, under lock and key, forever, by everyone else who ever owned me. I felt this amazing spirituality with him from the very beginning. I thought it was a lot with Kevin and Brent, but they could not meet up to this level. I never felt this connected with both of them. It had to build up from what I remember, more with Brent than Kevin, but it was something that had to form. It did not then or could never build up to this level, partly because of this connection, the intensity. I felt scared. I was attracted to other people in small quantities, but that is all where it stood. It stood no more than that, even though there were only a few people I even looked at. I tried and tried looking at people. I actually had to force myself to, but I felt like I betrayed my heart since I didn't feel like this heartfelt connection with anyone. I thought perhaps I was too pure, or I was unattractive, or it's because I had too many problems and was very unsatisfied with myself—whatever or however—most of these are the first one was the truest. I've only liked three people a lot in my day.

But the point is that when I found Kevin, it was nice and sweet. I felt I could empathize with his situation, but he was never very open with me. Then when I met Brent, I really could not stand him from the beginning, but I felt kind of mean and tried being nice and open with him, and I was happy to see he was expressing himself to me. It made me feel connected to him in a way I was never connected to Kevin. Both were, in a different way, tangible with my heart.

But when I met Mark, it was nice, sweet and warm in the beginning. I had no resentment or annoyance with him, and he was open with me, spiritually, but I finally got some sharing of his past in small doses. He is really open with me about his emotions. I never had this with one person before. He makes me feel strong and weak in ways. I don't understand some things, whether they are inside of him or inside of me. I remember when he told me, "You just don't want to admit to yourself how close we are." That shattered a facade I was living, a wall I was building. I never was this close in so many ways to one guy before.

It really devastated me, about the Claudia thing. I knew when I first heard about the situation from Stacy, Maggie, Kristin, I knew it would cause me heartache. I don't know what happened. When I heard this, my heart crashed. It hurt. I hurt because I had genuine feelings for him. A problem I know of sincerity. It hurt because there was another person who I cared for that wouldn't care or love back. It felt like another intangible Katie-seeks-love mission. It hurt. But I decided to take this with a grain of salt. I would be open with him and see what he wanted to do. I knew that getting over someone you loved would hurt, and I really didn't know the situation, but I wanted to help him because he was such a beautiful person. I was willing to put these feelings to the side and just be a friend. I felt like I could really trust him more than anyone. I suppose a big part of this was a lot of hope and expectation to some degree. I felt like I could never be intimate with anyone emotionally and mentally. It really scared me. I prayed to God that this would help me restore my faith in this damned human race. So I said to myself this seems like a sincerely good person. I will push myself and risk everything to be and learn from him. I hated the place where I was trapped and basically I threw myself out the window in hopes for a pleasant landing. I had all these visions of how beautiful this girl was and how skinny. I compared myself not only to her, but to other girls who caught his interest. I was so meticulous with myself. I hated my body so much. I tried going on so many damn diets in the past eight months so I would be more beautiful to him and most of all to myself so I wouldn't have to compete. I failed miserably on all of them, whether purposely or accidentally I did. A lot of this had to do with my sincere need to be wanted and cared about. I always get like this if I care about someone, be this friend or relationship.

I'm trying to be rational here, but it all was destroying me, the lies, the affair, the competition, the self-hatred. I couldn't deal with all of this. I just tried to meet everything evenly, not to be passive, not be hurt, and I did get hurt because my heart was really there and so was my mind. It was so hard for me to pull myself out of one sick, isolated, insane world to another world which confronted my isolation and sickness, a world where I had to take on responsibility for someone else, and I did this. I sacrificed all the good and bad things of this world so I could be with him. Yes, I was defensive, but I had everything to lose. There was no friend or person or parent to catch me. No one was there except me, as usual, to pick up the broken pieces, and there is only so much one broken person who is tired and weak from all these internal and external battles can take. If I hurt him during the process—I got sloppy as he says—but I was on completely new ground. I still always tried to be careful, but the whole time it was so obvious what was going on. He was so obvious. It really hurt. It really did.

When I found out, I was completely heart-broken with the cheating. I risked so much. Well anyway, about five days later we went back out. It was way too soon. I was so burnt out and so was he. Afterwards, he couldn't touch me. I felt so misused and abused—all those feelings were there. I just felt so hurt. I didn't care if he touched me or not. My body was not connected to my heart anymore. It was horrible. I just wanted to break it off with him forever. It was all so suffocating, those emotions. I was so devastated that I wanted to kill myself. I never really went into depth about my suicidal feelings. I felt like my world fell apart again, but this time Katie used all her energy trying to get close to someone. She didn't have any strength to catch herself. No, not this time.

The pieces had to stay.

Well after all this, we are here. But I got really jealous, defensive, angry, resentful and physically assaultive with him. I hated him so much. I lost all my respect for him, but more for myself. Surprisingly I stood by myself no matter what state I was in. Joyce and Sara and Ken and Jenna and Carmen and Kristin, etc., were utterly amazing with me. They helped me out a lot because I realized that my world was still here, but a piece got chipped away for someone else to enter in my future.

But anyway, we made it to here. Communication is way better. Our friendship seems to be getting better. Physically I'm getting better. My trust is slowly creeping up again, etc.

But the only bad thing was that he still hung out and spoke to Claudia. I felt it was so inconsiderate, and I started hanging out with Jenna because I found her to be a good understanding friend. But otherwise, I felt so blackmailed and threatened. The ambivalent feelings were back on his side. It tortured me so much inside, especially because I slept with him. I felt so devastated and unrespected. I listened, however, to what he said. But it gets difficult to trust him now.

Especially since Claudia calls and mostly because I saw her this weekend. My heart broke all over again. I saw the way he looked at her. It killed me. He seems so elusive at times. He kept on staring at her. It made me so nauseous. I thought I was going to die. Well, I bolted out. He left me to go talk to her. If he didn't want to talk to her, he just wouldn't make an effort to, but he did. So I bolted out. She is a real slut as far as I'm concerned. They both are throughout this whole situation. But I'm here now. Anyway the party was amazing. Grandparents and other people were very nice. This woman Cory made me laugh hysterically. I also got mad at Mark because he just left me there, all alone. He apologized later. But still, duh! I realize he felt uncomfortable, but so did everyone else. Well anyway, later we got drunk with Chandler. It was really funny. We kept going downstairs to the bathroom with all three of us. Also we opened the attic for some odd reason and I went up and Chandler mentioned Claudia. So I started throwing things at them. I want to see what would happen if I stopped having sex with Mark. Let me try one weekend. I know I can do this. It is only sex. I want to see if he treats me differently.

But, over all, I have healed a good amount. I love him very much. I am putting and have put some big things behind me so we can move forward to a carefree life. HOPE

June 23

Today, Carl will pick me up around 7:30 PM, and we are supposed to go out somewhere. I discovered that I want to be a nurse, but I don't want to transfer to another college. I will instead major in biology. I think that this will make a big difference in my financial status. I am going to look around for nursing schools around here. I love science and math because all it is is factual. You are right or you're wrong. I want to minor in psychology and major in biology. This is what I'm going to complete at this college. I'm a little afraid, but overall I'm very excited. I intend to take every session possible. I'm a little nervous about the AIDS and other disease epidemics, but I think I will be fine. I will try to work away from this stuff and work with the elderly or children or something. The hours sound difficult, but I think I can do this. I love hospitals and the health-care profession. So I really want a job in this field. It takes a lot of pressure off the arts.

June 23

I spoke to Ken, my sponsor. It was nice but, when he says nice things about me, I don't take it as seriously all because I don't feel he really knows me.

I kept comparing myself to that 90210 girl Dawn. She's beautiful. I can't stop looking at her—she is so gorgeous. Long blonde hair, tall, nice shape and good skin, really pretty. But it's only her hair, otherwise she's not so pretty. There is another beautiful girl in front of me. She has the most beautiful eyes. She is more beautiful than Dawn could ever be facially. I wonder if I could grow my hair as long as hers. I wonder if mine would be as beautiful. I feel so anxious, like I have all this catching up to do. But anyway, the only attitude is a fuck-everything attitude. I'm sure if Mark would see this girl he would drool. But I hate when I do this to myself. I get so damned horrible—only when I'm in a relationship and when I like someone. It is so horrifying. I hate doing this to myself. It is truly the worst. I can't deal with all this crap. I've been playing piano for two years now. I've taught myself everything. I know. I've got compliments from piano and music teachers and students who walk by. I taught myself. I figured out this game, a good bit, but I really want to ask Ken more. He gave me one lesson on chords. I also taught myself dance and acting and drawing. Me and only me. I know if I want to get better, I need to learn more structure. However, I feel too damn free in this essence. Free to play, in the first meaning. I feel trapped in other instances with art. I need an independent kind of thing, a my-own-way. I have to claim this ground as my own—no one else's.

It's miserable when I held so much in about everything, even to myself, because I was afraid that someone might use it. But it's all true. It stands, and I do too. I'm thinking about transferring to Chicago. I'm not sure yet. A lot has to do with Mark. I love him very much, but I need to follow my dreams. I want to get the best education possible. I don't have good competition or motivation to keep myself going. I suppose I need to compete to always do better against myself. I step more, I step higher.

My heart feels like it's in chains. I'm tired of all these damn knots. Where the hell is it going to take me? Where? I need to be practical here with my goals, to gain perspective. This way I have an equation of sorts to get there. To battle the elusive, the mundane.

weight goal: do well with food—150 lbs.

academic goal: Intro to Psyc, Readings and Humanities—study and work hard on papers—> B

I need to be open with certain people. I seem so extremist in some ways.

All or nothing

I can't live an empowering balance this way.

I don't know what will happen with Mark. All I know is I'm very emotional and stressed right now. I need to do a Psych paper. I'd better find a good referenced paper. Here with Will's work. I need to tell Mark about what Emmons said today, about introverted people get hard on themselves because they see they lack certain social skills. I'm all essence; it's ok to be a certain way, but they turn it inward to shyness.

Oh, my baby sister is going to heaven, by an ocean. She can't walk. She can only run. Here hold my hands and don't let go, just watch the river flow, the stream, the ocean, let yourself breathe instead of bleed. Don't worry, you're all right baby, you're all right baby.

My sister's going to college—Akron. I am so proud of her. I can't lie anymore. I don't want to. I love her. I miss her. Where does this story end, God? Please help me get my life going. Please don't let me get sick. Please don't ever leave me.

The air is getting so damn stagnant is all my relationships. I really resent them. I really want to cut myself off from the world permanently. I suppose a lot of this has to do with my connection to myself. I hate myself. It's so frightening. I hurt myself so badly. When will this ever stop? When?

June 24

Well anyway, I hung out with Carl last night. I felt uncomfortable being with him because I wasn't sure if he likes me or not. So I boldly asked him. I basically said, "Carl do you like me more than as a good friend?" He said no, very sincerely. I also said because if you do, you know how much I love Mark. He said that he loves me as his little sister. There is nothing else there. He also said that any guy would be stupid to try and chase me. He also said that no guy would even try because I don't play people—especially because I talk often of Mark. Well I questioned everything before I went off to assume things. I'm very glad I did. He was annoying me a lot that night. I felt like he really wanted to connect with me, but there was honestly no point to it.

Well finally we got here. I'm really glad. I was sick of hearing all the whining about other women and friends, whatever. I'm not that close to care. I just really don't give a fuck. I have a lot more important things to focus on.

Well what else? Carl came inside for a few. He felt uncomfortable so he left. Whatever. Mrs Bellamy told me that Mark called to see if I was here or not. I thought it was nice, but I figured it had to do with the fact that he probably wanted to record something. I was right. Well he came in and asked me to go to Matt's with him. I didn't want to because I was tired and the fact that why did he have to. There was no reason. I felt really hurt, so I went to sleep. I felt myself drifting away from him. I felt so cut off from everything yesterday. Well actually about 2 AM. But I kept not wanting to see him until he left, then leave on Sunday before he got back. I just had this overbearing urge to run away. But he came in about 3–4 times. It just seems that he wants to spend time, we should—when it's convenient for him. I hate that because, no matter how hard my schedule, I make time always for him. He is on top of my list. But I'm not saying that I don't think I mean a lot to him. But I wish he would treat me the way he treats his friends. He always connects the way I want to. Well I feel like he was taking me for granted or ignoring me or something. It really hurt. I'm tired of b.s. So I made myself go out and talk to him despite everything. My stomach hurt so bad yesterday. I think it was because I was dehydrated. However, I started a water fight with him. It's all because he wouldn't let me get out of the kitchen. I got a lot of frustration out.

Well anyway, then I brought up Carl, and he got all pissy, moody, grouchy, cruel, etc. He asked if he was tall. God, in the scheme of our relationship, what the hell does it mean? I still don't get relationships. Why can't two people just mellow together. Why must all this chaos be? That's why I stayed out of relationships for so long, or in such short ones. I know it's possible, but it's so pure and beautiful. I don't want all this arguing and crass statements. There is honestly no point to it. I think with both of our personalities, we would have a great bond. I feel like we are both relaxing or something. It's nice. Well, I started crying and shaking after he said some really cruel things to me. "He's just like all my parents." You can't love someone and then try to hurt them. It doesn't make any sense. Well, we talked—he told me that he hated me crying. It's true. I hate crying so much, but somehow I feel he's used to it. That's a really negative sign. It's so hot and sticky here blah. Well, today is analyze book day—write about 3–4 pages on each one.

Well anyway, we ended up making up, and we made love. It was really beautiful. He makes me feel alive and free in most ways. When I'm with him, I forget that I have problems. I realize I'm a different person—on my own—separate from these problems. I love Mark. Well, he got offended when I told him I wasn't into the anal thing. Sometimes he gets so childish, but we both do. But I try to get out of it. I love him. I do want to please him. I always push myself to be physical with him. I mean, it's not that I don't want to; however, I make myself feel and think that there is something wrong with me if I don't want to. I have a lot of things to figure out. A lot. Well, I hated the fact that I ate 300 more calories, but I wasn't that mean to myself. I was cool. The first 3 days are the hardest. Well, I'm finally on day 4, makeup day. I can't wait to be alone in the house, doing my work. I love it.

Mark just said hi. He had a funny look on his face. I think he might not want to leave me or something. Ken wants to come over today. Blah. I don't want anyone here.

I'm hungry—mmm bagel. I need to exercise and look over these books. I'm so excited. Ken will be lending me some books, especially about nursing. I know I can condition myself in any situation to be fully alert and be mentally free. I feel very beautiful and strong right now. I have this inner loving feeling that is so deep and joyful. What an entity. I focus on the wrong things. I cannot change the past. No matter how much I think about it, it won't make it go away. Well that gives me peace of mind. I sincerely believe I'm above it in every way. It's not that I'm denying my feelings or anything. Yes, these things hurt me. But I survived all of it. There is no damn need to go over things so thoroughly. I suppose it is, but what else can I do? I lived it. That is all I was entitled to do in this world, and experience I did. But it wasn't fair; but I made it fair. I reached out and put myself out of each grueling experience. I freed myself physically from everything. But I need to free myself mentally. I experienced it all.

But then, what is always going on inside me? I can feel so damn restless and initiating talking about it. Obsessing aimlessly. It's ridiculous. But mainly I have inner fears and abuses. Things I do to myself. I act our horrible ways with myself. I act very unconstructive.

Whether it's lying to people, or stealing, or being cruel by hurting my body. Whether it's all the helplessness I had to accept—lack of control which both of these were imperative factors. But the truth lies in the fact that I can attain this peace of mind, by being true, taking responsibility and charge over my behavior, of taking back control, taking it back, acting free in the area of positive respectable construction vs. other methods of approach to me life.

It makes me angry that I let things paralyze me to such an unproductive extent. What is the basis for this? I don't need to stop for anyone on my way. It's hard. I feel I have to sacrifice myself to be close to people or make them love me. That's wrong. I don't owe that to anyone at all. It's wrong, and I won't lower my standards anymore. I can't believe I did. It's wrong—unfitting—and doesn't establish the environment I deserve. No, it doesn't. I refuse to put myself in situations that hurt me or make me feel uncomfortable. I can take control of any situation. I have the heart and brains to. . . . These dots look like tiny footprints.

I'm tired of these struggles. Some are so damn unneeded. Mark's acting all weird. I don't know why. Could it be separation anxiety? Blah, blah, blah.

Both Brett and Mark are completely spoiled brats.

I can't believe he hit me. Doesn't he realize that little things affect me so much. They are not little to me.

I started freaking about my food ever since yesterday. I went over 300 calories. I did the same today. I feel miserable primarily because I didn't exercise, sleep right. Mark arguing and also looked at pictures of Claudia. I'm so alone. I have all this stress. I hate having a problem with my food. I have to do something today to take control. Nap, exercise, books, shower, clothes, type a paper. I am so freakish about everything. I miss Mark. God, I hate when we get all weird with each other. Oh, I need to lay down. I feel so behind in everything. I have so much to do. Ahhhhh!

Ken might stop by.

I did so damn terrible with my food today. It was horrible. I want to kill myself today. I hate this. I would cry, but I'm afraid I'll never stop. I feel so hopeless. I called my sponsor though. That was very good. I can't lie about things like this. I just don't have it in me. I looked through Mark's yearbook. I read what Claudia wrote him. She sounds so different than me. She seems so free. I think that this was one of the biggest triggers today.

Can't you see this. I can't deal with this. I know the way I want to be with Mark. I wish I could be free sexually with him. I feel sometimes he resents me because I'm not at that unvictimized point or something. I know he loves me. I can see and feel it. It truly is frightening. I can't just love him back. It's too painful. I know the way he wants things to be with me. I want it too. But I just don't feel safe! I try and try and try, but I just don't. I am always looking out, or getting ready for someone to hurt me. It's terrible. Us fighting doesn't make it easy at all. I cannot. I don't know how to stop it. I don't know how, how to end this miserable story. My character written desire, she still stands, I hate pitting myself, but I can't ignore everything either.

All I want to do is to be able to run into Mark's arms, carefree, care-fucking-free.

Oh God! Help me. I feel so damn alone. My shirt is drenched with tears. Oh God! I don't want to, I can't give up. I've made it too far. Please, please, somebody, help me!

I feel so trapped, bound, tied up, locked up, like I was when I was fourteen, thirteen, twelve, locked up in the house, never allowed out to be free, not allowed to run that often, felt trapped in my own body. Oh, why?

This story sucks. Oh, Mommy! Why? Oh, where were you? You selfish cunt. I need a Mommy. I feel so scared. I scare myself as much as anyone else. It doesn't make any fucking sense. None of it. It hurts the people who love me. I don't want to share or give this shit to anyone. It's like giving a broken doll to a child, a tease, a fucking tease. That's all you were Mommy, a fucking tease. Always bringing and offering things to me, but taking it away. God, you played this game too. I wish I could collect all my tears in a bottle. I think I'll put them in a vial and save them, so I can touch them. I want to give the vial to Mark. I want him to hold it. I love him so much with every part of my heart. I've never loved anyone except my Mom like this—and sister at times. That's it. No one else—ever! I never thought I'd feel so deeply. Why? Why God?

Please take all this pain away. So it doesn't hurt Mark, and I don't use it to hurt myself. I keep wiping my tears on this page, but then they disappear. Why do things disappear? I want to hold onto them because they mean so much to me, because they are real. I'm so afraid of you God. I hate fear. I hate all this crap.

Mark's Mom, a few weeks ago, was talking about "embracing the light," a book about a woman who experiences the world after death. She said that God would punish people by taking responsibility of feeling what they did to other people. I hope my father feels it! I don't want his spirit to be free to come and visit me—if he does at all—it's my right—I don't want his presence in my life.

I know a lot of problems occur in the fact with me and Mark because we feel so much, and tradition is making us, well me, I'm only talking about myself, feel all bound because it's scary that love, you are chained to someone. I don't want that aura in the relationship. It is irrelevant.

I haven't made Mark laugh that much. I hate that. I can make people laugh, feel good, very well. I don't think I make him laugh enough. I know I can. That's not the problem. The problem is that I've focused so much—we've focused so much on our problems, and it deserves the rightful validation. But so do the good things in life, that true freedom, not bound to any one extreme thing. It's beautiful, whole, circle of roses.

I just don't want to fight over stupid things. It's not beneficial. I mean, we need to get all sorts of things out, but it all depends on how it's communicated. I believe you should think about things like this especially if you love someone and try to love yourself. I always, ever since I can remember, always tried to make things better for people close to me and far away. I just everyone in the world to be happy, not just a few people, everyone, in the meaning of peace of mind.

I really hate Claudia. I just had to say that. I hate them both for what they did to me. I had to say that too. They are both to blame. I never just resented her for it. That would be so completely wrong and unfair. But, I don't hate Mark now. I did a lot before. Well, it wasn't that I hated him as a person, but what he did and how he hurt me.

I feel a lot of what has been and still is falling into perspective for the last few months. It still chokes me up sometimes when I think of it. I remember I couldn't have orgasms for a long time after he told me. I'd fake it so much. I felt like I didn't have any choice anymore. The thought crossed my mind that it didn't matter if he used me because I felt so misused already, like a piece of meat, like I was when my parents did things to me. But I kept going back in hopes that they would stop and because I loved them. I really thought they were protecting me from even worse things out there. Stupid! I was so fucking innocent! I was too with all my relationships! I knew how a good healthy relationship was supposed to work. I knew I always knew how to treat people. I always treated people so well. That's why so many people confessed things to me. I'd make them feel safe. Everyone I ever me told me that I make them feel unjudged for the things they told me. I've been told so many dark secrets. It's sad that there is so much pain. Well, at least I can do something to ease the world's pain a little bit by being a nurse or a doctor.

Despite all the ways I was mistreated, I still do love people. I honestly have had a hard time with myself this year, trying to make myself not care. It was just as destructive as the first extreme—loving too much. But now I just care, not to a point where it destroys me, but a real honest wholesome point.

I really want to help Mark feel better, more connected to good things. Sometimes he still confuses me so. A lot of that has to do with the fact that I haven't been connected or let myself be connected to my instincts (lately, past year). I always thought it made me vulnerable, but I realized it made me strong instead. It really kept me whole for a long time. It helped achieve a focus when I thought there was none. Well, I don't want to lie or be unconnected to my true self, not me, mind, self.

It is my priority. I know all my other relationships will fall into place, with people and other things. This is where the peace lies—power, knowledge, strength, like Sun Tzu said: When you truly know yourself, that is when you can know other people. This is where the heart becomes whole, where the balance with God begins, all in relationship to yourself.

I miss Mark so much! He's so beautiful, tangible, real, most loving man I ever met in my life. I have never met anyone who cared more about me, romantically, etc. I pray, dear God, please protect him from all harm. Let him rest beautifully, his heart laying on angels' wings beside him with soft white (hyperallergenic) feathers, making him feel so safe, light, peaceful, whole. Let his sweet heart, mind and body heal here so that, when he rises, he feels whole.

It stay for ever. Let my kisses cover him with a warm soft breeze that can touch his soul in ways I truly only am able to send my dreams to. Please let his sadness leave and peace come into existence with joy.

I prayed to day that both . . . wouldn't come by, and they didn't. Thank you.

    Food: oatmeal 1/2 cup cooked
               1 peach
               8 oz skimmed milk
   lunch tuna and lettuce
               stay away from sugar

I'm on the plan now—wheat and sugar and pretty fat-free. Anyway, 10 PM I was downstairs, playing piano. I got really scare, and I ended up carrying a book around the house to bash someone's head in. A rat just went up my nose—ahhh! Thank God for little suicidal rats.

Today, right after the Bellamy family left, I went into the kitchen, and Fido opened the drawer and was pulling pipecleaners out with her mouth and dropping them on the floor—so cute.

I don't mind the How Plan—lots of protein—great for skin and hair, etc. It's kind of nice to be alone, but I keep picturing some manic psycho cat killer rapist breaking in the house, killing and raping the cats—sick but funny.

I really want to marry Mark. Even though I try to be rational and realistic in my heart, my little heart wants to stay in his arms forever. I really do. I don't ever want to lose him to someone else. It really would kill me inside to lose another person I love. I wish I could physically express myself to him.

I know all the diets that I have tried have all revolved around the fact I don't want to lose him. I would stop eating for him. I would've done it by now. But he really says he doesn't want me losing any weight. He's such a polite person. I know he's just trying to be nice. I know he likes really skinny girls, but I'm here at this weight now. Another adventure for love through weight loss. I'm sick. It's making me sick just thinking about it. I can't deal with it. It's way too much.

I know being physical is important to him. It's also very very important to me. I know I have desires like other women who haven't been abused, but I wish I wasn't so damn afraid to express myself. I do try, but the crap was really beaten out of me—for natural instinctual physical things when I was young. My mother made me feel so horrible and like a slut for doing nothing. She kept on yelling at me, calling me a slut, telling me I was raped and I was lying about it all along. Every day she would ask me and then tell me that I was raped. A few times I put makeup on, she called me a whore, slut, a prostitute. I could have so easily become a prostitute, but I wanted to save myself, all of me, for that special someone. Mark was my first for everything. I feel it kind of makes me very vulnerable to him. I'm glad I waited. I could tell from the beginning that he was the highest quality person. I'm glad I shared these things with him, even though I question if he thinks less of me because of this.

It hurts me a lot to know that Mark doesn't want to marry me. It makes me cry a lot, but I have to accept and appreciate what affection, little or a lot, they are willing to give. I feel like I'm some sort of bum begging for scraps. I guess that's really all I'm allowed to get in life. I mean, why would he want to marry me? Yes, I love him very much but, and I know he cares for me a great deal, but look at me. I don't think I'm ugly, but I've been scarred in so many ways. I mean I've been misused and abused, damaged, tortured, wounded, etc. I feel like a wounded animal. And most of all I've been so damn defensive with him. I lost my good way of communicating and connecting to him and others, especially him. That's what matters the most. I have and had a lot to lose because I didn't really have much left to hold on to. But, look at me, I have a horrible disorder. I have a really hard time sharing sexual pleasure with him. I get jealous so easily. I'm ready to hurt myself so easily, react so immaturely. It's just that my heart can't take any more pain. I can't tolerate frustration and jealousy and feeling like I'm second best. I really demand a lot of attention. I wish I didn't. I always try to keep things to myself so I don't hurt anyone. I've always done this, and Mark gets so angry at me when I do this. I don't understand. I'm not a hassle that way. I'm no bother to him. My foster parents loved me this way. Look at the way I'm talking. It scares me. I need to cry.

My darling Mark just called. He's so sweet. I love him so wonderfully. I just need to get outside everyday as much as possible. It is so depressing inside, especially if you are inactive. I'm also going on the How Eating Program starting tomorrow. It's not a diet—kind of strange but beautiful. Daddy Ken wants me to do this. I'm going to dress up nicely for Mark Sunday night. Maybe I'll do a striptease for him. I found me schedule book—woohoo. I am willing to die for Mark. It's sad, but beautiful—sad if he doesn't feel the same way. I just want to have fun—that is all I want to do with him—just be happy. I know we have a great time together.

Well, I just have to say something important. I have written in this journal in all moods—have had the world in many perspectives, bit even though I've been angry at Mark and said I hated him, I never meant it. I have always loved him through everything.

June 25

I sit here with my untamed piano, untamed mind, untamed heart, with the music I only know, within myself. My mother is alive! Screaming viciously, laughing viciously, Jekyll and Hyde. Mommy Dearest, dearest, looks like my name.

My untamed music flows from inside, when I take the cuffs off, my mind set free, let off its duty to control.

Passion is the brink-pit that falls below the faulty earth, like a volcano, there it flows, in the moist safe darkness where even flowers cannot see it. My voice has come to stand by me now, above the ground. I stand guard to protect what they don't know exists, but can feel something, underneath my skull, discrete mannerisms, a raging whore, who wants to be beaten to a bloody pulp.

It is hard for me to carry these words into my journal. I anger with my beast. My mother holding one breast, my father clutching the other, the bind what my lover tries to touch, he hopes escape, he whispers escape from his soft lips, yet my heart is left with no protection.

I now lay in a bath of blood clutching my poetry to my chest. I hold my breasts bundled safely. The blood tries to exchange with my own, my skin acts as the barrier, that a fetus has with its mother, only exchanging food but never touches, exchanges with my mother's blood.

Parent naked tall ghosts, look down at me, like aliens, so I close my eyes, towards the fear and pretend to sleep peacefully. My music is untamed, that's why it's pure. My heart is untamed. That's why I'm pure and true.

Smoke alarm went off because eggs boiled. Pow, out on wall, devil dog hound of hell comes down street with look like master.

Fido chases me around the house because tuna. Fido sits on chair where I set up to do paper, with face positioned to blow on me. Blinds fell off when smoke alarm went off. Prank phone calls, nobody talks. Fido stares at self in mirror. Somebody peed on floor. Fido got catnip bag, got high. Boring birds still talking, don't get it, what is there to talk so much about. Cleaned toaster oven and bird cage, cat bowls and placemat. Found a bug that popped. Touch it, made a little crack or pop sound and flipped in the air, tried killing it with Fantastic.

While walking dog back, old woman stopped in car and started talking to dog. We both looked at her like we don't get it.

Ken stopped by, a little weird. I found out that the manager's Steve, the weirdo. Ken keeps telling me how attractive I am and if he weren't married and younger, steal me away. What's your point? Duh! Nice and polite but weird. I've been sneezing so much.

    Yum!!!
    Mark and my 8 month anniversary today.
    Told me more about HOW and have to write out
    Breakfast 1 oz cereal
            8 oz skim
            1–2 meat
            4 oz yoghurt
            1 fruit
    Lunch 4 oz protein
            2 cups salad or
            1 cup veg and 1 cup salad
    Dinner 4 oz protein
            2 cup veg
            1 cup salad

MA 1 oz cereal
    8 oz milk
    1 fruit

I love Mark.

Had dream, resolution dream, talk to Mom, as girlfriend. She wanted to get life on. She knew she was sick, apologized, familiar sense about her, as if it were me. I told her didn't tell Mark. My Mom was alive, restless, now alive and better, decision, do. I want to add her to my life. Weird dream. I have to tell Mark my Mom's alive. It was sad, painful and beautiful.

Pretty sluggish today. Have to bring trash out. Felt a little gross today. Not much at all. I'm so tired. Mark, come home tomorrow night.

P.S. I just wrote a new piano piece. It's all evolving before me, incredible. I have to write some more poetry. I wish I'd brought my book.

It's weird how last week I was looking up on how to make hair grow faster. And this week Ken wants to go on HOW which has a majority of protein which makes my hair grow fast.

> [There followed a "score" for a dance.]
> First when there's nothing
> but a slow blowing down
> and your fears seem to hide deep inside your mind
> all alone I have cried
> silent tears full of pride
> in world made of steel, made of stone
> what a feeling
> dream believer
> I can have it all
> now I'm dancing for my life
> take your passions and make it happen
> just come on through and I'm dancing through my life
> I made a new piano piece.

> shattered dreams I have known
> but I want to be
> I will stand on my own stand strong I won't go wrong
> follow my way because I will always stay
> by my side with no dismay on my own
> here I cry, here I laugh
> but my heart will always fast
> my freedom inside my mind will always be mine
> I will try, again, never to look where I fall
> but only where I begin

the music is my own, the rhythm, the pace
it won't be my last fast
here I go again, further ahead than where I once began
I begin

Little affirmation, simple/pure lyrics. Who says I can't? No one.

June 26

I awoke to police sirens. It's so confusing. I'm petrified. Reminds me of my Dad. When neighbors would call police on him, when he was beating my Mom. I was so scared all the time. Every time I thought would be the last I'd see my mother. I figured one of these times he would actually kill her, or vice versa. The first always seemed more likely. Oh, I hate this terror. I hate it so much. I think I'll make a pot of coffee or something. I hate this fear. I'm so afraid someone is going to come down here and hurt me. Not the police but my biological father. Oh, all the nights being afraid. He would sometimes disappear for a few days after each beating. We would be scared all the time. I slept with a knife under my pillow in my heart. A car just came by. It was mellow to hear the tires roll against the pavement. There are two people, man and woman, fighting outside. I wonder if the police are there. I'm afraid to look. They have Spanish accents. Oh, my breathing is so fast and shallow. Ahhhhh! Oh, I'm so frightened. I refuse to sleep tonight. I can't do it. Arg!
12 AM
Ewwwww! A love bug just flew into my hair. Kitty!!!!! Bramble most stubborn baby! But so cute. He got scared because of police and ran to my room. I felt bad and gave him a pretzel. Wow, Kitty just made a purr/meow sound. Yes. I heard him. Finally. Now he's drinking, such a loud slurpy durp. I need to laugh. Ha! ha! ha! ha! I'm so scared about this paper, almost 3 book themes down, 5–6 more to go. Need to lay down again, try to sleep.

    Schedule—try to sleep till 6 or 7 AM
              7–9 themes HOW breakfast
              10–12 write paper
              1–8 type paper

   everything covered
    I'll be o.k.
   There are people who just dream and there are people who live them.

I cannot deny the reality of life and my heart, mind, soul, etc., by zoning out and hiding. If I start to do this, I have to get out and move to gain perspective. Trigger, need, respond.

June 26

I had to feed Bramble two whole pretzels today. I made him go up and down stairs.

I had to put Fido outside in the porch because she was chasing me around again with Tuna. Well, me with Tuna. Kitty was licking faucet. I turned the water on a tiny bit, so a drip came out, and she was overjoyed with her slurp grin. I hate this fucking paper. I have to let myself brainstorm through it once and add things in. It had better make 20 pages. I hope Mark lets me borrow his typewriter. These birds are still talking. What is so damn interesting to talk about? But they seem happy. Oh, sweet simplicity, how I crave thee.

Ken called today and apologized if it made me uncomfortable when he kissed me. I'm glad I was honest with him and that he brought it up. I think I have some sort of hangover.

Kitty is attempting to go out to the front porch. So careful and graceful about watching out for Fido. I love this cat. I want to take her home with me. Even though Fido is so affectionate with me and gives me all this attention, I think I identify a lot more with Kitty, but not completely. I'm so sad, overwhelmed, unfocused. How am I going to get a good grade on this paper? Oh, so stressful and anxiety-stricken. Please God, help me with this paper. Help me create a paper of the highest quality and depth. I've already got a format.

I hate this heavy, stuck feeling. I hate it. I always run from situations that give me this feeling. I don't want this stuck, tied-down way I get when people get close to me. I hate it. It's so damn uncomfortable. I don't deal well with this. I feel a PTSD-attack coming on. It's not good. I need to get out, somehow, run away, be free.

I'm so frightened. I'm freaking out. I need to get out of here NOW! I hate this. I need to go to the park or something, but I don't know what direction that would be in. I want to hide somewhere.

I can't help but think about people dying that are very close to me. If anything would happen, I don't know what I'd do. I risk so much when I let people get close to me—weak or strong—who gives a fuck—it's a very scary place to be.

I've been numbing out—that is not a good thing. I have to stay conscious and focused about everything. I need to but some herbal tinctures for depression. I have given up all breads, pasta, sugar and slowly giving up caffeine and fake sugar. I need to do it. There honestly—in my heart—I know no other way of being better. This is the best. I want to purify my mind and spirit and body.

I hate the way I've been reacting to situations, but I've been getting a lot better. My focus is good. It used to be on how to prevent someone from hurting and controlling me. I left me unfree. Then it was how not to hurt anyone, anytime. That's ridiculous and puts my heart out to people who don't deserve someone else's heart. Now it's to be free with myself and my life to be happy. I know the other two will fall into place around this theme. I haven't gone outside yet for a long walk. However, I will tonight around 8:00 PM. I need to move around. I know I can't be perfect. So I won't try. It is a shallow empty pursuit is life anyway. There is no sense. It is being true to my dreams, heart, mind, circumstances, instinctual calculation—this is where my other actions will come from—the energy source being my soul. This is peace. I do open myself to the true fact of possibly being wrong and mistakes, but not willing to accept this would prevent me from establishing rewarding experiences and growth.

I wish Mark would write me more. Words on paper mean so much to me. Oh well! I suppose I can't have ANYTHING TANGIBLE. I've discovered that Bramble is a—well, I renamed him—Froggy-Doggy because of his long tongue.

June 27   2:00AM

I feel so suicidal. People still don't understand me—thought a few did. Well obviously, not really. I want to do. My heart hurts. Everything I ever wrote about marriage and relationships are true. Everything bad I've ever saw and learned as a child is true. I'm so hurt. Mark still doesn't understand me. I feel like time is running out for me. He told me his Mom has been acting all prissy. I suppose she's right. I won't be the one Mark will love that much to want to marry. Why do I dare to dream when all is truly here—my reality. Nobody would ever want to keep me. Just thinking about it made my heart happy for a little while. I suppose that's all I'm meant to have with people I love, just a little while, until something better and fresh, untainted, untouched by bad things, someone who doesn't need to fight. So hard to stay here, somewhere, anywhere, to live some life force.

I'm so hurt! I know everything I say, I never said good things about these guys to make him jealous. JUST facts about what he wanted to know, and I only speak in ideas of comparing situations and experiences—wrong or right—I do not lack empathy for anyone, but I do compare degree of losses, number of losses—wrong or right. That is what I see as survival. But I know someone else would see something different as survival or strength. But this is what I truly declare it to be. In my heart and mind, this is my definition. It does not tear down another's—people—people.

Mark got in a huge fight with me. He said that he couldn't deal with going out with me anymore. Basically, to sum it up is that we had a really bad time communicating about what we both really need to talk about and comment on. I love him so much. I want the same thing he does. I have dreams too. I so much want us to connect on everything, and I know we can. I hate when either one of us gets jealous. It hurts our relationship. I have gotten so much better since I've realized this. We are both so young. We question (take apart) everything to see how it works. We have to or we would live our lives blindly like other people around us.

Thank God we got back together. I knew it is so stupid to let my insecurities play such a huge part in my life and relationships. How else do I intend to get over them—by going against my fears—insecurities.

Basically, the point here is I love him. Sometimes I get paralyzed when we are together, and I am overwhelmed with such deep utter love and caring for him.

God, I need to draw so badly. O promise from this point on, I'll never keep anything from. I lay Steve, Kevin, Scott, Mom, Dad down to rest. Melissa and etc.

PEACE OF MIND ACHIEVED WHEN LET GO!!

June 28

Mark just left. I feel sad because I don't ever want to leave him. The way I've survived through the years is establish the strong understanding that I will leave someday on the (fear) they will leave someday. I look in his eye, and I feel forever in my heart. But how can I think such a way? He's not mine to keep. I wish he was. I wish we'd always be together. I love him so much. I feel the strongest feeling of wanting to marry him.

But we are both so young still. Life has so much to offer us in the future, changes, etc. I know he wants to be with lots of people (girls). I really don't care about that for myself. However, I understand the need to experiment with experience. One must know what's out there before you make a solid choice of one way of living or so. I don't want to interfere with his plans of getting married when he's 40. I'm not going to be one of those women who hound their lovers with intimidation, anger, and whatever else they do to trap them. It's not my personality. It's stupid. I don't want to *make* someone commit. It's not fair at all. But I do think of marriage often. It's all romantic in every way. The idea of both of us finishing school, learning about and loving each other more. Late twenties or early thirties getting married, being able to have our own careers and be financially set. Give him a beautiful family and living quietly for the rest of our lives. With some sort of central partner and home base where we both can be safe and at peace.

I just can imagine sharing these things with him. I know we both need time to ourselves, to grow and become more whole and discover what we want. I really want him to think of these things—or basically want him to love me as much as to commit himself. I can't help it. Maybe I'm old fashioned. I think marriage is the ultimate declaration of love.

It makes me cry when I think about it. I try to be realistic in the situation. However, my heart is very real in these beautiful dreams and desires. I'll try to clear my head of such things. It's not fair, and it is too early.

Mark is such a wonderful lover. He's gentle and then very intense. He is so sensitive to everything that is going on with me. I've masturbated to him all weekend. I'm sure he'd love to know that I feel a lot more free with my orgasms. It's a very free sensation to feel more at ease with my sexuality. I like when he gets rough with me and takes total control of the entire situation. I feel the sensation overcome my body because I'm not fighting him, and he is so passionate. I feel that he really wants me this way. He said he wants me to dance for him. I really want to but not yet. I want to go away with him somewhere when I do. There are so many things I want to do with him and to him, I really want to make him scream. I feel so passionate toward him which is very rare for me. I usually start getting scared, but I don't feel that way. I want to excite him so much. But how I wish we could have a huge bed. Then we can roll around so much. I really love being with him. I love him so much. I want to go away with him for a few days and . . . make love all day and night, until we are both unable to take it anymore.

That would be wonderful. I know I wouldn't feel inhibited in any way. Hmmmm! Ohhhh Mark!. In EVERYWAY. SUCH A BEAUTIFUL PERSON.

I snapped so bad at Mark today. It was so damn pointless. I was frustrated that he wasn't getting his paper work done. I could [have] acted better. I just couldn't help but get frustrated. I know how hard it is to stay on top of paperwork. It is so easy. It doesn't take much effort anymore like it used to. I think he can be so self-sabotaging. It is sad. I don't think he has his perspective down. There is, well are, these disgusting maintenance men who don't look, but stare at me. What's their problem? Ever seen a damn girl before, for God's sake? I'd beat the shit out of them if I could. Just because I could. This I'm sure is the reason these dorks stare at me. I just act like a complete snot—just. I just want people to leave me the fuck alone.

I don't know how to approach the Emmons absence issue. He told me not to worry about it. I really hate him today. He annoys the shit out of me. So does Trixie partially. She can be so damn superficial. I'm glad I started not to give a shit or thought to losing weight anymore. Well, all I have to do is write out Emmons's paper—skim reading and study, take final and it's all over. I don't want an F. And write a note about the absences. Jerk! He told me not to worry about it.

I am feeling so damn deep and close to Mark nowadays. So safe. Well, secure. Such an odd feeling. I don't know I've ever felt like this with anyone before. It almost sounds like the perfect cheesy line. Whatever. I just want to cut to the base.

I feel amazingly close and connected with him. It's very exciting. It's pouring outside. Blah.

But it is so beautiful. I hate magazines nowadays. It makes me so nauseous looking at them. It couldn't be 4:00 PM already. I hope Mark fills out those forms and sends it in. I'll follow it through up here. I have to take a nap since I'll be studying all night. I want an A+ on this quiz and an A+ on this paper. I pray God, please let me do well in his class—well, these classes. I feel myself changing and maturing so much lately. I feel so much more at peace with myself. I'm so incredibly happy and overwhelmed with this.

I called Joyce. Everything seems a lot more clear. I like being assertive with people.

I hope Mark. Wait, I have to call Registrar to check processing of the letter throughout the system of Medicaid withdrawal for Mark. Well, I have to go. I can't really focus on getting some [?]. I have to go.

Whatever!

I knew Mark must be dying to read my diary. I guess I would be too. There is so much in here concerning him, but. However, it is so damn repetitious. I have to move on to a different degree of expressing myself.

Well, I just sent Mark his card. I talked to Mary Florence. I've been calling her Florid to her face. She seemed highly annoyed at this, but anyway she did help me make the connection with Mark.

Anyway, this weekend, as I mentioned a little before, Mark wanted to break up with me. It really broke my heart. I have put so much thought and time into "us." I always spent so much time trying to figure out what would make him happier, help him, why he acts the way he does. I felt so lost. But, despite that, I knew I'd survive somehow. I'd deal with this situation the way I've dealt with all the others.

About two weeks ago, after Mark dropped me off, I came to school around 11 PM at night. It was terrible. I felt so frightened for a while. I turned around when I was walking down the hall, and there was a skinny guy with his tie untied walking in small fast steps, moving closer to me. I turned around, acted calm and gave him the biggest don't fuck with me look ever. Today I sat down in the student center, in the hallway upstairs, and he was sitting at the other end staring at me. I gave him the bitchiest look ever. He was trying to intimidate me. Despite how I act, I don't get intimidated that easily. I knew it was him. I recognized him so clearly. I don't think I told Mark about this, but I wonder if somehow I brought this upon myself. I don't want to seem all paranoid because of what happened last year on campus. I'm a bit worried. I don't know how to report him. All he does is watch me outright, viciously. I'm a bit afraid of what happened last year being some sort of prediction for this year, a setup of sorts.

I suppose it will go away, somehow.

I am amazing sensing things about people. I have a strong intuitive sense. I very rarely think situations exist like this unless they truly do.

I'm frightened. He almost fits last year's description of the same guy.

I don't know what this all means. He has a very angry sense about him.

If anything happens, if it does, I'm dead. My life is over. All the safety net I've manipulated will fall apart in the courtroom. Things will come up and be said.

The police have records of what happened last year. I wouldn't want that to be brought up again in any kind of way.

But then again, I crave this to happen for some reason. I don't know why. Maybe because I associate love with hurt, sometimes. Not all the times, but sometimes. As equally I love, the depth of hurt is the same too, black = white— same percentage—doesn't mean it's true for everything, but it is somehow. I've been somehow conditioned by my mother to feel and think this way. I feel like I'm suffocating every time I think of my mother, my past, my love for her. I HATE YOU, GOD, FOR HURTING HER AND ME! I HATE YOU FOR THE PAIN OF THE WORLD. For every cry a child makes out of pain to every adult woman and man's cry out of pain. My HEART CAN'T understand you logic here. I CANNOT DENY MY OWN HEART AND TRUTHS. THAT IT IS WRONG—THAT UNFAIR CRIMES HAVE TO BE ABOLISHED— THAT THE CRY OF THESE PEOPLE HAVE TO BE HEARD. I [HATE] THIS FUCKING SYSTEM. IT DOES NOT benefit the good of the people. WHERE IS THE FUCKING TRUTH, THE SOLUTION TO THE PROBLEM. AHHHHHHHHHHH!

Commentaries

4 The Complexity of Suicide
Exploring Katie's Diary Through a Bioecological Lens

John F. Gunn III

One of the most fascinating things about suicide, from my perspective, is the duality of suicide. I see suicide as immensely complex and yet, at the same time, simple. This stems from considering the ultimate versus the proximal causes of a suicide death. In referencing the ultimate cause of suicide, I am speaking of the most basic motivation—which I, and many others, would argue is to escape from pain. That, in itself, is not complicated. We can all understand the desire to escape from pain although many of us in the field, myself included, do not understand what it is like to desire to escape from the type of anguish that motivates an individual to die by suicide. The proximal cause of suicide, however, is immensely complex. Proximal causes are less abstract than ultimate causes and relate more directly to an individual's decision to die by suicide. Knowing that suicide is about a desire to escape from pain (assuming that is the ultimate cause) is less useful than understanding the connection between events and experiences in an individual's life and the development of *their* pain.

In this chapter, I am seeking to illuminate the complexity of suicide by examining the diary left by Katie. Much of the work in suicidology is criticized as being "psychocentric," that is, the pathologizing of human problems as being predominantly a psychological/individual issue (Marsh, 2020). When attempting to understand suicide, we often look to the characteristics of the individual. Were they mentally ill? Did they seek help? Had they experienced recent loss? Were they engaging in self-harming behaviors? Many of the questions we ask focus solely on how the *individual* contributed to their death, thereby ignoring situational factors. I would never argue that we should abandon understanding suicide at the individual level, but I would stress the importance of considering the individual within their ecological settings. In order to do this, I draw heavily from Bronfenbrenner's bioecological theory (Bronfenbrenner & Morris, 2006) in discussing the themes found in Katie's diary. I will outline this theory in greater detail later followed by a discussion of the themes gleamed from Katie's diary. Examples will be drawn directly from the first month of her diary which can be seen in Chapter 3.

DOI: 10.4324/9781003125655-5

Bronfenbrenner's Theory

Bioecological theory places human development within the context of a series of nested ecological systems that influence an individual at various levels. Figure 4.1 illustrates these nested ecosystems. At the center is the *individual* whose biological and dispositional characteristics cannot be ignored. The *microsystem* refers to the environments that the individual directly interacts with, such as friend groups, family, work environment and so forth. The *mesosystem* refers to the interactions between microsystems, such as the interaction between friends and family. The *exosystem* refers to the environment that does not directly influence an individual but that still impacts them. For example, a spouse's work environment does not, necessarily, directly impact an individual, but it nevertheless can influence an individual through its impact on their spouse. At the greatest abstraction from the individual is the *macrosystem* which encompasses culture, social, economic and legal environments in which an individual dwells. Finally, the *chronosystem* places all of this within the context of time, such as developmental period and historic events.

As can be seen, bioecological theory allows an examination of an individual's life within the context of these various ecosystems. It is with a focus on this framework that I will examine the themes within Katie's diary, drawing examples from the first month of the diary presented in Chapter 3.

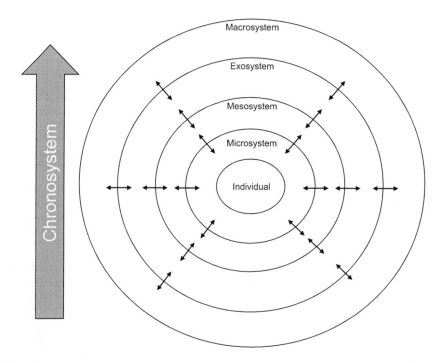

Figure 4.1 Outline of Bronfenbrenner's bioecological model

Themes Within the Diary

Individual Themes

Depression

I shall start my discussion of the themes within the diary with individual-level factors that Katie highlights in her writings. Katie's history (discussed in Chapter 2) establishes that she was diagnosed with a mood disorder, and you see this expressed periodically in the first month of her diary. The opening line of the diary states, "I am so depressed and suicidal. My body feels restless and tired." She talks about being "sad, overwhelmed, and unfocused" and there are constant references to despondency and crying, although these are frequently tied to interpersonal interactions. Among college students, as Katie was, there is a strong relationship between depression and suicide, with suicidal thoughts common among those with depression (Garlow et al., 2008). I do not wish to oversell the relationship between mental illness and suicide, however. It is certainly true that the two can be related, but many who die by suicide do not have a diagnosed or documented mental illness meaning that mental illness is insufficient in explaining why people die by suicide (Schmutte et al., 2021).

The IPTS (see Chapter 5) places loneliness or a lack of belonging front and center in explaining suicidal behavior. Katie makes consistent references to being lonely:

> "I feel so unbelievably lonely and battered."
>
> (June 8, year 1)
>
> "I don't feel I have any friends. I feel so alone."
>
> (June 14, year 1)
>
> "I feel so unabandoned and unconnected with everyone."
>
> (June 14, year 1)
>
> "I feel this cold isolation feeling, abandoned, alone, with nowhere to go, no one to go to."
>
> (June 16, year 1)

It is impossible to read through Katie's diary and not get a sense of her feelings of isolation and lack of belonging. Katie also expresses a lot of devaluation of herself, frequently writing about hating herself ("I hate myself"), being a failure ("I have failed and lived a hollow existence") and being concerned with being a burden, another important factor of the IPTS ("I don't want to bother anyone with my battle" and "I repress so much in order to be coherent—not a burden"). Generally speaking, the IPTS finds robust support in the field, and Katie in relation to the IPTS is discussed at greater length in Chapter 5.

Katie's devaluation of herself extends to her constant references to her body image and her eating disorder. Early in June of year 1, Katie wrote "I really hate my body" then later that month when referencing Mark's affair:

> I had all these visions of how beautiful this girl was and how skinny. I compared myself not only to her, but to other girls who caught his interest. I was so meticulous with myself. I hated my body so much. I tried going on so many damn diets in the past eight months so I would be more beautiful to him and most of all to myself so I wouldn't have to compete. I failed miserably on all of them, whether purposely or accidentally I did. A lot of this had to do with my sincere need to be wanted and cared about. I always get like this if I care about someone, be this friend or relationship.

Throughout the diary, Katie obsesses over her eating and her weight, experiencing lows whenever she perceives herself as eating poorly and higher moods when she feels she has done well. She compares herself to other girls she sees in college, convinced that Mark is more attracted to them. This is exacerbated by the fact that Mark, in fact, cheated on her previously. In a similar entry to the one mentioned earlier on July 7, year 1, Katie talks more about "pretty and thin" girls who catch Mark's attention more. Eating disorders and, to a lesser extent, perceiving your body image negatively have been previously linked to suicidal thoughts and behaviors (Brausch & Gutierrez, 2009; Runfola et al., 2014).

In addition to these, a number of other risk factors for suicide at the individual level are highlighted throughout the diary, though to a lesser extent. At one point, Katie references feeling "so bound up inside and trapped in the feelings of my childhood, trapped, not able to move" and references wanting to feel free (e.g., "Every morning I want to feel my freedom" and "Where the hell is my freedom"). Feeling trapped, as if there is no escape from one's circumstances, has been previously linked to suicide (Taylor et al., 2011). Indeed, a sense of being trapped is a central component of the Integrated Motivational Volitional (IMV) model of suicide discussed in greater detail in Chapter 7. Also referenced in this first month of Katie's diary are feelings of pain (e.g., "I'm sick of numbing out my feelings. I'm in such pain and disarray" and "Please take all this pain away"). Psychological pain (often referred to as psychache) has a long history in suicide research and is often associated with suicidal thoughts and behaviors (Mento et al., 2020). Psychological pain is a central theme of many theories of suicide such as the 3ST of suicide discussed at length in Chapter 6.

Micro-Level Themes

By far the most common themes throughout the first month of the diary are tied to Katie's more immediate environment. Many of Katie's diary writings focus on interpersonal conflict and issues with her relationship with Mark. Katie perceives herself as struggling to connect with people (e.g., "I have a hard time getting along with people") and often feels harmed by them (e.g.,

"People are so mean and selfish"). Although interpersonal stressors such as these are present, the majority of themes that emerge from the micro level are surrounding her relationship with Mark. Katie's writings regarding Mark fluctuate frequently. Some writings paint Mark as instrumental to her happiness:

> "He makes me feel alive and free in most ways. When I'm with him, I forget that I have problems."
>
> (June 24, year 1)

> "I am feeling so damn deep and close to Mark nowadays. So safe. Well, secure. Such an odd feeling. I don't know I've ever felt like this with anyone before. It almost sounds like the perfect cheesy line."
>
> (June 28, year 1)

However, though at times Katie seems to feel that Mark is her salvation or her respite from her pain—at other times, he is portrayed as instrumental in her suffering:

> "Mark will probably read this and hate me. I don't care. He is so emotionally abusive at times and doesn't realize it. I know it comes from the way he treats himself—it hits people he's close with."
>
> (June 16, year 1)

> "I really thought he loved me. I guess it's because my heart wanted it so. I hate the way I've treated him, but I was so angry with him. It's all over."
>
> (June 16, year 1)

> "It really devastated me, about the Claudia thing. I knew when I first heard about the situation from Stacy, Maggie, Kristin, I knew it would cause me heartache. I don't know what happened. When I heard this, my heart crashed. It hurt. I hurt because I had genuine feelings for him."
>
> (June 22, year 1)

> "MARK DOESN'T LOVE ME. Well I am blowing things out of proportion here. Hm. He got all mad at me because I called him last night. 4:00 AM . . . Bad day—thought about Mark not wanting to be with me and lots of other stuff."
>
> (July 9, year 1)

On at least one occasion, there may have also been an incident of interpersonal violence when Katie says, "I can't believe he hit me." This comes up shortly after referencing Mark, giving the impression that he struck her at some point. Their relationship is certainly one of the most common themes throughout the diary and, in the first month, Katie's pain over the affair and conflict in their relationship is made evident throughout. Relationship difficulties, especially unresolved issues, can have a negative impact on well-being and have been linked to suicidal thoughts (Till et al., 2016).

Chronosystem Themes

Another major theme, and perhaps one that is even more common than her relationship with Mark, is in the trauma experienced by Katie in her past. Katie was sexually abused and emotionally abused by her parents, and these themes are common throughout the first month of her diary:

> "I suppose a big part of the upset lies in the past."
>
> (June 8, year 1)

> "I hate all this crap. Why can't life just fucking move on completely. . . . I don't need my mother in my life anymore. I never needed someone who was so sick and raped me—my mind, heart, soul. Buy why do I love and miss her so much?"
>
> (June 14, year 1)

> "I also had flashbacks, and Mark held me. I was shaking so badly."
>
> (June 22, year 1)

> "I feel like I'm carrying this feeling of abuse—it sucks . . . OH MOMMY. WHERE ARE YOU!! I FEEL DADDY'S SICK PRESENCE HERE. ALL DONE."
>
> (July 1, year 1)

The trauma Katie experienced in her past is carried with her, and these brief exerts do not do justice to the extent to which Katie references her abuse and its aftermath. Like the other factors highlighted thus far, sexual abuse in childhood is linked to both experiences of mental distress (such as depression) and suicidal thoughts and behaviors (Molnar et al., 2001).

Macro-Level Themes

Macro-level themes, such as cultural or societal risk factors, are harder to gauge in the diary, perhaps simply because these are less commonly discussed in journals and diaries. However, it is possible to look back over the themes discussed so far and draw connections to societal and cultural factors. Katie's anorexia and negative view of her body may be psychological in nature, but it is influenced heavily from the greater society in which she lives. Women are inundated with images of the "ideal" body type in advertisements and other forms of media. They are exposed to a culture that shames people for being fat or makes judgments about their health or self-control based on their body size. As a survivor of sexual abuse, Katie has to deal with not only the trauma of her abuse but also the messaging surrounding cultural and societal ideals surrounding women and sexuality. She talks about being made to feel like a "slut" by her mother. Katie is indisputably a victim and yet, with cultural messages of the importance of purity of the female body and restrictions on female sexuality, she is unshielded from feelings of shame.

Interactions Across Systems

If you look back at the figure highlighting Bronfenbrenner's bioecological theory, in addition to the various spheres of influence, there are also arrows connecting them all together. These are arguably the most important to consider. These systems do not exist in isolation but rather interact and influence each other. An individual's experiences of depression may be exacerbated by interpersonal stress, such as that experienced when a significant other betrays them sexually with another, but so too can an individual's depression make it harder to connect to and interact with others. Couple this with a society that regularly discriminates against individuals living with depression and you start to see the complexity of human behavior and the factors that influence. Suicide is no exception to this.

Consider Figure 4.2, which takes the themes that have been discussed in this chapter and places them together in the various spheres of influence. Though certainly not exhaustive, we can see how these themes may influence Katie and her ultimate death by suicide. Katie expressed feeling like a burden. She frequently spoke of feeling lonely and in intense pain, from which she felt she could not escape. She also had a very negative perspective of her self-worth and her body, making constant references to her supposed failures to eat properly or lose weight. These individual-level factors alone would cause a great deal of distress, but couple these with the fact that she was dealing with relationship issues, such as Mark's infidelity and trauma of childhood sexual abuse and you get a clearer picture of Katie's life and her decision to die by suicide.

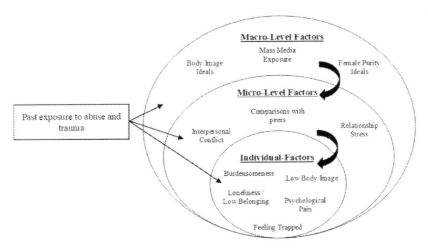

Figure 4.2 Themes from Katie's diary

Conclusion

This chapter set out to highlight how a bioecological viewing of Katie's diary, with a focus on the first month of her diary (provided in Chapter 3), might provide a context for her death. Often in suicidology, we focus wholly on the internal workings of the mind, taking a psychocentric approach to explaining suicide (Marsh, 2020). However, although an individual's psychology is important in understanding their suicide, their choice does not exist in a vacuum. Instead, individuals are nested within an immediate environment, surrounded by peers, in a larger cultural context and with life histories. Katie, like all people, was a complex individual whose suicide is no less complex.

Throughout my reading of her diary, I attempted to draw out relevant material, but it is important to keep in mind that what material stood out to me may very well differ from that which is noted by others. As a researcher without lived experience and a man with a significant amount of privilege, the details that drew my attention may certainly not draw the attention of others, and there are almost certainly things I have missed. You, the reader, may see what draws your attention.

References

Brausch, A. M., & Gutierrez, P. M. (2009). The role of body image and disordered eating as risk factors for depression and suicidal ideation in adolescents. *Suicide & Life-Threatening Behavior, 39*, 58–71.

Bronfenbrenner, U., & Morris, P. A. (2006). The bioecological model of human development. In W. Damon & R. M. Lerner (Eds.), *Handbook of child psychology, vol 1: Theoretical models of human development* (6th ed., pp. 793–828). New York: Wiley.

Garlow, S. J., Rosenberg, J., Moore, J. D., Haas, A. P., Koestner, B. S., Hendin, H., & Nemeroff, C. B. (2008). Depression, desperation, and suicidal ideation in college students: Results from the American Foundation for Suicide Prevention College Screening Project at Emory University. *Depression & Anxiety, 25*, 482–488.

Marsh, I. (2020). The social production of psychocentric knowledge in suicidology. *Social Epistemology, 34*, 544–554.

Mento, C., Silvestri, M. C., Muscatello, M. R. A., Rizzo, A., Celebre, L., Bruno, A., & Zoccali, A. R. (2020). Psychological pain and risk of suicide in adolescence. *International Journal of Adolescent Medicine & Health*, early online access.

Molnar, B. E., Berkman, L. F., & Buka, S. L. (2001). Psychopathology, childhood sexual abuse, and other childhood adversities: Relative links to subsequent suicidal behaviour in the US. *Psychological Medicine, 31*, 965–977.

Runfola, C. D., Thornton, L. M., Pisetsky, E. M., Bulik, C. M., & Birgegard, A. (2014). Self-image and suicide in a Swedish national eating disorders clinical register. *Comprehensive Psychiatry, 55*, 439–449.

Schmutte, T., Costa, M., Hammer, P., & Davidson, L. (2021). Comparisons between suicide in persons with serious mental illness, other mental disorders, or no known mental illness: Results from 37 U.S. states, 2003–2017. *Schizophrenia Research, 228*, 74–82.

Taylor, P. J., Gooding, P., Wood, A. M., & Tarrier, N. (2011). The role of defeat and entrapment in depression, anxiety, and suicide. *Psychological Bulletin, 137*, 391–420.

Till, B., Tran, U. S., & Neiderkrotenthaler, T. (2016). Relationship satisfaction and risk factors for suicide. *Crisis, 38*, 7–16.

5 Katie From the Perspective of the Interpersonal Theory of Suicide

David Lester

The 21st century has seen several new theories of suicide proposed, and the theory that has captured most interest is the Interpersonal Theory of Suicide, also known as the Interpersonal-Psychological Theory of Suicide (IPTS), proposed by Thomas Joiner (Joiner, 2005). Joiner proposed that two socio-psychological factors were present in those who chose to die by suicide: thwarted belongingness (i.e., perceptions of disturbed interpersonal relationships) and perceived burdensomeness (i.e., believing one is a burden on others). These alone were not enough, however, to explain death by suicide. Those who die by suicide also had to have the acquired capability for suicide which involved two factors: increased pain tolerance (so that they can endure the pain that might be involved in the suicidal act) and a reduced fear of death.

While research into the IPTS model has been generally supportive (Chu et al., 2017), the theory has been criticized on several grounds. Some have claimed that thwarted belongingness is not a new idea. Emile Durkheim (Durkheim, 1897) proposed that too little social integration was a risk factor for suicide, resulting in a type of suicide which he called *egoistic suicide*. Similarly, Raoul Naroll proposed that suicide was more likely in those who were *socially disoriented*, that is, those who lose or lack basic social ties, as, for example, through divorce (Lester, 1995; Naroll, 1963). However, feeling that one is burden to others, although mentioned peripherally in the past in connection with suicide, had not, prior to Joiner's theory, become a major focus for understanding suicide. Finally, the concept of the capability of dying by suicide explained a number of past experiences of suicide that increase the risk of suicide, such as childhood experiences of abuse, experience of combat in war and previous non-lethal attempts at suicide. Many of these criticisms have been recently outlined by Hjelmeland and Knizek (2020). One criticism that the theory's claim to explain *all suicides* is an overreach has been explored by Gunn and colleagues (2012). In a sample of 261 Australian suicide notes, they found that thwarted belongingness was present in only 30.7% of the notes and perceived burdensomeness in only 10.3%. Only 4.2% of the notes had both themes present, thereby casting doubt on the generalizability of Joiner's theory to all suicides.

In order to explore whether the IPTS throws light on Katie's suicide, I will use a more recent broader description of the theory by Van Orden and colleagues (2010). Van Orden and colleagues, while maintaining the original conceptualization of the IPTS, expanded upon the original model by (i) introducing the role of hopelessness and (ii) elaborating the original definitions of thwarted belonging, perceived burdensomeness and the acquired capability for suicide. In this new model, hopelessness, a well-known risk factor for suicide, is seen as a stepping stone between thwarted belonging, perceived burdensomeness and the desire for suicide. Both perceived burdensomeness and thwarted belonging can result in the development of hopelessness, which then leads to the development of the desire for suicide.

Additionally, thwarted belonging (conceptualized by the phrase, "I am alone") is divided into two broad dimensions: *loneliness* and *reciprocal care*. Loneliness is conceptualized as feeling disconnected from others, while reciprocal care is conceptualized as having no one to turn to and not supporting others. Loneliness is related to living alone, having few social supports, feeling lonely and having a non-intact family unit, while reciprocal care is related to social withdrawal and experiential factors such as childhood abuse, family conflict, domestic violence and prison and jail time.

Perceived burdensomeness is also broken into two broad dimensions: *liability* and *self-hate*. Liability is conceptualized as viewing one's own death as more valuable to others than one's life, while self-hate is hating oneself. Liability is associated with distress from homelessness, incarceration, unemployment, a sense that one is unwanted or expendable or a belief that one is a burden on their family, while self-hate is associated with low self-esteem, self-blame and shame and general agitation.

The acquired capability for suicide is still viewed as being divided into the general dimensions of lowered fear of death and an elevated tolerance of physical pain and affected by experiences including a family history of suicide, serotonergic dysfunction, impulsivity, exposure to the suicide of others, combat exposure, previous suicide attempts and childhood maltreatment.

Can we find these risk factors in Katie's diary?

Katie and the IPTS

This is the first entry in Katie's diary, and it appears to show two of the components of the IPTS.

> I am so depressed and suicidal. My body feels restless and tired. I don't know who to turn to for help. I don't want to bother anyone with my battle. I've been acting out in all sorts of ways. I just feel like crying. I presume that all has to do with the fact that I love Mark [romantic partner] so deeply. I think he cares for me but, however, I don't know if it's true love for him. It definitely is for me. I really want to marry him so badly. I don't care if he reads my journal at all. I am just so stressed out. I haven't done any of my work. I have a hard time getting along with people. I really hate my body. I really hate my life where it is, with everything I am. I decided

Katie From the Perspective of the Interpersonal Theory of Suicide

to start exercising today. I need to do it every day. I leave all my life's frustrations there out on the track. God give me strength. Help me today. I feel so unbelievably lonely and battered.

For thwarted belongingness, Katie tell us that she feels lonely, she has no one to turn to (reciprocal care), she has trouble getting on with others and she doesn't trust that Mark loves her. For perceived burdensomeness, she hates her body and her life, she does not want to bother anybody and she is restless (agitation). She has low self-esteem, and she has hurt Mark.

> It sucks to let, for me to allow, to waste my life away. It's absolutely horrible. There is such a desolate feeling with this relapse. It sickens me.
> One of the main reasons I cried today was because of all the ways I have affected Mark. I hate it. It hurts me that my pain hurts someone else.

She is not hopeless yet (she has plans to improve) but, with one year before her death, she is already at high risk for suicide.

Katie's diary covers 13 months, and the quotes from her diary will be number by month.

Perceived Burdensomeness

Katie talks of being a burden throughout the diary:

> He [Mark] may want to leave because of all my burdens (month 3)
> [I'm]—sick of being a burden or acting like the embodiment of a problem or problem(s) (month 5)
> but it really made me feel like I was a burden versus a part of her life [a friend] (month 6)
> I just felt like such an utter burden to him [after breaking up with Mark] (month 6)

Katie tries to be less of a burden.

> I repress so much in order to be coherent—not a burden (month 2)
> I never want to be some sort of burden to people (month 2)
> I refuse to be a god damn burden (month 3)
> So stupid—thinking I was better than that, trying to fix myself so I'd be less of a burden for him (month 3)

Yet in the last month of her life, just 20 days prior to her death and 11 days prior to the last entry in her diary, the perception of being a burden is still strong, and she wrote: "I don't want to burden anyone at all anymore. I'm so scared of losing everything and everyone I love."

The IPTS theory does not distinguish between those who perceive themselves to be a burden and really are a burden to those in contact with them, especially friends and family members, and those who perceive being a burden but whose friends and family do not consider themselves a burden. Diekstra (1995) presented a case of a man in the Netherlands dying of cancer who wanted to end his life because he felt that he was burden to his family. Mr. L had cancer and was given no more than six months to live. He was a retired civil servant, a stubborn man with a defeatist attitude toward life. His wife was informed of his prognosis first and communicated this to her husband, after which he declared that he wished to end his life with medications. He felt that his life was useless, and he feared dependence on physicians, burdening his wife with nursing and the degeneration of his body. Mr. L's wife thought that it was too soon for him to die. Their relationship was still rewarding, and she saw that her husband could still enjoy some aspects of living, at least for a while. She did not want him to die in pain from the cancer, but she also feared that her husband might try to kill himself by other, more violent methods if he was not provided with medication, a situation that she would find traumatic.

At Diekstra's suggestion, Mr. L's wife told her husband that she thought it was too early for him to die and that she would miss him if he died at that moment. He was pleased to hear this and glad that he was still needed. He agreed to postpone the decision, but he wanted assurance that he would be given the medication when the appropriate time arrived. He was given this assurance, and he lived for two more months.

Was Katie a burden to others? She had no family in her present life, and toward the end of her life, she was becoming more isolated from friends and from Mark. Was she difficult to be with? To know this, we would have to ask Mark and her friends and hope that they would be honest. From her diary entries, she does seem to present problems for others in interpersonal relationships, but we must remember that people express thoughts and feelings in diaries that are cathartic and, on reading, seem more intense than they really are.

Katie showed self-hate in the first entry in her diary, noted earlier, saying that she hates her body and hates her life. Throughout the year, Katie says that she hates many aspects of herself and her behavior, including her jealousy, her frame of mind, her fear and terror, the impact she has on Mark and the way she has treated him, when she acts immaturely, her depressions (which make her feel hopeless), being mean to others, her emotions and her memories, her crying, what she writes in her diary, how much she sleeps, but especially her body and eating so much. She also hates God, her parents, her past pain and other people (and she mentions several specific friends and acquaintances).

The self-hate leads to self-destructive thoughts:

> I really hate myself so fucking much right now. I want to hurt myself so badly.... I hate this torture. I can't save myself right now. I want to rip up my stomach and arms so badly—with my nails—if I had any. I want to slash up my whole fucking body right now. I feel so unloved by everyone.... I HATE MYSELF. I WANT TO DIE! WHAT I DO ISN'T GOOD ENOUGH!!
>
> (month 2)

Katie also experiences shame, shame over her body, but also shame because her mother and father abused her, a common feeling in those who are abused as children who blame themselves for the abuse.

Thwarted Belonging

Katie had horrible experiences with her parents, experiences which made it difficult to have meaningful and healthy experiences with others in her life, including peers. She has a boyfriend but has strong ambivalent feelings toward him, both love and hate. The fact that he may have cheated on her with other women and that he may flirt with other women increases her ambivalence. However, it may be that Mark did not cheat on Katie and does not flirt with other women, but that this is a fear that Katie has. Studying a diary does not enable us to check facts, but the emotions expressed are real.

The ambivalence that Katie expresses toward the resources in her life (Mark and her peers) is a risk factor for suicide. Lester (1969) used a test devised by George Kelly (Kelly, 1955) to measure the people to whom one could turn for different crises (interpersonal, financial, career, etc.). Lester asked the participants to rate these people on two occasions separated by 15 minutes. On one occasion, they rated them for how much they liked the people; on the other occasion, they rated the people for how much they resented the people. The non-suicidal participants typically told the researcher to simply reverse the previous ratings (but they were told to complete the task nevertheless), and their second set of ratings was the reverse of the first set. The suicidal participants did not suggest the same reversal, and in fact, the people they rated as most liked were also rated as most resented. The suicidal participants were most dependent, therefore, on resources (people) that they liked and resented. This, of course, made it more difficult for the suicidal participants to turn to their resources for help when they were in crisis. This is the dilemma that Katie faced.

Katie has friends and acquaintances, but her state of mind makes her feel alone. She has no intact family unit, only a deceased father, a mother in a psychiatric institution and a sister who was separated from her. Interestingly, Katie's sister who gave me the diary worried that Katie expressed hatred toward her, and I was able to reassure her that Katie expressed only positive feelings toward her.

The revised version of the IPTS has the construct of reciprocal care, including the experiences of childhood abuse and family conflict in the past and social withdrawal in the present. These characterize Katie's past and present.

The Acquired Capability for Self-Harm

Katie has several factors that increase her capability for self-harm and suicide.[1] Her experience of childhood abuse is a major factor here. There is no evidence of previous self-harm or suicidal behavior, but her anorexia has subjected her to discomfort and pain and disordered eating has been linked to the acquired capability in previous work (Fink et al., 2013; Zuromski & Witte, 2015).

Katie's father was an alcoholic and abusive man, and Katie's diary indicates that he sexually abused her. Her mother divorced her husband, but then became schizophrenic and was hospitalized. Katie also indicates that her mother abused her, perhaps sexually, and Katie held her mother responsible for all her childhood trauma.[2] Katie and her sister were usually placed with different foster families, and Katie became anorexic and bulimic with frequent hospitalizations because of this.

Hopelessness

Katie expressed hopelessness throughout the diary. For example, "I did so damn terrible with my food today. It was horrible. I want to kill myself today. I hate this. I would cry, but I'm afraid I'll never stop. I feel so hopeless.... I hate it when my depressions get the worse of me. It makes me feel so hopeless. I make myself feel so hopeless" (month 1); and "It is all so damn hopeless. I hate that emotion. It is all so suffocating and killing—heart/hope killing" (month 9).

Yet 27 days before her suicide, Katie wrote, "That is the hope I believe in, that I do have control over my fate now as a fully grown, adult versus my circumstance as a child and nothing is hopeless, absolutely nothing." One wonders what happened in those 27 days and, especially, in the seven days between the last entry of the diary and her death.

Discussion

Some commentators on Joiner's IPTS have objected to his assertion that the theory is relevant to *every* suicide. Despite this, Katie's suicide is consistent with the IPTS in every way. Katie's diary has indications of thwarted belongingness, perceived burdensomeness and an acquired capability for suicide. What is interesting is that both Canetto (2004) informally and Pennebaker and Stone (2004) statistically showed that the mood in Katie's diary improved toward the end of the diary (and her life), and this makes the question of what happened in the week between Katie's last diary entry and her death by suicide of great interest, although we will never have this information.

Lester (2014) has analyzed several other diaries written by people who died by suicide, some qualitatively and some statistically, although none from the perspective of the IPTS. Many of the writers describe their disturbed interpersonal relationships, such as Cesare Pavese, Kenneth Williams, "Jim" and "Robert,"[3] providing evidence of thwarted belonging. Evidence for perceived burdensomeness is less apparent. For example, whereas Katie often viewed herself in her diary as being a burden, the word *burden* (in the sense of being a burden to others) does not appear in the other diaries studied. Of course, this does not mean that perceived burdensomeness was not present in their perception of themselves, but only that there is no evidence for this perception in their diaries.

One problem with the type of analysis of Katie's diary is whether the analysis helps us understand Katie rather than merely supporting the IPTS. Clearly, this chapter shows that Katie's suicide fits the parameters of the IPTS, but it also points to elements in Katie's thinking that indicate that suicidal behavior is likely. Although Canetto and Pennebaker and Stone, mentioned earlier, found that Katie's mood improved toward the end of the diary, the word *burden* appears on page 5 of the 175-page diary and on page 170. Her mood may have improved, but the risk factors for suicide did not change. Not only do we want to understand Katie, but we also want to prevent suicide in others, our significant others, our friends and colleagues and, for some, our patients. Hopefully understanding Katie will help us in this endeavor.

Notes

1. There is no indication from her diary that Katie had a reduced fear of death.
2. Children of alcoholic fathers often blame their mother for not protecting them from the father.
3. Some of the diaries analyzed were from ordinary individuals and given to Lester by friends or relatives of the suicide. They were given assumed names for the book in order to preserve their anonymity.

References

Canetto, S. (2004). Why did you kill yourself Katie? In D. Lester (Ed.), *Katie's diary: Unlocking the mystery of a suicide* (pp. 41–54). New York: Brunner-Routledge.

Chu, C., Buchman-Schmitt, J. M., Stanley, I. H., Hom, M. A., Tucker, R. P., Hagan, C. R., . . . & Joiner, T. E. Jr. (2017). The interpersonal theory of suicide: A systematic review and meta-analysis of a decade of cross-national research. *Psychological Bulletin, 143,* 1313–1345.

Diekstra, R. F. W. (1995). Dying in dignity. *Psychiatry & Clinical Neurosciences, 49*(supplement 1), S139–S148.

Durkheim, E. (1897). *Le suicide*. Paris, France: Felix Alcan.

Fink, E., Bodell, L., Smith, A., & Joiner, T. (2013). The joint influence of disordered eating and anxiety sensitivity on the acquired capability for suicide. *Cognitive Therapy & Research, 37,* 934–940.

Gunn, J. F., Lester, D., Haines, J., & Williams, C. L. (2012). Thwarted belongingness and perceived burdensomeness in suicide notes. *Crisis, 33,* 178–181.

Hjelmeland, H., & Knizek, B. L. (2020). The emperor's new clothes: A critical look at the interpersonal theory of suicide. *Death Studies, 44,* 168–178. https://doi.org/10.1 080/07481187.2018.1527796

Joiner, T. E. (2005). *Why people die by suicide*. Cambridge, MA: Harvard University Press.

Kelly, G. A. (1955). *The psychology of personal constructs: Vol 1 and 2*. New York: WW Norton.

Lester, D. (1969). Resentment and dependency in the suicidal individual. *Journal of General Psychology, 81,* 137–145.

Lester, D. (1995). Thwarting disorientation and suicide. *Cross-Cultural Research, 29,* 14–26.

Lester, D. (2014). *The "I" of the storm*. Warsaw, Poland: De Gruyter.
Naroll, R. (1963). *Thwarting disorientation and suicide* (Unpublished discussion paper). Northwestern University, Chicago, IL.
Pennebaker, J., & Stone, L. D. (2004). What was she trying to say? In D. Lester (Ed.), *Katie's diary: Unlocking the mystery of a suicide* (pp. 55–80). New York: Brunner-Routledge.
Van Orden, K. A., Witte, T. K., Cukrowicz, K. C., Braithwaite, S. R., Selby, E. A., & Joiner, T. E. (2010). The interpersonal theory of suicide. *Psychological Review, 117*, 575–600.
Zuromski, K. L., & Witte, T. K. (2015). Fasting and acquired capability for suicide: A test of the interpersonal-psychological theory of suicide in an undergraduate sample. *Psychiatry Research, 226*(1), 61–67.

6 Using the Three-Step Theory to Understand Katie's Desire for Suicide

E. David Klonsky and Oscar F. Cetnarowski

Can we understand suicide? This is a complicated question, not only because suicide is complex, but also because some may feel that something destructive and hurtful like suicide does not deserve understanding. We offer a counter-perspective. Millions and millions of people have died by suicide. If we do not understand suicide, then we do not have a full understanding or appreciation of human nature. Moreover, if we do not understand suicide, we are limited in our ability to help people who are suffering and considering suicide.

Katie's diary presents an opportunity to examine the weeks and days before a young woman's suicide in unique detail. This chapter considers Katie's experiences through the lens of the Three Step Theory (3ST) of suicide (Klonsky & May, 2015). We believe the 3ST can bring some measure of understanding to Katie's suicide and, more generally, help people understand and prevent suicide.

The Three-Step Theory of Suicide

The 3ST of Suicide was published in 2015 as a concise and evidence-based explanation for suicide. According to the 3ST: (a) the combination of pain and hopelessness causes suicidal desire, (b) suicidal desire becomes strong when pain exceeds connectedness and (c) various contributors to the capability for suicide facilitate the transition from strong suicidal desire to a potentially fatal suicide attempt. The first two steps of the theory, which describe the conditions under which suicidal desire is present and becomes strong, comprise the focus of this chapter. We elaborate these steps in the following paragraphs.

Step 1 of the 3ST suggests that the combination of pain and hopelessness causes suicidal desire. While people are biologically wired to fear and avoid death, we are also biologically wired to avoid pain. If a child touches a hot stove, they learn quickly not to do it again. Similarly, if one's experience of life is that it is aversive, miserable or otherwise painful, they will experience a powerful instinct to avoid the pain that life has to offer. We intentionally do not specify the sources of pain, as the list would essentially be infinite, and what causes pain for one person may cause hope for another (e.g., the end of a difficult relationship). The key point is that people are creatures of behavioral conditioning. If someone's experience of something is that it is primarily aversive or painful, they will have a powerful instinct to avoid this experience. This principle applies to all kinds of experiences, including life itself.

However, pain alone is not sufficient to cause suicidal desire. If someone finds life painful but has hope for a better future—perhaps they hope that through time or effort they can achieve a less painful, more enjoyable life—then their focus will be on achieving this better future. In contrast, if someone finds life painful and becomes hopeless that this can change, they will experience a desire to stop being alive. Thus, it is the combination of pain and hopelessness that cause suicidal desire.

Step 2 of the 3ST addresses the situation when suicidal desire becomes strong. For many people with suicidal desire, the suicidal thoughts are occasional or modest, whereas for others, suicidal desire becomes persistent and strong. The 3ST suggests that suicidal desire becomes strong when pain exceeds or overwhelms connectedness. Connectedness is defined broadly and can refer not only to valued relationships but also to a community, job, pet, cause or any sense of meaning or purpose that keeps one invested in living. In short, whereas pain provides a push away from life, connectedness is what makes life worth living. Thus, even if someone experiences frequent pain without any hope that the pain will abate, sufficient connectedness can make their desire to live greater than their desire to die. In this scenario, there will still be occasional or modest desire for suicide as a result of pain and hopelessness, but the desire to live will remain predominant. In contrast, if someone has pain and hopelessness, and their pain exceeds their connectedness (or their pain is so intense as to remove their ability to appreciate connections that were otherwise valued), the desire to die outweighs the desire to live. In this scenario, suicidal desire becomes strong.

Thus, from the perspective of the 3ST, if we want to understand someone's suicidal desire, we must understand their pain, hopelessness and connection. The remainder of this chapter views Katie's diary entries through the lens of the 3ST. We characterize the nature, intensity and sources of Katie's pain, hopelessness and disconnection, and thereby seek to understand why Katie made the decision to die.

Understanding Katie's Desire for Suicide

Katie's Pain

There is no doubt that Katie's experience of pain was intense and frequent. Pain was such a common part of Katie's life that she had "So many words for pain." Sometimes Katie characterized her pain in straightforward terms, such as "I'm in a lot of pain," or "I'm really hurting." At other times, Katie's pain took different forms, such as "anxiety," "turmoil," "scared," "absolutely awful," "tired and dry" and "lost . . . the most awful feeling in the whole world."

Perhaps not surprisingly, Katie's pain had many sources. A key source of pain was her unhappiness with her body. Katie wrote of experiencing "hate" toward her body and of her desire to get rid of "this disgusting excess weight." When Katie did not meet her weight-loss goals, she wrote of feeling "shameful," "so damn awful" and "ripped up about it." At the same time, Katie saw losing weight as a path toward happiness: "I need to get skinny and it will make me very happy." Thus, in Katie's experience, her inability to achieve a desired body weight caused her great pain and prevented her from achieving happiness.

A second key source of pain was her relationship with her boyfriend Mark. Katie was frequently pained by both her impact on Mark and the impact Mark had on her. In one instance, she wrote, "I've worn him out, and it hurts me so badly," and in another, "it kills me that I hurt him last week." At the same time, Katie was often hurt by Mark: "he hurt me too very much by the way he treated me and spoke to me." Katie experienced many "horrible turbulent" times with Mark, frequently lamented the "pain" that he caused her, and in a moment of reflection about her relationship with Mark stated, "I hate it all."

Other sources of pain included tumultuous relationships with friends. For example, Katie had appreciated her friendship with Joyce, but over time this relationship ended up causing Katie to be "hurt" and feel "awful." Katie often felt let down or betrayed by close friends. As a result, she wrote: "My sincere love for my friends brings the most pain once it's been tainted."

Katie's efforts to engage with life were consistently paired with experiences of intense pain. At a fundamental level, people are creatures of behavioral conditioning. If something is paired with pleasure or reward, we seek to do it more; if something is paired with misery or punishment, we seek to avoid it. For Katie, her efforts to engage with life were consistently met with pain and anguish. Under these circumstances, it is human nature to want the pain to stop and to look for ways out.

Katie's Hopelessness

According to the 3ST, pain does not translate into suicidal desire as long as there is hope. Frequent and intense pain, such as that experienced by Katie, creates a powerful desire to escape from the pain. But if someone has hope that the future can be better and less painful, their focus will be on achieving that future. In contrast, if someone is in pain and hopeless that things can get better, their desire to live lessens, and suicidal desire emerges.

We see this dynamic in Katie's diary entries. She experiences pain regularly and intensely but at times has enough hope to look for a way out and to seek a better future: "That is the hope I believe in, that I do have control over my fate now as a fully grown adult versus my circumstances as a child and nothing is hopeless." Katie has experienced tremendous pain both as a child and as an emerging adult. Though she continues to struggle with pain as an adult, Katie reasons that, as an adult, she has increased control over her circumstances and thus hope for a better future. Consequently, in this moment, Katie is responding to her pain not through thoughts of dying but with an eye toward creating a better future. At other times, Katie's hope in the face of pain comes through her faith in God. For example, "This too shall pass, and I truly believe so. Choice and thought before action are great gifts from God himself," and "Please, dear God, let things pick up in my life beautifully." When she can find hope, Katie responds to her pain by focusing on how she can create a better future.

However, Katie's sense of hope is not stable. Whereas sometimes she feels she has more control of her circumstances and future, at other times, she does not: "I don't have any control whatsoever in my life at all. It's absolutely terrifying." Katie also has moments in which she explicitly loses hope: "I've become negative. There does not seem to be a route back to optimism at all." In short, Katie is frequently meeting the ingredients specified in Step 1 of the 3ST that cause of suicidal desire. She frequently experiences the combination of pain and hopelessness.

Importantly, the 3ST does not expect a steady, continuous path from hope to hopelessness. On the contrary, pain and hopelessness are assumed to ebb and flow, similarly to other forms of emotion and distress such as depression and anxiety. What matters most for suicide risk are the peaks. It is at the peaks of pain and hopelessness when suicidal desire becomes most acute. Thus, when seeking to understand someone's suicidal desire, the question is not simply what led them to become hopeless, as if hopelessness is a destination at which one may or may not arrive. Instead, hopelessness, like pain, ebbs and flows over time with one's internal experiences and external circumstances. The question, then, is how often and how intensely peaks of pain and hopelessness occur together. The more frequent peaks of pain and hopelessness co-occur, the more often individuals will experience periods of suicidal desire and each period of suicidal desire represents a potential suicidal crisis, an opportunity for suicidal desire to progress to a suicide attempt.

In Katie's case, it is clear that peaks of pain and hopelessness are frequent. For all the times she responds to her pain with hope, there are times when she feels hopeless in the face of pain. Thus, from the perspective of the 3ST, Katie would be expected to have frequent periods of suicidal desire.

Katie's Connectedness

According to the 3ST, connectedness is what makes life worth living. Specifically, if one's connectedness exceeds one's pain, then the desire to live will exceed the desire to die. On the contrary, if pain exceeds or overwhelms connectedness, and one loses hope that life can get better, there is no more reason to bear the pain, no more reason to stay alive.

For Katie, connectedness began as an uphill battle. She was raised as a foster child and lacked stable, warm family connections. She described her foster family members as being "all so abusive to me," and associated her family life with feeling "alone, abandoned, rejected, and neglected." Probably as a consequence of this, Katie placed tremendous value on other sources of connection in her life. These included friends, her boyfriend Mark and God.

It is hard to exaggerate the intensity of Katie's desire for meaningful friendships. In one entry she writes, "There are just some things that I am so in need of. And a good number of encouraging friends would help along the way." In another, she writes, "I need some real and good friends, really bad." She makes references to various friends throughout her diary entries. Unfortunately, her friendships seem to bring more pain than meaning or happiness. Katie alludes to various instances in which she felt bullied or mistreated, although it is difficult to determine the extent to which some of the perpetrators were considered by Katie to be friends. In contrast, it is clear that Katie felt a deep connection to Joyce. Even after concluding that Joyce "hurt me so badly" and is "stupid, valueless," Katie acutely feels the loss of their relationship. After severing her friendship with Joyce, Katie felt "awful" and "torn up inside," and writes "I miss Joyce already."

Katie's desire and struggle for connectedness are amplified in her feelings toward Mark. Mark is her romantic interest throughout her diary entries. Katie looks to Mark to fulfill a variety of connectedness needs: to "love him," to be her "best friend" and to give her a "secure place." Given all the tumult in her life, it is not surprising that Katie feels: "I have nothing else to really hold on to right now, and I don't feel rooted at all anywhere." Because Mark is Katie's primary source of connectedness, it is especially difficult and painful when this relationship does not work out. Mark is not fully committed to Katie and shows interest in other women, including a woman named Claudia. This betrayal and relationship disruption shakes Katie to her core: "I gave up everything for Mark. I forced myself to be close to him despite all the pain and trust he killed in me. I hate it all. I never really felt safe with him after that."

Katie also strives to maintain a connection to God. As discussed earlier, one function of this relationship is to give Katie hope. However, God also represents an important source of connection for Katie. She writes of "healing my connection with God," and gaining "incredible strength from God." Katie also grapples with whether God is real and, at one point, apparently separated herself from religion. However, she concludes that "what I can perceive of Him, and touch of Him is real" and that she will focus on these parts of God for "extra help and support." In her darkest moments, Katie looks to God not just for hope but also for connection.

Conclusion

The final entry in Katie's diary contains an earnest request to God that reads like a prayer. It begins with the preface "Please dear God" and expresses many yearnings. These include "Let things pick up in my life beautifully . . . Please let our [hers and Mark's] relationship become awesome and wholesome . . . Please help me overcome the challenges that I face everyday in life . . . Please let me feel an ever-encouraging life force in my everyday existence." And finally, "Please help me through this and next week especially; things are so hard right now." In her time of deepest pain and hopelessness, Katie reaches out for hope and connection one more time. With nowhere else to turn, she reaches out to God. She imagines the relationship she has always wanted to have with Mark. She imagines a day-to-day existence characterized by encouragement, beauty and awe rather than pain and hopelessness. One more time she aspires for a future with connection and meaning rather than pain.

We might surmise that over the next nine days—between the time of this final entry and Katie's death by suicide—her pain did not abate, her life did not improve and that, in the absence of hope and connection, her pain simply became too much to bear.

Suicide is a difficult and painful topic. But it can be understood in part as reflecting a basic aspect of human nature. At a fundamental level, we are biologically and psychologically wired to avoid pain. When pain becomes intense, we become desperate for escape. Katie worked extremely hard to maintain hope and build a life worth living despite her pain, before it became too much. May we learn from her example. May we come to understand that a desire to die is a natural consequence of intense pain and hopelessness; that a desire to live comes from connectedness to people and sources of purpose and meaning and that, if we wish to reduce suicide, we must find ways to ease people's pain, increase hope and enhance connectedness and, in turn, ensure that all people have lives that feel worth living.

Reference

Klonsky, E., & May, A. M. (2015). The Three-Step Theory (3ST): A new theory of suicide rooted in the "ideation-to-action" framework. *International Journal of Cognitive Therapy, 8*, 114–129.

7 Understanding Katie's Experiences From the Perspective of the Integrated Motivation Volitional Model of Suicidal Behavior

Tiago C. Zortea and Rory C. O'Connor

Katie's suicide was a tragedy. The pain and desperation expressed in her diaries illustrate the complexity of a problem that ravages the lives of many young people worldwide annually. The question why Katie took her own life is a difficult one to answer directly, particularly given the interplay of so many factors contributing to the deterioration in her mental health and the escalation in her suicidal thoughts that culminated in her death. Such difficulties in understanding suicide are not new. Indeed, it is the pursuit of such knowledge that has galvanized scientists, clinicians, policy makers, people with lived experience and other professionals for decades. Despite the advances that we have made, many challenges remain. One approach to make sense of suicidal thoughts, attempts and deaths is through the conceptualization of such experiences from the perspective of theoretical models of human behavior. Through developing, employing and testing theoretical models of suicidal behavior, scientists hope to improve our understanding of these experiences which may help us to prevent unbearable tragedies such as Katie's.

Several theoretical models have been developed to explain the etiology of suicide risk (O'Connor & Nock, 2014), but only three models aim to explain which factors differentiate those who think about suicide from those who attempt suicide: the Interpersonal Theory of Suicide (IPTS) (Joiner, 2005; Van Orden et al., 2010), the 3ST (Klonsky & May, 2015) and the Integrated Motivational-Volitional (IMV) model of suicidal behavior (O'Connor & Kirtley, 2018). These frameworks are known as "ideation-to-action" models, because previous suicide theories did not clearly establish which factors and contexts could be associated with suicidal thinking and those associated with suicide attempt or suicide death (O'Connor & Portzky, 2018). This is important because not all individuals who think about suicide will act upon those thoughts, and most of the traditional suicide risk factors in psychiatric research do not suggest any consistent differences between those who think about suicide from those who will attempt to take their own lives (Klonsky et al., 2016).

In this chapter, we will focus on the IMV model of suicidal behavior (O'Connor, 2011; O'Connor et al., 2016; O'Connor & Kirtley, 2018). The IMV model provides a comprehensive framework for conceptualizing the processes involved in the development of suicidal thoughts as well as those associated with the translation of suicidal thoughts into a suicide attempt (Figure 7.1). By incorporating other contemporary theories of suicidal behavior, including the Cry of Pain model (Williams, 1997) and the Interpersonal Psychological Theory (Joiner, 2005; Van Orden et al., 2010), the IMV model theoretically maps out the interaction between specific psychosocial components that are critical for the emergence of suicidal thoughts and behaviors. This process is understood to have three phases: the pre-motivational phase (background factors and triggering events), the motivational phase (ideation/intention formation) and the volitional phase (behavioral enaction).

The current chapter endeavors to understand Katie's suicidogenic process through the lens of the IMV model. By doing so, we aim to gain some insights into how Katie's life events, experiences and interactions with the world escalated to resulted in the most devastating outcome. We hope that our reflections may be useful in making sense of the pain that results in too many young women dying by suicide each year. This chapter is structured in three main sections, each one discussing specific aspects of Katie's diary from the perspective of the IMV model.

Vulnerabilities, Traumatic Experiences and Triggering Events: The Backdrop to Katie's Suicidal Experiences

Across the five books of her diary, Katie describes a series of events that can be conceptualized as the pre-motivational phase of suicide risk from the IMV viewpoint. The pre-motivational phase of the IMV model establishes the biopsychosocial context in which suicidal thoughts emerge (see Figure 7.1). As a diathesis–stress framework, the IMV model posits that the emergence of suicidal thoughts results from the interaction of vulnerability factors (biological or psychological) and stressful events. Biological vulnerability factors, such as impairments in the serotonergic and hypothalamic-pituitary-adrenal axis stress response systems (Van Heeringen & Mann, 2014), and epigenetic processes (Lutz et al., 2017), have been shown to play a role in suicide risk when activated in stressful conditions. Such biological factors may render someone to be hypersensitive to the experience of emotions. Indeed, this hypersensitivity seems to be a constant across Katie's experiences: "I'm going absolutely crazy. I've calmed down since I've spoken with Mark. I hate all the anxiety I feel. It is all absolutely awful. The turmoil, at times like this, seems absolutely endless." Consequently, when facing a negative interaction with someone or interpreting an event as threatening, the intensity of the physiological/emotional responses can be higher than what someone who is less sensitive would experience, and the distress may last longer, being more difficult to regulate. The combination of such biological vulnerability with stressful life events and exposure to strenuous environments may result in significant maladaptive psychological traits, which can be resistant to change over time.

As previously reported (Lester, 2004), Katie had an extremely difficult upbringing. She was sexually abused by her father, experienced and witnessed

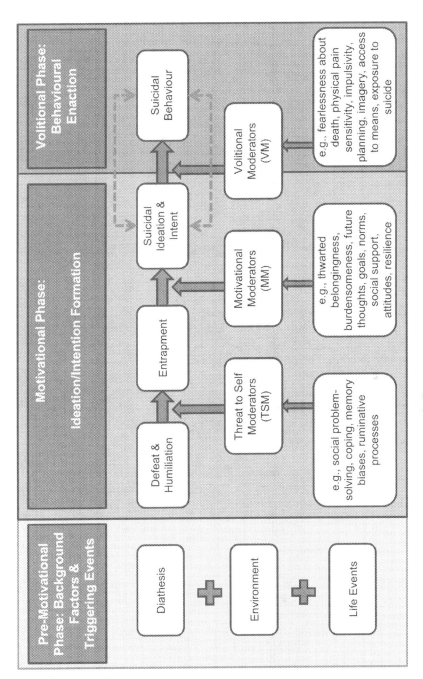

Figure 7.1 The integrated motivational-volitional model of suicidal behavior (O'Connor & Kirtley, 2018)

domestic violence. In addition, she was placed in foster homes as her mother had intense psychotic experiences, which resulted in institutionalization in a psychiatric hospital. Katie herself was hospitalized on several occasions due to a severe eating disorder that she developed when she was taken away from her mother and placed in foster care. She was frequently depressed, and her sister would sometimes worry that Katie suffered from hallucinations, given her "eccentric" religious ideas. Across all five books of her diary, Katie reports frequent experiences that are characteristic of post-traumatic stress disorder such as flashbacks, intense nightmares of difficult life experiences, reliving repetitive and distressing sensations and imagery and feeling sick or trembling. The complex constellation of past negative experiences and biological and psychological vulnerabilities place Katie in a dangerous position according to the pre-motivational phase of suicide risk (O'Connor & Kirtley, 2018).

> I awoke to police sirens. It's so confusing. I'm petrified. Reminds me of my Dad. When neighbors would call police on him, when he was beating my Mom. I was so scared all the time. Every time I thought would be the last I'd see my mother. I figured one of these times he would actually kill her, or vice versa. The first always seemed more likely. Oh, I hate this terror. I hate it so much. I think I'll make a pot of coffee or something. I hate this fear. I'm so afraid someone is going to come down here and hurt me. Not the police but my biological father. Oh, all the nights being afraid. He would sometimes disappear for a few days after each beating. We would be scared all the time. I slept with a knife under my pillow in my heart. A car just came by. It was mellow to hear the tires roll against the pavement. There are two people, man and woman, fighting outside. I wonder if the police are there. I'm afraid to look. They have Spanish accents. Oh, my breathing is so fast and shallow. Ahhhhh! Oh, I'm so frightened. I refuse to sleep tonight. I can't do it. Arg!

Katie's account depicts a tumultuous, highly violent, volatile and unpredictable parental environment, in which family members' lives were frequently at risk. The exposure to such an environment seems to have resulted in an anxious and defensive way of responding to triggers that became conditioned. The detailed images described (and probably mentally visualized) by Katie in the extract mentioned earlier were activated by waking to police sirens. These images seem to be accompanied by strong feelings of anxiety, fear, difficulties in regulating her emotions and sleep difficulties. Across Katie's writings, it is possible to identify several occasions where current events trigger extremely negative feelings and maladaptive strategies necessary to cope. These make it difficult for her to deal with everyday demands, her distressing thoughts and managing her emotions.

From a stress-diathesis paradigm perspective, although an individual may possess certain levels of vulnerability, they are unlikely to become suicidal unless they are exposed to specific stress-inducing factors. These factors can be environmental/social variables such as socioeconomic inequalities (Platt,

2016), the impact of economic recessions (Chang et al., 2013) or adverse life experiences, both when experienced in adulthood (Bagge et al., 2012) or during childhood (Cleare et al., 2018). Adverse childhood experiences, such as sexual, physical or emotional abuse, have been associated with the development of biological and psychological vulnerability by triggering persistent alterations in neurobiological systems and, consequently, increasing sensitivity to stressful life events during adulthood (Jeronimus et al., 2013; Sánchez et al., 2001).

The exposure to extremely negative experiences also seems to be associated with insecure patterns of interpersonal relationships. From her writings, Katie seems to have had extremely ambivalent perceptions about important relationships (such as with her boyfriend Mark and others close to her). She repeatedly questions individuals' worth as romantic partners or as significant others, but at the same time, she worries about losing her attachment figures and remains vigilant to signs of rejection. In her own words, "I have such a problem with loss. Fear of losing someone. Fear of loving someone. Fear of trusting someone." This approach to relationships can be understood as attachment anxiety (Simpson & Rholes, 2012), a pattern very likely to have been developed throughout her interactions with parents and those she was closest to during childhood (Bowlby, 1988; Zortea et al., 2020). These patterns seem to have been intensified after she was cheated upon by her boyfriend Mark, with whom she had a troubled relationship.

> My love for Mark is so great. I don't know where my heart would be if I never met him. I honestly think I would've killed myself by now for some reason. I wish we were rich and could just run away somewhere beautiful together. I would be so happy then. I want to get away from this world of madness—death & pain. I hate it. I want to be solely with him & only him. I had a horrible nightmare. Mark hated me and got so sick of my problem that he went with Claudia again. I was trying to fix everything and make everything easier for him, but he just was so malicious & didn't want me anymore. I was walking around in the rain & crying. I was trying to reach out to people and make myself feel better—it was so horrible & I just couldn't. I snuck into his house & walked up the stairs. I could hear her giggling & him laughing. I burst in, jumped on the bed & grabbed them both & him them in the face. Mark jumped off, & I just kept on beating Claudia's face in so hard. Then Mark, I think, told me to stop, grabbed my ankle & dragged me to the edge of the bed & told me that he hated me so much. I looked at him & realized I was fighting for him & I didn't want him back anymore. I hated him too & just left. It was so horrible to think that [it] all really happened around this time of the year. I wonder if some of this dream had to do with Angela & Gerald & when he cheated on her. I really hate this time of the year. I truly get so damn depressed. I feel like its too late to salvage what I had with Mark—the past. I guess it means I can't change it, so I need to concentrate honestly on right now, and then I have a really strong sense of freedom.

In her account, Katie expresses an extreme emotional dependence on Mark, in which the theme of suicide appears associated with Mark's absence in her life. In the nightmare, Mark's infidelity seems to be triggered by her problems, which gives the impression that she is to be blamed for him cheating on her. The contents of the nightmare highlight Katie's fear of being abandoned, particularly given the potential consequences of Mark's absence. When trying to manage the distress that emerged from her relationship with Mark, Katie describes coping strategies that are emotion-focused or hypervigilant. These seem to sustain and even escalate her existing apprehensions, fears and ruminative tendencies. These characteristics of attachment anxiety and relationship difficulties constitute key factors that help us to understand the psychological vulnerability present in Katie's life as outlined in the pre-motivational phase of suicide risk. As attachment theory researchers propose (Simpson & Rholes, 2012), those who have a more anxious approach to close relationships generally generate negative explanations for their attachment figure's ambiguous behaviors when facing a difficulty. Such challenging situations can be so emotionally distressing that they usually respond defensively and destructively in return. They often display higher levels of anger, hostility or coercive attempts to seek reassurance from their attachment figures. These patterns are common across Katie's diaries and may have contributed to her increased vulnerability for suicide risk (Zortea et al., 2019).

Katie's insecurities and decimated self-esteem also manifested itself through her eating disorder. Although partially explained by her fear of being abandoned by Mark, Katie's eating disorder was always accompanied by thoughts of social comparison. Other girls' body shape was constantly used as a reference and source of self-criticism.

> I had all these visions of how beautiful this girl was and how skinny. I compared myself not only to her, but to other girls who caught his interest. I was so meticulous with myself. I hated my body so much. I tried going on so many damn diets in the past eight months so I would be more beautiful to him and most of all to myself so I wouldn't have to compete. I failed miserably on all of them, whether purposely or accidentally I did. A lot of this had to do with my sincere need to be wanted and cared about. I always get like this if I care about someone, be this friend or relationship.

Within the context of the IMV model, evidence suggests that social comparison is associated with suicidal thoughts via perceptions of defeat and entrapment (Wetherall et al., 2019a, 2019b). From this perspective, it is possible to understand that the thoughts and behaviors associated with her eating disorder seem to have had a coping and self-regulatory function, in that they helped her to reduce feelings of insecurity, fear of abandonment and low self-esteem. However, as a maladaptive strategy, Katie's health was compromised, and other effects on her mental health also emerged from the eating disorder. Although stressful environments and adverse life experiences have been recognized as critical risk factors for suicide, not all those who are exposed to such experiences will develop suicidal thoughts. Hence, as outlined in the pre-motivational phase of the IMV model, it is the diathesis–stress interaction that is vital to understand the vulnerability to suicide risk. In her diaries, Katie describes a range of negative events and the stressful environment that she was exposed to, and these contextual factors may have triggered a wide range of biological and psychological vulnerabilities. It is the debilitating effects of such interactions that increase the likelihood that an individual will enter the motivational phase and develop suicidal thoughts driven by feelings of defeat, humiliation and entrapment.

The Cycle of Risk: Katie's Trapped Life and Her Recurrent Suicidal Thoughts

It is not clear when Katie first thought of taking her own life. In her diaries, they seem to be almost omnipresent since the beginning of her writings. Hence, it is not possible to infer which contextual factors were primarily associated with Katie's first suicidal thoughts. It is interesting, however, to observe that the processes suggested by the IMV model as main drivers of suicidal thoughts are clearly present across her diary.

As a key influence on the IMV model, the Cry of Pain framework of suicidal behavior (Williams, 1997) posits that the emergence of suicidal ideation is predicated on perceptions of entrapment, triggered by experiences of defeat and/or humiliation. Such insight was extended from Gilbert and colleagues' work on the etiology of depression (Gilbert & Allan, 1998). The IMV model adopts Williams' hypothesis that, in the aftermath of failing to escape from a defeating and/or humiliating experience, perceptions of entrapment arise, and the odds of suicidal ideation are increased if there is insufficient hope of being rescued, for example, when social support is absent (Williams et al., 2005). The IMV model assumes that sensitivity to signals of defeat and/or humiliation are determined by pre-motivational factors (diathesis–stress processes).

Feelings of defeat and humiliation are also present across Katie's diaries. Her attempts to desperately find a solution for the sources of her suffering (pre-motivational factors) through different ways of coping seem to be continuously thwarted. Such perceptions of failure seem to be generalized by Katie to all aspects of her life, which seems to make her feel lost, with no purpose and meaning. This seems to have been facilitated by some of Katie's personality and cognitive functioning factors, which from the IMV model's viewpoint are understood as "threat-to-self moderators" (see Figure 7.1). These include dichotomous thinking, cognitive rigidity, hopelessness, perfectionism and dysfunctional attitudes (Ellis, 2004) and are thought to emerge from her developmental traumatic experiences.

> Dear God, I tried. I really did with what I knew. But I guess it just wasn't good enough. Honesty just scares people, doesn't it? Why do I

have this sin of being abused? Why does it hurt so badly when something little or big touches my heart? Why do I still run from my heart? Why are people so mean still to me? Why can't people love me? Why can't people want to treat me and spend time with me like I am above and separate from what's happened to me? Why can't people treat me like a friend? Why do people still use me? Why do I bother to try so hard when people can't accept where I have come to so far? Why do people treat me like I'm the problem and it's my fault without realizing it? Why do people get angry when you tell them the truth? Why don't you make all of this go away?

The questioning expressed in this account is not isolated in Katie's diary and provides an illustration of a "cycle of risk" where she feels unable to foresee a solution, a way out from such an overwhelming set of experiences. She seems to be lost, misunderstood, tired and defeated. It seems that, every time when Katie faces a relationship problem with Mark or other acquaintances, the symptoms of her eating disorder re-emerge, and she re-lives flashbacks of past traumatic events. She seems to enter a spiral where, the more she tries to make sense of things, the worse and more trapped she feels. Such a sense of entrapment emerges from the circular and endless nature of trying-and-failing, fueled by threat-to-self moderators (see Figure 7.1). One of these moderators is memory bias. Given that Katie was exposed to a large range of harrowing experiences throughout her upbringing, her approach to solving interpersonal problems seems to be biased by the negative memories she has about the past, when those close to her abused and abandoned her. It seems that she can only remember failures and negative events. These autobiographical memory biases also seem to contribute to Katie's worries and rumination about herself and the interminable nature of her problems.

> Where does freedom go? I feel so bound up inside and trapped in the feelings of my childhood, trapped, not able to move. Laying motionless on the floor because it's told it's safe. Is it really safe? Every morning I want to feel my freedom. Argh! Oh, still frustrated, oh so frustrated. Nothing is resolved!

Such entrapment seems to be manifested both internally and externally. The former includes the psychological difficulties caused by the traumas she was exposed to throughout her childhood: Katie feels unable to deal with her memories, feelings of the past, to regulate her own thoughts and emotions. On the other hand, external entrapment is evident through interpersonal encounters in her life where she has no control, such as Mark's attitudes toward other women, his infidelity, her acquaintances' offensive jokes or commentaries or even the difficulties to escape from a world where she is constantly comparing herself with other girls.

I feel so trapped, bound, tied up, locked up, like I was when I was fourteen, thirteen, twelve, locked up in the house, never allowed out to be free, not allowed to run that often, felt trapped in my own body. Oh, why?

It kills me still inside—this pain angers me—blinds me—tortures me. I have given so much sensitivity in a careful fashion. I had to deflect the attention from the depth that my heart truly cared for him (Mark). Maybe it was all because I was so sad. I'm scared about absolutely everything in my life. I feel so alone &, when the bridge of intimacy is being crossed, I feel baffled, tormented, abused, unsure of the safety, and I once again throw myself to the wolves for love—truth, love & truth. I want and crave such a wholesome existence.

According to the IMV model, entrapment is perhaps one of the most dangerous psychological states one can experience, particularly in a recurrent way, as such a state may act as a bridge between defeat and suicidal ideation. This happens when the individual feels defeated and unable to escape from the problems and the pain: the psychological state of entrapment. Evidence has shown the role of entrapment in increasing suicide risk (O'Connor & Portzky, 2018), particularly in the presence or absence of other key factors known as "motivational moderators" which increase the likelihood of the motivation for suicide developing, that is. suicidal thinking and intent (see Figure 7.1). Consistent with the Cry of Pain framework, O'Connor and Kirtley (2018) proposed that entrapment can be experienced externally or internally, where the latter is related to being ensnared by feelings and thoughts of suffering, whereas the former concerns the motivation to escape from the context that produces the pain (Gilbert & Allan, 1998; Williams, 1997). An important distinction between entrapment and hopelessness is that the latter relates to a sense of pessimism about the future (Beck et al., 1985), and the former assumes the existence of an underlying motivation to escape—"flight motivation" (Gilbert & Allan, 1998).

When trapped, the individual may adopt a series of strategies to escape from the psychological and contextual complications that led to one's pain. These strategies (either internal or external—motivational moderators) can include reaching out for social support, increasing interpersonal connectedness and belongingness and reassessing goals, norms and values with the support of others. In the presence of such motivational moderators, there is a reduced likelihood that suicidal thoughts will emerge. However, the absence of such moderators may increase risk. Within the IMV model, motivational moderators also incorporate the main factors from the IPTS (Joiner, 2005), namely, perceived burdensomeness (the perception that one is a burden to others, regardless of existing contrary evidence) and thwarted belongingness (the perception of interpersonal exclusion and lack or belongingness). Across Katie's journals, it is possible to identify a constant feeling of being a burden to Mark and other people. Katie's attachment anxiety, manifested through a constant demand for reassurance and emotional validation, seems to be seen by her as a dependence pattern that burdens Mark, which is heightened by his infidelity and inappropriate statements of interest for other women.

> I refuse to go be dependent on Mark at all. I would have to break up with him, most definitely. I can't do this to him anymore. My life—I would need lots of time to myself. I don't want to burden him anymore. My heart is in such numb reality, yet it quivers at the thought of losing. Why have one person you love when you are bound to lose everyone and everything you've ever loved?
> God, I feel like such a burden to everyone. It's awful.
> I need to pray now and cry. I don't want to burden anyone at all anymore. I'm so scared of losing everything and everyone I love. I feel too tangled up in everyone else and my past. I need to pray to words that do not touch this page so they can be set free.

The fear of losing everyone and everything, the self-blaming process that sustains the feelings of burdensomeness and the perception of being lost seem to be strongly connected with Katie's sense of loneliness. As analyzed by Ellis (2004), she is continuously mindful of her struggles with dealing with interpersonal issues—a view that is endorsed in the police report following her death, noting that Mark had declared that Katie "did not really have any friends that she hung out with." In her diary, Katie recognizes that her interpersonal difficulties seem to be directly related to her past traumatic experiences and partially guided by negative autobiographic memory biases.

> Is it so wrong to want to have a family? It's always been such a big dream for me. But my old family life seems to come up now, being alone, abandoned, rejected and neglected. My voice doesn't seem to carry me very far away from things of this sort. It's all such treacherous ground, I suppose. Uncertainty and doubt creep into what I have now, and I have the things I've been through. It has affected my life with people. It's alienated me from simply honesty, open personality. I wish I could live free not to have to worry about a thing and not long internally for some sort of unity and security by being close to someone. I guess as long as I feel this and have felt this, everyone I know has rejected this and me along with it. So I guess I will still continue to punish myself sometimes for such cravings, and everything will come full circle, everything. So I can see what I have been starved for and what I starve and what starves me—if any of this makes any sense. I'm scared, but I have to tell myself I'll be all right because I've always been by myself, and I need to hold myself and carry myself for a little while.

It is the interaction of these moderating factors with defeat and entrapment, experienced concomitantly in the presence of pre-motivational variables, that increases the likelihood that suicidal ideation and intent develop (Gooding et al., 2015; Littlewood et al., 2016; O'Connor, 2003; Owen et al., 2018; Rasmussen et al., 2010; Russell et al., 2018; Taylor et al., 2011). The complexity of all the aforementioned interacting factors discussed so far seems to be the driving force behind Katie's suicidal thoughts and feelings. On several occasions, she writes about the desire to kill herself, which is accompanied by a variety of emotions including sadness, anger, guilt and the overwhelming feeling of being tired of trying to find a solution to her pain. The perceptions of entrapment seem to go alongside her thoughts of ending her life:

> I feel so unable to find solace in anything. I have all these dreams for our future (with Mark), but they are only dreams as I found out before. There really seems to be nothing for me. I could easily kill myself. No one would notice. Everyone has seemed to get the most out of me they wanted. I feel so used in every way possible. I work so hard with him (Mark) and everyone, but it doesn't seem to get me anywhere. He is just a boy, after all. His loyalties are so selfish. I really hate him so much, maybe because I've grown so damn dependent on him. I feel so out of balance. I'm in so much pain.

The Last Straw: On Katie's Volitional Process of Ending Her Life

The last phase of the IMV model is the transition from suicidal ideation/intent to enactment (suicide attempt). This transition is facilitated or obstructed by a specific group of factors entitled "volitional moderators." In the most recent version of the IMV model (O'Connor & Kirtley, 2018), the understanding of which factors may constitute volitional moderators has been expanded—as outlined in Figure 7.2. The volitional phase of the IMV model integrates components of the acquired capability of suicide framework (increased physical pain tolerance and fearlessness about death), proposed by Joiner in his IPTS (Joiner, 2005). However, according to O'Connor and Kirtley (2018), volitional moderators can be environmental (e.g., having access to means of suicide), psychological (e.g., formulating a suicide plan, mental imagery, fearlessness about death), social (e.g., exposure to suicide or suicidal behavior of other people) or physiological (e.g., physical pain sensitivity/endurance) in nature. O'Connor and Kirtley (2018) provide a comprehensive summary of the current empirical evidence that yields support for the hypothesis that the factors depicted in Figure 7.2 act as volitional moderators, increasing the likelihood of a suicide attempt.

An important feature of the IMV model is the representation of the cyclical relationship between suicidal thoughts and repeat suicide attempts in Figures 7.1 and 7.2 (see the dotted lines). This is based on the assumption that people who have attempted suicide once are statistically more likely to engage in suicidal behavior again (Hawton et al., 2012). It is understood that individuals who have attempted suicide in the past and are at current risk may have a recurrence of suicidal behavior triggered by a lower threshold of defeat and

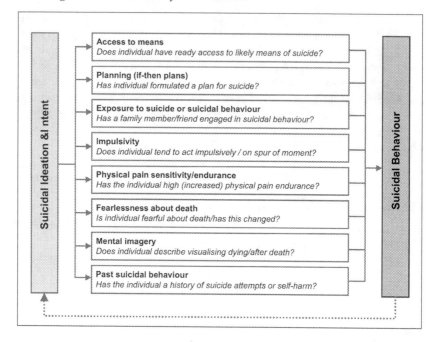

Figure 7.2 Volitional moderators that may increase the likelihood of suicidal thoughts being translated into a self-harm (including suicide attempt) (O'Connor & Kirtley, 2018)

entrapment (O'Connor & Kirtley, 2018). Although volitional factors represent key elements for understanding the transition from suicidal thinking to suicidal behavior, these seem to be the most difficult aspects to be identified in the investigation of Katie's suicide.

As pointed out by Lester (2004), there is no indication that Katie had a history of suicide attempts. However, her writings suggest that she used to self-harm and was also exposed to her boyfriend's self-harm on some occasions:

> He called me a slut because I referred to Brent as my X. I felt so depressed and cheap because of what I remembered the past year. I got up, said you're right and cut my wrist. Then he ran over to stop me and then he started screaming—saying he was sober—and started cutting himself. I fought him physically to make him stop and get the knife away. I tried every tactic I knew to make him stop. He cut himself, so the only way I made him stop was I started cutting myself. I cut my breast and my shoulder. I realized I didn't truly want to die and that I had a choice—I didn't want to cut my body. I didn't really want to hurt myself at all. It made him stop. Then I pulled him and got aggressive and made him go on the couch with me and cry it out. I cried so much. I couldn't bear seeing him cut himself like that, and the fact I saw my very fear from the time I got to know about his depression better.

> I carried in my heart his pain all year—his turmoil—his conflicts. I rarely showed face for what I carried in my heart. I cared for him so deeply with all of me, but I didn't show him so openly or freely. It made me too vulnerable and almost sold all of my pride. I'm so glad that night is over.

The situation described by Katie sounds extremely disturbing and traumatic, with both Mark and herself at heightened risk. As posited by O'Connor and Kirtley (2018), the non-fatal self-harm (including suicide attempt) of others may increase the chances that an individual models or imitates a loved one's suicidal behavior (O'Connor et al., 2014; Pitman et al., 2014). In fact, this seems to be what is happening in Katie's description. In addition to the use of self-harm as a means to communicate pain and exert some influence on someone else's behavior, one of the "side effects" of exposure is the increased salience and cognitive accessibility of suicide and self-harm such that an individual is more likely to attempt suicide when they encounter stressors. Similarly, Katie seems to suggest that her mother had taken her own life, although according to Lester (2004), she used to prefer telling other people that her mother was dead: "Talked to Mimi Jones. It was nice—told her my mother killed herself. I hate my mother so much. I kill her over and over again through my word to thoughts."

The absence of information in Katie's diary about the presence of most volitional moderators (Figure 7.2) limits the extent to which we can properly explore her suicide through the lenses of an ideation-to-action framework. However, the sense of entrapment and non-resolution of issues in her life are frequently present in her words. In the nine days before her suicide, Katie left a long note of prayer, in which she begs God to meet some of her deepest needs. It is likely that the failure to meet these needs was related to the unbearable pain she was carrying.

> Please let me feel an ever-encouraging life force in my everyday existence from the time I wake to the time I sleep. Let my voice become strong and defined along with my character—strong, warm, distinct, good, downright real. And let my nurturance be doubled or even tripled when I do what is right and let the times, I fall be soft so I can pick myself up on what I worked so hard on and have overcome.

Katie's Legacy for Suicide Prevention

Through a close reading of Katie's diary, we are able to get some sense of understanding the factors associated with her tragic death. Katie's death was not inevitable, and her words give us some clues about how to prevent someone from taking their own life. These include the provision of continuing mental health care, particularly for those more vulnerable and affected by a history of emotional and sexual abuse, domestic violence and psychological disorders. Psychoeducation, the general efforts to reduce stigma about mental health conditions, the provision of information about help seeking and the implementation of suicide prevention and surveillance systems within educational institutions could also be useful. (Katie died by suicide at student accommodation.) With hindsight, it is reasonable to hypothesize that Katie would have benefited from these strategies, particularly from tailored mental health care and psychological services support. Finally, an important lesson learnt from this tragic event is that suicide is not inescapable, and that its prevention demands help and provision of support at the earliest stages of someone's mental health difficulties.

References

Bagge, C. L., Glenn, C. R., & Lee, H.-J. (2012). Quantifying the impact of recent negative life events on suicide attempts. *Journal of Abnormal Psychology, 122,* 359–368.

Beck, A. T., Steer, R. A., Kovacs, M., & Garrison, B. (1985). Hopelessness and eventual suicide: A 10-year prospective study of patients hospitalized with suicidal ideation. *American Journal of Psychiatry, 142,* 559–563.

Bowlby, J. (1988). *A secure base: Clinical applications of attachment theory.* London, UK: Routledge.

Chang, S. S., Stuckler, D., Yip, P., & Gunnell, D. (2013). Impact of 2008 global economic crisis on suicide: Time trend study in 54 countries. *BMJ* (Online), *347*(7925), f5239.

Cleare, S., Wetherall, K., Clark, A., Ryan, C., Kirtley, O., Smith, M., & O'Connor, R. (2018). Adverse childhood experiences and hospital-treated self-harm. *International Journal of Environmental Research & Public Health, 15*(6), 1235.

Ellis, T. E. (2004). Thoughts of Katie: A cognitive perspective. In D. Lester (Ed.), *Katie's diary: Unlocking the mystery of a suicide* (pp. 81–96). New York: Brunner-Routledge.

Gilbert, P., & Allan, S. (1998). The role of defeat and entrapment (arrested flight) in depression: An exploration of an evolutionary view. *Psychological Medicine, 28,* 585–598.

Gooding, P., Tarrier, N., Dunn, G., Shaw, J., Awenat, Y., Ulph, F., & Pratt, D. (2015). The moderating effects of coping and self-esteem on the relationship between defeat, entrapment and suicidality in a sample of prisoners at high risk of suicide. *European Psychiatry, 30,* 988–994.

Hawton, K., Saunders, K. E. A., & O'Connor, R. C. (2012). Self-harm and suicide in adolescents. *The Lancet, 379,* 2373–2382.

Jeronimus, B. F., Ormel, J., Aleman, A., Penninx, B. W. J. H., & Riese, H. (2013). Negative and positive life events are associated with small but lasting change in neuroticism. *Psychological Medicine, 43,* 2403–2415.

Joiner, T. (2005). *Why people die by suicide.* Cambridge, MA: Harvard University Press.

Klonsky, E. D., & May, A. M. (2015). The Three-Step Theory (3ST): A new theory of suicide rooted in the "ideation-to-action" framework. *International Journal of Cognitive Therapy, 8,* 114–129.

Klonsky, E. D., May, A. M., & Saffer, B. Y. (2016). Suicide, suicide attempts, and suicidal ideation. *Annual Review of Clinical Psychology, 12*(1), 307–330.

Lester, D. (2004). Who is Katie? In D. Lester (Ed.), *Katie's diary: Unlocking the mystery of a suicide* (pp. 15–18). New York: Brunner-Routledge.

Littlewood, D. L., Gooding, P. A., Panagioti, M., & Kyle, S. D. (2016). Nightmares and suicide in posttraumatic stress disorder: The mediating role of defeat, entrapment, and hopelessness. *Journal of Clinical Sleep Medicine, 12*, 393–399.

Lutz, P.-E., Mechawar, N., & Turecki, G. (2017). Neuropathology of suicide: Recent findings and future directions. *Molecular Psychiatry, 22*, 1395–1412.

O'Connor, R. C. (2003). Suicidal behavior as a cry of pain: Test of a psychological model. *Archives of Suicide Research, 7*, 297–308.

O'Connor, R. C. (2011). Towards an integrated motivational-volitional model of suicidal behaviour. In R. C. O'Connor, S. Platt, & J. Gordon (Eds.), *International handbook of suicide prevention* (1st ed., pp. 181–198). Chichester, UK: John Wiley & Sons.

O'Connor, R. C., Cleare, S., Eschle, S., Wetherall, K., & Kirtley, O. J. (2016). The integrated motivational-volitional model of suicidal behavior: An update. In R. C. O'Connor & J. Pirkis (Eds.), *International handbook of suicide prevention* (2nd ed., pp. 220–240). Chichester, UK: John Wiley & Sons.

O'Connor, R. C., & Kirtley, O. J. (2018). The integrated motivational-volitional model of suicidal behaviour. *Philosophical transactions of the Royal Society of London: Series B, Biological Sciences, 373*(1754), 20170268.

O'Connor, R. C., & Nock, M. K. (2014). The psychology of suicidal behaviour. *The Lancet Psychiatry, 1*(1), 73–85.

O'Connor, R. C., & Portzky, G. (2018). The relationship between entrapment and suicidal behavior through the lens of the integrated motivational: Volitional model of suicidal behavior. *Current Opinion in Psychology, 22*, 12–17.

O'Connor, R. C., Rasmussen, S., & Hawton, K. (2014). Adolescent self-harm: A school-based study in Northern Ireland. *Journal of Affective Disorders, 159*, 46–52.

Owen, R., Dempsey, R., Jones, S., & Gooding, P. (2018). Defeat and entrapment in Bipolar disorder: Exploring the relationship with suicidal ideation from a psychological theoretical perspective. *Suicide & Life-Threatening Behavior, 48*, 116–128.

Pitman, A., Osborn, D., King, M., & Erlangsen, A. (2014). Effects of suicide bereavement on mental health and suicide risk. *The Lancet Psychiatry, 1*(1), 86–94.

Platt, S. (2016). Inequalities and suicidal behavior. In R. C. O'Connor & J. Pirkis (Eds.), *International handbook of suicide prevention* (2nd ed., pp. 258–283). Chichester, UK: John Wiley & Sons.

Rasmussen, S. A., Fraser, L., Gotz, M., MacHale, S., MacKie, R., Masterton, G., . . . & O'Connor, R. C. (2010). Elaborating the cry of pain model of suicidality: Testing a psychological model in a sample of first-time and repeat self-harm patients. *British Journal of Clinical Psychology, 49*, 15–30.

Russell, K., Rasmussen, S., & Hunter, S. C. (2018). Insomnia and nightmares as markers of risk for suicidal ideation in young people: Investigating the role of defeat and entrapment. *Journal of Clinical Sleep Medicine, 14*, 775–784.

Sánchez, M. M., Ladd, C. O., & Plotsky, P. M. (2001). Early adverse experience as a developmental risk factor for later psychopathology: Evidence from rodent and primate models. *Development & Psychopathology, 13*, 419–449.

Simpson, J. A., & Rholes, W. S. (2012). Adult attachment orientations, stress, and romantic relationships. In P. Devine & A. Plant (Eds.), *Advances in Experimental Social Psychology* (Vol. 45, pp. 179–328). New York: Elsevier.

Taylor, P. J., Gooding, P. A., Wood, A. M., Johnson, J., & Tarrier, N. (2011). Prospective predictors of suicidality: Defeat and entrapment lead to changes in suicidal ideation over time. *Suicide & Life-Threatening Behavior, 41*, 297–306.

Van Heeringen, K., & Mann, J. J. (2014). The neurobiology of suicide. *The Lancet Psychiatry, 1*(1), 63–72.

Van Orden, K. A., Witte, T. K., Cukrowicz, K. C., Braithwaite, S. R., Selby, E. A., & Joiner, T. E. (2010). The interpersonal theory of suicide. *Psychological Review, 117*, 575–600.

Wetherall, K., Robb, K. A., & O'Connor, R. C. (2019a). An examination of social comparison and suicide ideation through the lens of the integrated motivational: Volitional model of suicidal behavior. *Suicide & Life-Threatening Behavior, 49*, 167–182.

Wetherall, K., Robb, K. A., & O'Connor, R. C. (2019b). Social rank theory of depression: A systematic review of self-perceptions of social rank and their relationship with depressive symptoms and suicide risk. *Journal of Affective Disorders, 246*, 300–319.

Williams, J. M. G. (1997). *Cry of pain: Understanding suicide and the suicidal mind.* Harmondsworth, UK: Penguin.

Williams, J. M. G., Barnhofer, T., Crane, C., & Beck, A. T. (2005). Problem solving deteriorates following mood challenge in formerly depressed patients with a history of suicidal ideation. *Journal of Abnormal Psychology, 114*, 421–431.

Zortea, T. C., Dickson, A., Gray, C. M., & O'Connor, R. C. (2019). Associations between experiences of disrupted attachments and suicidal thoughts and behaviors: An interpretative phenomenological analysis. *Social Science & Medicine, 235*, 112408.

Zortea, T. C., Gray, C. M., & O'Connor, R. C. (2020). Perceptions of past parenting and adult attachment as vulnerability factors for suicidal ideation in the context of the integrated motivational: Volitional model of suicidal behavior. *Suicide & Life-Threatening Behavior, 50*, 515–533.

8 Katie's Implicit Life Plan for the End of Summer

How Implicit Prospection May Influence the Course of Events

Dmitri I. Shustov, Olga D. Tuchina and Anastasia U. Borodkina

I need a good plan to follow always

(July 16)

Today, hopelessness, the core concept describing the suicidal state of mind and the main component of Beck's negative triad (Beck et al., 1974), is operationalized as a deficit in positive future thinking (Beek et al., 2009). Indeed, lack of positive images of one's future and future selves, which may be characteristic of suicidal thinking (MacLeod et al., 2005; O'Connor et al., 2015), implies a certain termination of all life plans or the endpoint of planning. A person wants to interrupt or to complete his/her life journey and, at the point of suicide, killing oneself to achieve this seems to be the only option.

There is also an alternative view on this issue. For instance, Hillman (1993) believed that suicidal ideas and the need to terminate one's present life could symbolize the need to change the current life trajectory, a symbolic attempt to break away from the old life and to start a "new" one from scratch. This interpretation may also imply that suicidal people do have positive life alternatives (Baumeister et al., 2018; Cole & Kvavilashvili, 2019), but crises and distress may prevent them from becoming aware of and accessing these options (Brown et al., 2020).

Based on the reports of attempted suicides, Grof and Halifax (1977) described cases of "spiritual rebirth," when people ceased having suicidal ideation any longer. At the same time, clinical experience proves a history of suicide attempts to be the most significant predictor of a repeated suicide (Bostwick et al., 2016). Despite the existence of multiple life plans and possible future identities (Rathbone et al., 2016), suicidal consciousness may be preoccupied with attempting suicide again and again. However, we have to ask why living through such a tragic experience as a suicide attempt does not become a powerful remedial factor facilitating life changes for most people?

In this chapter, we use Katie's diary to elucidate the dim outline of her unconscious life plan for the end of summer. Our analysis rests on David Ingvar's neurocognitive concept of "memory of the future" (Ingvar, 1985;

DOI: 10.4324/9781003125655-9

Schacter et al., 2017) and Eric Berne's psychological concept of a hamartic life (Berne, 1972). These authors believe that people build some plan of their personal future which is stored as a memory and which can be retrieved. It is argued that most of our thoughts about the future embrace these spontaneous pre-made "memories of the future" that are "automatic, fast and undirected" (Cole & Kvavilashvili, 2019; p. 7), which emerge in response to external and internal stimuli. We believe that these involuntary memories of the future are not only prone to spontaneous recall and becoming explicit, but they can also bias the actual content of voluntary (deliberate and slow) future thinking, just like implicit memory (Szpunar, 2010).

It is worth clarifying that future thinking has certain mechanisms, structure and forms (D'Argembeau et al., 2012; Conway et al., 2018; Schacter et al., 2017), as well as a neural substrate in the brain's default mode system (Spreng et al., 2009). A contemporary taxonomy (Szpunar et al., 2014) singles out four major forms of future thinking, namely, "simulation (construction of a detailed mental representation of the future), prediction (estimation of the likelihood of and/or one's reaction to a particular future outcome), intention (the mental act of setting a goal), and planning (the identification and organization of steps toward achieving a goal state)" (p. 18415). These forms interact very closely in real life but can be measured independently by various psychometric methods.

Our own clinical experience of working with suicidal clients and people with alcohol dependence, as well as some theoretical and empirical works (Fukukura et al., 2013; Gerrans & Sander, 2013; Shustov & Tuchina, 2019; Shustov et al., 2019), shows that future thinking implies planning and the existence of two alternative plans, that is, an explicit (conscious) and an implicit (nonconscious) plan. A negative explicit voluntary plan is recognized as a suicidal plan (i.e., planning a suicide method, time, and site; precautions to avoid being saved; a suicide note and a will). The existence of this plan may be revealed during a professional interview, recognized as such, and become a relevant reason for intervention (Stefansson et al., 2012). Unfortunately, this does not prevent suicide even in the immediate future (Luoma et al., 2002). A different effect may be produced by diagnosing an implicit suicidal plan that people have been constructing for many years and whose details include not only past and present individual failures and traumas but also a history of trauma and suicide within generations of relatives, acquaintances or fictional characters (O'Reilly et al., 2020). An implicit plan may become explicit shortly before a suicidal attempt, or it may be activated involuntarily, that is, impulsively, so that the suicidal individual may not be aware of the overall meaning and roots of his/her actions (Lim et al., 2016). As an example, a suicide whose history we studied (Shustov, 2016) stated in his note, "*I do not know why I am doing this . . . there may be some people later who will explain this.*"

Clarifying "the details" of an implicit plan (i.e., a "memory of the future" that might bias explicit planning and lead to a fatal result) with a suicidal client can take place during psychotherapy. In our opinion, gaining awareness into the details of implicit life scripts that imply a tragic life ending can empower the client to re-decide the tragic life plan (Shustov et al., 2019). A recent study that we carried out in alcohol-dependent clients with and without suicidal ideation provided partial evidence for the hypothesis that clients who failed to reflect on their personal and family history and were unaware of its contribution to their own life journey and planned future had worse remission quality, that is, higher addiction severity in terms of health-related behavior planning (Tuchina et al., 2020).

Our Method

The aim of our analysis is to identify specific features of Katie's future thinking based on the content analysis of her diary and to identify regularities that could have implications for further research and psychotherapy of clients with suicidal ideation.

At the initial stage, three experts (a psychiatrist and two psychologists, all experienced in working with self-destructive clients) analyzed the five books of Katie's diary. These books covered time periods of various durations: Book 1 covered 2.5 months; Book 2 covered 4 months; Book 3 covered 1 month; Book 4 covered 3 months and Book 5 covered 1 month, roughly. In order to trace the evolution of Katie's future thinking, we decided to use Katie's division of her diary into books based on the assumption that starting a new book or completing an old book might have coincided with specific periods in Katie's intrapsychic dynamics rather than with physical characteristics of the books alone. (For example, Katie could get rid of an unwanted diary and suddenly start a new one—see her entry of May 30, Book 5: "I've decided to take this journal back and throw out the Victorian one the W's gave me. I hated the way it was starting to sound—absolutely awful. Now I have a new one so I can start all over.")

The experts identified 1,252 future-oriented statements in Katie's diary which constitute the pool of statements subject to the content analysis. The experts waited to discuss and code for several weeks after the pool of statements was generated so as to control for the effect of recognizing statements as belonging to a specific book.

At the second stage, following the primary analysis of the data, we conducted a comparative study of Katie's future-oriented statements in Books 3 and 5. In order to understand, how Katie's future thoughts in Book 5 differed from the other Books, we compared her future thinking in Books 5 and 3 as the latter encompassed a comparable period of time, and, just like Book 5, included no explicit suicidal future thoughts. The choice of Book 3 was also determined by the fact that the frequency of implicit suicidal future-oriented statements in Book 3 was not significantly higher than in Books 1, 2 and 4, but when compared to Book 5, the frequency was significantly lower, with a corresponding increase in the frequency of neutral statements (Type 1).

Measures

1. **Future-oriented statements.** In line with the aim of the study, three types of statements were singled out.

    Type 1: **neutral future thinking** ($N = 1,003$) included Katie's future thinking that was not directly or indirectly related to suicide planning: for example, "*I would love to level out at 130 lbs. I will just eat healthy and stay active. I don't want my metabolism to screw up at all*" (8/11). These statements could embrace both negative and positive explicit plans: "*I'm saving up for some sort of extensions during August to make my hair long again*" *(February)* (Note that Katie died in June).

    Type 2: **explicit suicidal future thinking** included statements ($N = 46$) that were related to explicit, verbalized suicidal intentions and plans, e.g., "*I want to kill myself on my birthday. I have to (6/15)*"; "*If she ever died I'll kill myself. I really would*" (10/17).

    Type 3: **implicit suicidal future thinking** ($N = 203$) included statements that conveyed Katie's suicidal planning in a covert manner, e.g., "*I am willing to make a permanent change in my life (8/10)*"; *[addressing God]* "*Don't let my soul and body die & wither away. Give me strength to make it through this summer with flying colors*" (9/30).

2. **Self-defining future projections** (SDFPs) are "mental representations of plausible and highly significant future events that provide with core information for one's understanding of self" (D'Argembeau & Mathy, 2011, p. 111). In order for a statement to be coded as an SDFP, it had to describe some plausible event in Katie's future vividly and in quite a detailed way; to be personally significant, to be present quite frequently (i.e., to occur in the text of the journal at least twice or join into a whole thematic cluster like "marriage" or "becoming a beauty"); to be linked to strong emotional experience (either positive or negative) and to reflect Katie's central life themes or conflicts and to be linked to other events relating to this theme. This event could not be marked as imminent. An example is

    I want to marry him and spend the rest of my life with him. I want to have a family with him. He will be the most incredible father when he gets much older. I want to spend the rest of my life just making him happy. I know he would just want me to do what's best for myself—in conjunction with sensitivity toward his feelings. I want to have his baby one day, when I get much older (9/2).

3. **Specificity** of future thinking was assessed using Singer and Blagov's manual (Singer & Blagov, 2002). However, for the purposes of the study, we measured only two categories: specific and generic future events, with generic ones including both episodic and generic narratives according to Singer and Blagov.

    Specific future-oriented statements included unique, short-term events not exceeding 24 hours, which usually could be traced in time and space. They had to be perceived as wholesome. These events often included indication of time and site of occurrence, embraced multiple details that allowed for imagining the environment and the participants for this event. Specific events could contain generic statements. However, this did not preclude coding them as specific provided that all the other conditions were observed. *"I can't wait to see Mark tomorrow night. I really want to dance for him tomorrow night. I love Mark" (7/22).*

Generic future-oriented statements included events that evolved throughout several days or longer time periods ("first semester," "vacation," "a year after finishing school," etc.) and abstract events (i.e., the generality of similar events—"every winter"—when the abstraction of repeating experience was emphasized). *"I guess I could start charming everyone and not expect crap from them. But hopefully I'll get a good social rep. I think I'm going to start hanging out with Maggy more. I'll see where the friendship goes from there" (2/5).*

4. **Thematic content** was assessed in line with Thorne and McLean's manual (Thorne & McLean, 2001) for coding of autobiographical narratives. Each future-oriented statement was coded as reflecting the theme that seemed to be most prominent in it. For the purposes of the study and in line with Katie's main life themes (see also Pennebaker & Stone, 2004), we singled out additional subcategories under the general one of achievement (Thorne & McLean, 2001). In this way, we measured the following thematic categories of Katie's future thinking:

   A. **Life-threatening event** (death, illness, suicide, and murder of a human being or an animal): *"I'm so afraid someone is going to come down here and hurt me. Not the police but my biological father."*
   B. **Recreation/exploration** (spending time with friends, experiments, traveling, hobbies, etc.): *"Am supposed to go to New York with Mark and his friends."*
   C. **Relationship** (positive/negative episodes of inter-relational communication, interacting with one's partner, family, etc.): *"Maybe he will always love her. Well, I need to separate to save my own life."*
   D. **Shame/guilt** (right/wrong action) (the focus is on experiencing hard feelings of shame, guilt, non-okness, moral failure, or vice versa, moral superiority): *"It makes me want to scream and kill him. I feel like I'm transferring feelings from all the asshole men onto him. I hate it because he is so different—like a sweet flower—should be untouched by my rages."*
   E. **Substance use.** *"I'm getting a drink. I don't want to feel to bound. I want to feel free to protect myself."*
   F. **Achievement.**
      1. **Weight and looks**: *"I really want to lose so much weight. I want to be 130 lbs. That's all, and I'll take it from where I am—145."*

2. **Professional and financial**: "*I have to get a normal job this summer. I wonder what I got on my report card. If I got all B's I will Thank you God forever for putting me back on top where I belong.*"
3. **Recovery and mental well-being**, including various coping strategies (crying and praying to get relief): "*I just have to keep my eyes and heart and words and spirit open and on true and wonderful things in life. Appreciate everything for what it is worth. Nothing lasts forever. But to let oneself dive into the experience of everyday will create a feeling of aspirations and vitality.*"

G. **Unclassified.** Most often these included routine events in the imminent future like taking a taxi.

5. **Temporal distance.** As far as the horizon of planning was concerned, we singled out **short-term** future thinking (day—year) and **long-term** future thinking (coming in over a year). We also counted statements with an indefinite time range (not specified in the statement and unclear from the context).
6. **Form of explicit future thinking**. In line with the contemporary taxonomy (Szpunar et al., 2014), Katie's statements were qualified as reflecting simulation, prediction, intention and planning.

    A. **Simulation** is the construction of detailed mental representations of alternative hypothetical scenarios (or reconstruction of real scenarios) that people are ready to use depending on circumstances (Szpunar et al., 2014), e.g., "*And please let Mark call soon, because I want to go to sleep soon and be uninterrupted. Please let us unleash, and a spiritual and emotional relationship emerge.*"
    B. **Prediction** is a fundamental mental function that allows the brain to continuously generate predictions that anticipate the relevant future (Bar, 2009, p. 1235). "*And Mark, sweet Mark, well, if we will last or will not, whatever will happen? . . . I don't think I have anything to fret if we decide to stay together.*"
    C. **Intention** is defined as an instruction that people give to themselves to perform some behavior or to achieve a certain goal and can be shaped as a statement, "I intend to do/achieve X" (Prestwich et al., 2015, p. 321). "*I would never leave. I can't hurt the people I love. I would only leave if it was for the best.*"
    D. **Planning** is the ability to identify alternative ways of achieving the preset goal by choosing the most appropriate among them and thinking over the probable consequences of each alternative (Haith, 1997). "*This break, I've decided to exercise every day and study. I want to lose a lot of weight by next semester. The only pity is that my hair will probably not grow that fast. I will eat a lot of protein, however. I*

refuse to eat bread or fat, only low-fat protein, so my hair will not be affected that badly. Same thing with my skin. I need to buy vitamins, E, A, C and calcium."

The same future-oriented statement could include all the four forms, as it is difficult to imagine, for example, planning as isolated from simulation, prediction and intention. Nevertheless, some statements could be qualified as simulation or prediction alone unless they had signs of other future thinking forms.

Because of the nominal nature of the data, we compared frequencies using contingency tables with chi-square (χ^2), Yates' chi-square and Fisher's exact tests as appropriate. In case of multiple comparisons, the adopted significance level ($p < 0.05$) was adjusted accordingly. The qualitative data (the number of characters without spaces in Books 1–5) were compared using the Kruskal–Wallis test; pairwise assessment employed the Mann–Whitney test.

What We Found

At first, we measured the frequency of the future-oriented statements (character count including spaces) in Books 1–5 as a percentage of all the other verbal material (the total character count including spaces) in each Book, respectively (see Figure 8.1).

The percentage of future-oriented statements as measured in characters plus spaces was almost similar in Books 1–4 ranging from 27% to 32% and increased significantly in Book 5 to 52%. These findings are important as they contradict the common view that potential suicides suffer from deficits in the future time perspective which hinders access to future-related verbal material which, in turn, leads to experiencing difficulties in imagining self-relevant future (especially positive) (Hirsch et al., 2006; MacLeod & Conway, 2007).

Table 8.1 presents the frequency of future-oriented statements independent of their character count. We found out that the Type 1 statements ("neutral future thinking") had an even distribution in Books 1–4, ranging from 80.7% to 82.7%, but in Book 5, their frequency decreased abruptly and significantly down to 67.5%.

The Type 2 statements ("explicit suicidal future thinking") had similar frequencies in Books 1, 2 and 4 (3.8–5.4%), and disappeared in Books 3 and 5. The lack of straightforward references to the suicidal plan in Book 5 was astonishing.

The Type 3 statements ("implicit suicidal future thinking") frequency in Books 1–4 was also comparable (from 13.1% to 17.2%) but doubled in Book 5 (32.5%). It appears that the Type 3 statements replaced the Type 1 statements in Book 5.

In general, the distribution of the future-oriented statements of all types in Book 5 differed significantly from their distribution in the other books. This highlights the fact that Katie's last period of life was somewhat unusual judging by the results of our "future thinking" analysis.

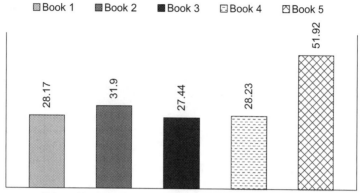

Future thinking symbol count, % of book's total symbol count

Figure 8.1 Katie's future-oriented statements, % of all the other statements in Books 1–5

Table 8.1 Distribution of future-oriented statements by types in Katie's diary, N (%)

Future-Oriented Statements	Book					Total
	1	2	3	4	5	
Neutral (Type 1)	410 (81.3)	301 (80.7)	72 (82.8)	139 (82.7)	81 (67.5)	1,003 (80.1)
Explicit suicidal (Type 2)	19 (3.8)	20 (5.4)	0 (0)	7 (4.2)	0 (0)	46 (3.7)
Implicit suicidal (Type 3)	75 (14.9)	52 (13.9)	15 (17.2)	22 (13.1)	39 (32.5)	203 (16.2)
Total (100%)	504	373	87	168	120	1,252

In order to identify which future-oriented statements accounted for the decrease in the Type 1 statements in Book 5 (as these statements could have had a suicide prevention effect), we compared the structure of the future-oriented statements in Books 3 and 5. The results of this comparison are presented in Table 8.2 and Figure 8.2.

Table 8.2 shows that **the general distribution of various categories of future-oriented statements** in Books 3 and 5 indicates a prevalence of **generic statements,** that is, non-specific, lasting for over 24 hours or having an indefinite time perspective and frequently embracing abstract self-images in the future. For example, "*I will, I want to separate myself from Mark*" (12/30); "*I feel as if I'm addicted to his touch, but I'm afraid things will go sour here*" (1/1). It should be mentioned that over-generality of future thinking and autobiographical memory is a characteristic feature of psychopathology, including depression (Gamble et al., 2019).

There were almost no statements with an explicit temporal distance exceeding one month. Long-term plans explicitly marked by the period of 5–10 years were mentioned once in Book 5. The average time perspective of planning in

Table 8.2 Katie's future thinking in Books 3 and 5

Future Thinking Variable		Book		p
		3	5	
Specificity	Specific	28 (32.2%)	48 (40%)	0.25
	Generic	59 (67.8%)	72 (60%)	
Temporal distance	Short-term	31 (35.6%)	50 (41.7%)	0.38
	Long-term	0 (0%)	2 (1.7%)	0.51
	Indefinite	56 (64.4%)	68 (56.7%)	0.27
	Day	19 (21.8%)	19 (15.8%)	0.27
	Week	4 (4.6%)	5 (4.2%)	1
	Month	4 (4.6%)	8 (6.7%)	0.77
	Year	2 (2.3%)	3 (2.5%)	1
	5–10 years	0 (0.0%)	1 (0.8%)	1
Self-defining future projections (SDFPs)		6 (6.9%)	24 (20%)	**0.015***
SDFP theme	Achievement	5 (5.7%)	18 (15%)	**0.044**
	Relationship	1 (1.1%)	6 (5%)	0.24
Explicit future thinking form	Simulation	42 (48.3%)	81 (67.5%)	**0.005**
	Prediction	47 (54%)	48 (40%)	**0.046**
	Intention	49 (56.3%)	47 (39.2%)	**0.015**
	Planning	4 (4.6%)	19 (15.8%)	**0.013**
Thematic content	Achievement in general	27 (31%)	55 (45.8%)	**0.03**
	Achievement in weight and looks	7 (8%)	26 (21.7%)	**0.01**
	Achievement in recovery	6 (6.9%)	17 (14.2%)	0.12
	Academic and financial achievement	14 (16.1%)	12 (10%)	0.19
	Relationship	23 (26.4%)	43 (35.8%)	0.15
	Life-threatening events	6 (6.9%)	3 (2.5%)	0.17
	Recreation/Exploration	**12 (13.8%)**	**6 (5%)**	**0.04**
	Shame/Guilt	**17 (19.5%)**	**10 (8.3%)**	**0.03**
	Unclassified	2 (2.3%)	3 (2.5%)	1
Statements containing negations		34 (39.1%)	51 (42.5%)	0.62

*Note: Differences that are significant are marked in bold.

Books 3 and 5 covered 3–3½ weeks. It is worth emphasizing that Katie mentioned this period of 3–3½ weeks eight times (!) in Book 5 (and on two more occasions in Books 1 and 2). This time period occurred almost exclusively in statements describing Katie's wish to separate from Mark and astonish him with the change in her looks, "*I really want this separation for the next 3½ weeks. I need a change, time to grow and do my own stuff and conquer some fears of my own*" (6/9).

Book 5 contained more statements qualified as ***SDFPs*** (D'Argembeau et al., 2012). Thematically SDFPs were related to gaining an ideal self-image and achieving perfection. For example, Katie wrote:

> *I just want to take a vacation for myself—make the next 5–6 weeks a very very spa experience. I decided to drop my summer bio class anyway, but I've*

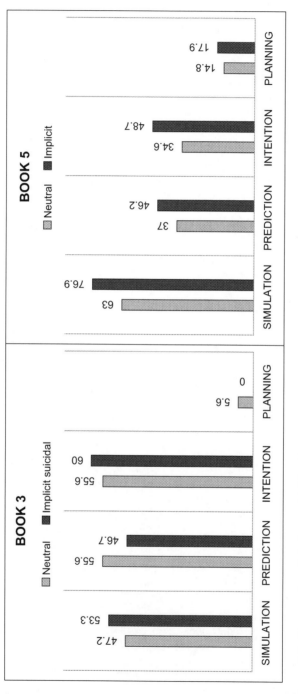

Figure 8.2 Forms of explicit future thinking in neutral (Type 1) and implicit suicidal (Type 2) future-oriented statements in Books 3 and 5

decided not to tell a soul, till probably mid-through, and just concentrate on losing weight. I've never quite had an opportunity like this. I intend to shed so much weight that it is absolutely shocking by the end of the summer.

(5/30)

I want my body to become so strong, not weak at all. I really want a strong body. I could care less about waifishness, but muscles make the human body (meaning women) absolutely beautiful.

(6/2)

The frequency of future-oriented statements containing negations of all kinds was quite high in both Books (about 40%), for example, "*I have to just say for the record that **I'm not going to try to kill myself by doing this**—only perhaps the old Katie, so a new isolated individual one could rise up and emerge*" *(5/30)*. These statements could, in fact, express concerns that an aversive event might actually come true. In this sense, it may be useful to pay attention to such statements as "*However, now my life, I want, I don't need to go and kill myself at all*" *(Book 3)*. Even though we did not code them as expressing explicit suicidal intention because our coding procedure presumed that formally these statements should be qualified as implicit rather than explicit suicidal future thinking, they may nonetheless be considered as marking suicidal ideation. This finding explains the lack of explicit suicidal future-oriented statements in Book 5. It appears that straightforward explicit suicide planning and verbalization of these intentions on paper evoked fear in Katie, and she expressed this planning through negations. However, this is just a hypothesis.

The frequency of statements qualified as ***simulation of future events*** increased in Book 5 as compared to Book 3. These simulations rarely ended in further assessment of their probability (**prediction**) and **intention** formation (both prediction's and intention's frequency decreased in Book 5), for example, "*And I guess I secretly wish for that sort of love from Mark—to want to give me a secure place and always want to be with me*" or "*I'm so scared, as if someone is going to come in and kill me.*"

On the other hand, the frequency of statements perceived as **"action plans,"** which included goals, plausible ways and stages of achieving them, and sometimes even alternative results increased in Book 5 (perhaps a result of planning of weight loss and improving her looks), for example, "*I will get to 130, then to 120 and then to 115 and then to 110, 100. Maybe then people will take me seriously. I want my weight to drop, not my grades.*"

As far as **thematic content** is concerned, the frequency of Achievement statements in Book 5 increased resulting from a significant upsurge in statements related to beauty and weight loss (Weight and Looks) and a non-significant rise in statement describing her achievements in mental recovery, well-being and use of certain adaptive coping strategies (prayer and crying), for example, "*So I need* to be perfect. I have nothing else to really hold on to right now, and I don't feel rooted at all anywhere. So I want to focus on my grades, work and weight."

There was also a significant difference in the frequency of Recreation/Exploration statements and Shame/Guilt statements (reflecting inner conflicts in relation to behaving in the right or wrong way) (see Table 8.2). The quality of the narrative (which we did not assess separately) seemed to change as well. Statements that described future involvement in social events, rest and entertainment became less eloquent, shorter in length, more concrete and excluded mention of other people. For instance, whereas Katie was considering various alternatives and using emotionally colored language while thinking over her free time in the nearest future in Book 3 (*"I really want to do something fun tomorrow. Hiking? Mall? Too far away. Bowling? Who knows? Movie, no. Too much money. Diner, boring—eating food. The Lakes. Oh God, please help me organize my day right and let everything fall into place—a good place in my life. Maybe go back to Dover?" (1/8)*), in Book 5, her free time plans were restricted by sleep (two mentions out of six), a lonely walk (two mentions), cleaning (one mention) and going out with Mark once (*"I think I'll take a little snooze" (5/30); "I want to walk around casually"* (6/11)).

Regarding the statements that reflected Katie's intrapersonal conflict (feelings of shame and guilt), we observed not only a decrease in their frequency but also a shift in their focus from an external object on to her own self and her own deficiency, for example, *"I've decided to transfer all my insecurities, jealousies and anxieties into this book. I do not feel at all that sharing these things with Mark would better our relationship" (Book 3)* versus *"I don't want to burden anyone at all anymore. I'm so scared of losing everything and everyone I love" (Book 5)*.

Future-oriented statements of other thematical categories also suffered a loss of external interests related to enjoying life and interacting with other people and revealed a smoothening of inner conflicts. The focus shifted from actual interpersonal connections and encounters to an intra-personal preoccupation with her own perfection or imperfection. This is illustrated by Katie's relational statements about Mama W in Books 3 and 5 which switched from Katie's planning of long-term and happy family communication (*"I don't want to give up Mama W at all. I want her so badly to give me away at my wedding. I want her to be the grandmother to her grandchildren, my children. I want to give her everything I couldn't give to my own mom as she gets older. Sweet freedom" (Book 3)*) to an actual break in relationship and, perhaps, some relief due to freeing herself from the need to maintain interpersonal connections (*"I will talk to Mama W later. She can't fix this, and I don't want her to, but I want to be able to see her still. I can't though. I know her children come first. I know this will be a lot less hassle, money and rides" (Book 5)*).

Pennebaker and Stone (2004), who compared Katie's lexical material to a control group of students' essays, found similar tendencies in the last period of her life and identified an even lower decrease in the use of socially-oriented language which seemed to be quite low as compared to the controls.

Contrastive Analysis of Neutral (Type 1) and Implicit Suicidal (Type 3) Future-Oriented Statements in Books 3 and 5

Although the percentage of **SDFPs** increased from 6.9% in Book 3 to 20% in Book 5 (Table 8.2), when we compared future thinking plans (explicit neutral vs. implicit suicidal) in these two books, we found no significant difference. It is interesting that, although the majority of SDFPs (67%) in Book 3 were fully explicit, the rest of them had an implicit suicidal plane *(e.g., "I'd give almost anything to be skinny, except my life or the people I love. Oh, how I wish I never had this horrible eating disorder"; 12/18)*. Implicit suicidal SDFPs in Book 5 were a little more frequent and usually discussed the possibility of achieving Katie's ideal, *"I just want to take a vacation for myself—make the next 5–6 weeks a very very spa experience. I decided to drop my summer bio class anyway, but I've decided not to tell a soul, till probably mid-through, and just concentrate on losing weight. I've never quite had an opportunity like this.* **I intend to shed so much weight that it is absolutely shocking by the end of the summer"***(5/30)*.

Figure 8.2 illustrates the differences between the **forms** of explicit future thinking if compared by types of future-oriented statements.

Figure 8.2 shows that the difference between some forms of explicit future thinking remained significant in the Type 1 statements but disappeared in the Type 3 statements where all forms of future thinking were distributed more evenly, and almost equal levels of prediction and intention were observed.

The theme of **weight and Looks** neutral statements in Book 5 (6.9% ($n = 5$) in Book 3 versus 19.8% ($n = 16$) in Book 5) seemed consistent with a higher frequency of **Achievement-related** SDFPs and might correspond to Katie's strong urge for exterior perfection in the last month of her life (Book 5). This assumption is partially supported by a significant decrease in Recreation/Exploration Type 1 statements (16.7% ($n = 12$) in Book 3 and 4.9% ($n = 4$) in Book 5). At the same time, there were no Recreation/Exploration future thoughts among the Type 3 statements in Book 3, and their percentage in Book 5 was as low as 5%, that is, most Recreation/Exploration statements in both books had no implicit plan.

The theme of intrapersonal conflictual experience (Shame/Guilt) "calmed down" in Book 5 as compared to Book 3 in both the Type 1 (13.9% ($n = 10$) vs. 4.9% ($n = 4$)) and the Type 3 future-oriented statements (46.7% ($n = 7$) vs. 15.4% ($n = 6$)). This decrease in ambivalent feelings may also relate to the cathexis of a dominant theme of gaining perfection. Interestingly, Pennebaker and Stone (2004) also noted that during the last month of her life (Book 5), Katie used negative emotional words far less frequently in contrast to an upsurge in her use of positive emotional words.

Whereas the temporal distance of the Type 1 statements in Books 3 and 5 did not differ, there was a change in the Type 3 statements. All implicit suicidal statements in Book 3 ($n = 15$; 100%) had an indefinite time perspective in contrast to 59% ($n = 23$) of these in Book 5. At the same time, a fair number of the Type 3 statements marked as short-term appeared in Book 5 (38.5% ($n = 15$) *vs.* 0% in Book 3).

This difference may be a result of the fact that, in Book 5, the implicit suicidal plan started approaching the surface (conscious awareness), became more accessible and got a specific time frame of 3–3½ weeks, at which point Katie could have achieved her explicit goal of "*perfection*" and "*a very clean and fresh look*," and her implicit goal of a dramatic separation from Mark and parental figures, and "permanent" transformation in death. Some indirect evidence for the existence of this implicit goal is found in Pennebaker and Stone (2004) who observed that although words related to eating correlated positively with the frequency of words related to anger, sports and numbers (calorie counts) and had a negative correlation with references to other people since the summer of year 1 until May of year 2, in June eating words correlated positively with sadness, body-related language and sleeping.

In summary, the frequency of Type 1 (neutral) statements in Book 5 declined because of a decrease in predictions and intentions (Szpunar et al., 2014). We also identified some deficits in the thematic content of Katie's future-oriented thoughts. As compared to Book 3, there was a decrease in Katie's Recreation/ Exploration statements and statements reflecting feelings of Shame/Guilt, moral purity, or failure in Book 5. At the same time, the frequency of the Type 3 (implicit suicidal) statements increased significantly in Book 5. Katie also generated more SDFPs (D'Argembeau et al., 2012), which reflected intensification of simulating representations of herself as having lost weight and having achieved perfection.

Discussion

We believe a statistically significant prevalence of future thinking in Book 5, one month prior to her suicide, to be a most important finding of our analysis of Katie's diary from the perspective of future thinking. As mentioned earlier, many authors have noted a relationship between suicidal ideation and future thinking deficits, such as an inability (difficulty) to imagine oneself in the long-term perspective, or a reported prevalence of negative pessimistic mental representations of the future and a lack of positive self-images (Hirsch et al., 2006; Jager-Hyman et al., 2014; Laghi et al., 2009; MacLeod & Conway, 2007; MacLeod et al., 2005; O'Connor et al., 2015). Our study shows that, at least one month prior to her suicide, Katie's future thinking was quite intensive. This intensity may result from a strong competition between several contradictory implicit plans for the future (i.e., a negative suicidal one and some positive plans) and the necessity to make a choice. Other researchers who studied Katie's diary (e.g., Pennebaker & Stone, 2004) performed a month-by-month lexical analysis of several word categories and found an increase in question mark frequency in Book 5. To account for this, one can assume that Katie's pre-suicidal consciousness found itself at a crossroads of her futures, "sets of multiple alternative possibilities, some of which are incompatible with each other" (Baumeister et al., 2018, p. 224).

Another important finding that we arrived at while analyzing Katie's future thinking from the perspective of the existence of an explicit (voluntary) and implicit (involuntary) suicidal plan (Cole & Kvavilashvili, 2019) was lack of straightforward suicidal statements in Book 5 or, in other words, the absence of an explicit suicidal plan at least before she ceased writing in her diary. (Incidentally, Katie left no suicide note.) Taking into account what happened to Katie in the actual course of events, this fact might bear evidence that her suicidal intention and its implementation in June were sudden and impulsive. Our analysis identifies the dominance of an implicit suicidal plan that could suddenly (involuntarily) become conscious and guide Katie's explicit tragic choice. Such activation of the implicit material could be explained in terms of the dual-process model (Cole & Kvavilashvili, 2019; White, 2011), and in terms of the life script concept and/or intergenerational transmission of the tragic suicidal experience (O'Reilly et al., 2020; White, 2011).

At the same time, we noticed quite straightforward future-oriented statements with negative connotation ("*I'm not going to try to kill myself by doing this*" 5/30) in Book 5, which denied the existence of an explicit suicidal plan. These future thoughts looked similar to Katie's statement that she made ten months before her death and that resembled a no-suicide contract (Drye et al., 1973; Stanford et al., 1994) made to oneself: "*I promise not to kill myself and do stupid things to myself*" (8/17). We can but acknowledge that Katie failed in an attempt to build an explicit no-suicide plan. She may have lacked enough details and positive scenes and selves to project into the future, as well as being devoid of sufficient professional support from the outside.

There were few statements that described Katie's long-term plans in Book 5, and most statements that could be considered long-term (like becoming happy and healthy) were not coded as such (were indefinite) and were overgeneral. They were more like references to the plans rather than fully-fledged plans, while representations of short-term future coded as 3–3½ weeks were frequent (occurred eight [!] times in Book 5) and described Katie's separation from Mark and plans to become beautiful through losing weight.

This most impressive discovery of Katie's remaining life duration is one of the main components of Katie's implicit plan. In other words, whereas Katie's consciousness did not predict dying within 3–3½ weeks (or the last month) and her explicit suicidal planning did not embrace this term (there were no straightforward explicit statements about dying or killing herself within these dates), her implicit suicidal plan limited Katie's future thinking with this time frame of a month. Pennebaker and Stone (2004) also paid attention to the fact that it was within this last period when Katie stopped talking about herself using the future tense verbs. In this regard, we may assume that an engaged reader (e.g., her therapist) studying Katie's diary from the perspective of future thinking and aware of her suicidal story could have noticed this and asked a straightforward question what such a frequent use of this 3–3½-week period meant to her. As we have mentioned it earlier, gaining awareness into an implicit structure of the probable future in the context of the past traumatic experience may exert a positive effect on behavior (Tuchina et al., 2020). Moreover, Katie, who was extremely sensitive and talented, expressed this idea in her diary too, *"If I go back & remember where I came from, I can define where I am today—so I can take control of tomorrow"* (11/1).

Regarding SDFPs, Katie's SDFPs mirrored her dreams of an ideal self and perfection and clustered mostly around getting slim and weight loss plans. (There was also a long hair theme.) There was a significant increase in Weight-and-Looks future-oriented statements in Book 5 as compared to Book 3. Katie kept projecting a desirable range of weight on to the future, from 83 lbs (like *"Victoria Ince,"* September, year 1) up to 150 lbs (June, year 2), with the weight goal decreasing over time getting down to *"125 lbs by next September"* (4/6). One of the last weight-related entries was, *"I weigh 139. As least that is what I need, and I'm so very glad"* (6/20). Katie's autopsy weight was 143 lbs.

Let us remember Katie's early future-oriented statements that we qualified as implicit suicidal planning, for example, *"I can't starve till I'm dead"* (6/14) or *"I will diet till I die"* (10/2), and quite explicit suicidal future thoughts, *"I would give my life to be thin. I really would. It scares me to say this but it is all so true"* (9/28). Keeping in mind these statements, it may be assumed that Katie died having achieved her weight goal for some period and that she was afraid of losing this achievement and spoiling her ideal looks if she continued living.

Her other, more positive plan focusing on the retention of the achieved implied neither instantaneous transformation (*"all I want to do is make myself instantly beautiful,"* 12/18) nor ease of achieving a long-cherished dream (*"I will get so much thinner than her automatically,"* 6/7), and therefore, it failed to become a competitive alternative to the fatal plan. An ideal "angelic" image (as Katie put it) of a future Katie came with metaphors of flying, achieving weightlessness, making her body smaller (6/18), instant beauty and transformation (*"to be entirely different,"* 6/18), fading away and disappearing.

> *If I could slender myself, disappear, angelic form, model ideal, beauty. I can't take much more of this disrespect. I need to live. I want things to be good. I forced myself to run to him. Now run away is the ideal. I hate all these aggressive negative emotions. I hate it. I want to disappear. I want to fade away. I want to see my bone. What the fuck am I fighting for? Myself, really. I refuse to fight for anyone else anymore.*
>
> *(3/18)*

Her method for suicide (by hanging) was not stated explicitly in the diary in contrast to other multiple methods, and this might correspond to an implicit scaffold (Vygotsky, 1978; Williams et al., 2009)[1] of "weighing," "weight loss" or dying under the effect of "body weight." Interestingly, statements that describe details of hanging (suffocation, a belt, choking, etc.), but that never came together to construct the scene or the *knowledge* of a final suicide method, kept appearing throughout all the books of Katie's diary and their frequency varied from 14%, 1.6%, 22%, and 20% to 7.1% in Books 1–5, respectively, that is, some activation of the hanging-related verbal material took place in Books 3 and 4 and calmed down in Book 5.

It is also worth discussing the more positive explicit life alternatives that Katie had. These options related to obtaining an interesting profession, getting married and giving birth to children and gaining long-term rather than momentary beauty (*"I'll be beautiful the way I want to in about four years counting this month,"* 4/6). Unfortunately, Katie failed to maintain these plans at the most acute moment of realizing her need for transformation. A reason for this may be overload of her future thinking with traumatic scenes projected from the past. As van Beek argued, reconsolidation of the negative past (recalling and treating traumatic experience within a supportive environment) might not be sufficient for suicidal patients, as they need a fundamental change in their temporal scheme of perceiving and differentiating between temporal periods (Beek et al., 2009).

Conclusion

Studying diary entries, as well as clinical therapy sessions, can provide material for the unveiling of an implicit suicidal plan. Many authors emphasize the value of journaling as a therapeutic factor (Frisina et al., 2004), and state-of-the-art current approaches invite depressed and suicidal clients to focus on positive goals and to project positive mental representations of their personal future and enhance their specificity (Roepke & Seligman, 2016). Working on Katie's diary, we came to the conclusion that a client's life-time diary analysis should be carried out under the guidance of a therapist who would be able to identify and detail specific features of an implicit suicidal plan to the client and encourage her conscious effort to change the plan. In spite of the fact that negative representations from the past, failures and trauma infiltrate one's cognitive future, giving rise to feelings of fatality and hopelessness, there are always minimally conscious positive scenarios of the future which lose their competitive quality unless fueled by therapeutic support.

Note

1. Scaffolding is a process by which people integrate new information into semantic memory (our general knowledge system) and which enables integration of episodic details into a coherent scene during simulation of past or future (or even atemporal) events (Irish & Piolino, 2015). It also plays a pivotal role (Klein, 2016) in the emergence of autonoetic consciousness (D'Argembeau & Mathy, 2011; Tulving, 2002) that makes mental time travel at all possible.

References

Bar, M. (2009). The proactive brain: Memory for predictions. *Philosophical transactions of the Royal Society of London: Series B, Biological sciences*, *364*(1521), 1235–1243.

Baumeister, R. F., Maranges, H. M., & Sjåstad, H. (2018). Consciousness of the future as a matrix of maybe. *Psychology of Consciousness*, *5*, 223–238.

Beck, A. T., Weissman, A., Lester, D., & Trexler, L. (1974). The measurement of pessimism. *Journal of Consulting & Clinical Psychology*, *42*, 861–865.

Beek, W. van, Kerkhof, A. J. F. M., & Beekman, A. T. F. (2009). Future-oriented group training for suicidal patients. *BMC Psychiatry*, *9*, #65.

Berne, E. (1972). *What do you say after you say hello?* New York: Grove Press.

Bostwick, J. M., Pabbati, C., Geske, J. R., & McKean, A. J. (2016). Suicide attempt as a risk factor for completed suicide. *American Journal of Psychiatry*, *173*, 1094–1100.

Brown, T. I., Gagnon, S. A., & Wagner, A. D. (2020). Stress disrupts human hippocampal-prefrontal function during prospective spatial navigation and hinders flexible behavior. *Current Biology*, *30*, 1821–1833: e8.

Cole, S., & Kvavilashvili, L. (2019). Spontaneous and deliberate future thinking. *Psychological Research*, online, open access.

Conway, M. A., Justice, L., & D'Argembeau, A. (2018). The self-memory system revisited. In J. H. Mace (Ed.), *The organization and structure of autobiographical memory* (pp. 28–51). New York: Oxford University Press.

D'Argembeau, A., Lardi, C., & van der Linden, M. (2012). Self-defining future projections. *Memory*, *20*, 110–120.

D'Argembeau, A., & Mathy, A. (2011). Tracking the construction of episodic future thoughts. *Journal of Experimental Psychology: General*, *140*, 258–271.

Drye, R. C., Goulding, R. L., & Goulding, M. E. (1973). No-suicide decisions. *American Journal of Psychiatry*, *130*, 171–174.

Frisina, P. G., Borod, J. C., & Lepore, S. J. (2004). A meta-analysis of the effects of written emotional disclosure on the health outcomes of clinical populations. *Journal of Nervous & Mental Disease*, *192*, 629–634.

Fukukura, J., Helzer, E. G., & Ferguson, M. J. (2013). Prospection by any other name? *Perspectives on Psychological Science*, *8*, 146–150.

Gamble, B., Moreau, D., Tippett, L. J., & Addis, D. R. (2019). Specificity of future thinking in depression. *Perspectives on Psychological Science*, *14*, 816–834.

Gerrans, P., & Sander, D. (2013). Feeling the future. *Biology & Philosophy*, *29*, 699–710.

Grof, S., & Halifax, J. (1977). *The human encounter with death*. New York: E. P. Dutton.

Haith, M. M. (1997). The development of future thinking as essential for the emergence of skill in planning. In S. L. Friedman & E. Kofsky Scholnick (Eds.), *The developmental psychology of planning* (pp. 25–42). Mahwah, NJ: Erlbaum.

Hillman, J. (1993). *Suicide and the soul*. Dallas, TX: Spring Publications.

Hirsch, J. K., Duberstein, P. R., Conner, K. R., Heisel, M. J., Beckman, A., Franus, N., & Conwell, Y. (2006). Future orientation and suicide ideation and attempts in depressed adults ages 50 and over. *American Journal of Geriatric Psychiatry*, *14*, 752–757.

Ingvar, D. H. (1985). Memory of the future. *Human Neurobiology*, *4*(3), 127–136.

Irish, M., & Piolino, P. (2015). Impaired capacity for prospection in the dementias. *British Journal of Clinical Psychology*, *55*, 49–68.

Jager-Hyman, S., Cunningham, A., Wenzel, A., Mattei, S., Brown, G. K., & Beck, A. T. (2014). Cognitive distortions and suicide attempts. *Cognitive Therapy & Research, 38*, 369–374.

Klein, S. B. (2016). Autonoetic consciousness. *Quarterly Journal of Experimental Psychology, 69*, 381–401.

Laghi, F., Baiocco, R., D'Alessio, M., & Gurrieri, G. (2009). Suicidal ideation and time perspective in high school students. *European Psychiatry, 24*, 41–46.

Lim, M., Lee, S., & Park, J. I. (2016). Differences between Impulsive and non-impulsive suicide attempts among Individuals treated in emergency rooms of South Korea. *Psychiatry Investigation, 13*, 389–396.

Luoma, J. B., Martin, C. E., & Pearson, J. L. (2002). Contact with mental health and primary care providers before suicide. *American Journal of Psychiatry, 159*, 909–916.

MacLeod, A. K., & Conway, C. (2007). Well-being and positive future thinking for the self versus others. *Cognition & Emotion, 21*, 1114–1124.

MacLeod, A. K., Tata, P., Tyrer, P., Schmidt, U., Davidson, K., & Thompson, S. (2005). Hopelessness and positive and negative future thinking in parasuicide. *British Journal of Clinical Psychology, 44*, 495–504.

O'Connor, R. C., Smyth, R., & Williams, J. M. G. (2015). Intrapersonal positive future thinking predicts repeat suicide attempts in hospital-treated suicide attempters. *Journal of Consulting & Clinical Psychology, 83*, 169–176.

O'Reilly, L. M., Kuja-Halkola, R., Rickert, M. E., Class, Q. A., Larsson, H., Lichtenstein, P., & D'Onofrio, B. M. (2020). The intergenerational transmission of suicidal behavior. *Translational Psychiatry, 10*(1), #173.

Pennebaker, J., & Stone, L. D. (2004). What was she trying to say? In D. Lester (Ed.), *Katie's diary* (pp. 55–80). New York: Brunner-Routledge.

Prestwich, A., Sheeran, P., Webb, T., & Gollwitzer, P. (2015). Implementation intentions. In M. Conner & P. Norman (Eds.), *Predicting and changing health behaviour* (3rd ed., pp. 321–357). New York: McGraw-Hill.

Rathbone, C. J., Salgado, S., Akan, M., Havelka, J., & Berntsen, D. (2016). Imagining the future: A cross-cultural perspective on possible selves. *Consciousness & Cognition, 42*, 113–124.

Roepke, A. M., & Seligman, M. E. P. (2016). Depression and prospection. *British Journal of Clinical Psychology, 55*, 23–48.

Schacter, D. L., Benoit, R. G., & Szpunar, K. K. (2017). Episodic future thinking. *Current Opinion in Behavioral Sciences, 17*, 41–50.

Shustov, D. I. (2016). *Self-destructiveness and suicide in alcohol dependence*. Saint-Petersburg, Russia: Spetslit.

Shustov, D. I., & Tuchina, O. D. (2019). "Theodora" way station. *Transactional Analysis Journal, 49*, 292–307.

Shustov, D. I., Tuchina, O. D., & Lester, D. (2019). The social relationships of suicidal individuals. In D. Lester (Ed.), *The end of suicidology* (pp. 127–133). Hauppauge, NY: Nova Science.

Singer, J. A., & Blagov, P. (2002). *Classification system & scoring manual for self-defining memories*. New London, CT: Connecticut College.

Spreng, R. N., Mar, R. A., & Kim, A. S. N. (2009). The common neural basis of autobiographical memory, prospection, navigation, theory of mind, and the default mode. *Journal of Cognitive Neuroscience, 21*, 489–510.

Stanford, E. J., Goetz, R. R., & Bloom, J. D. (1994). The no harm contract in the emergency assessment of suicidal risk. *The Journal of Clinical Psychiatry, 55*(8), 344–348.

Stefansson, J., Nordström, P., & Jokinen, J. (2012). Suicide intent scale in the prediction of suicide. *Journal of Affective Disorders, 136*, 167–171.

Szpunar, K. K. (2010). Evidence for an implicit influence of memory on future thinking. *Memory & Cognition, 38*, 531–540.

Szpunar, K. K., Spreng, R. N., & Schacter, D. L. (2014). A taxonomy of prospection. *Proceedings of the National Academy of Sciences, 111*, 18414–18421.

Thorne, A., & McLean, K. (2001). *Manual for coding events in self-defining memories*. Santa Cruz, CA: University of California.

Tuchina, O. D., Kholmogorova, A. B., Agibalova, T. V., & Shustov, D. I. (2020). Implicit memory of the future in alcohol-dependent patients. In *Zeygarnik's readings: Diagnosis and psychological help in clinical psychology today* (pp. 637–641). Moscow, Russia: FGBOU VO MGPPU.

Tulving, E. (2002). Chronesthesia. In D. T. Stuss (Ed.), *Principles of frontal lobe function* (pp. 311–325). London, UK: Oxford University Press.

Vygotsky, L. S. (1978). *Mind in society*. Cambridge, MA: Harvard University Press.

White, T. (2011). *Working with suicidal individuals*. Philadelphia, PA: Jessica Kingsley.

Williams, L. E., Huang, J. Y., & Bargh, J. A. (2009). The scaffolded mind. *European Journal of Social Psychology, 39*, 1257–1267.

9 What Is the Meaning, Katie?
Katie's Diaries Read Through a Meaning-Making Lens

Birthe Loa Knizek and Heidi Hjelmeland

Prologue

In this chapter, we try to understand the mind of the suicidal Katie from the perspective of meaning-making. According to Frankl, human beings need a sense of meaning in order to endure suffering (Frankl, 1969/2014). Others have developed this line of thinking further and, recently, in the field of health promotion, meaning-making has attracted attention as a coping mechanism in times of hardship. Meaning-making describes the establishment of an internal order of the world which gives a feeling of predictability and control. Meaning-making is, however, an individual life-long process and goes on in everyday life in the encounter and relationships with others, but especially during traumatic events, where the universe of the individual is shaken. According to existential psychology, human beings are characterized by an innate drive to find meaning and values that make their life worth living. Failure to achieve a stable meaning system results in psychological distress and an existential void and makes the individual vulnerable for influences from their context.

Katie tries to achieve a stable meaning system in order to get control of her life. To achieve this, she needs a stable global meaning system consisting of beliefs about the world and her self, goals that she can aspire to and, finally, a general sense of purpose and a perception that she makes a difference. Katie struggles with all three elements in a global meaning system that makes the world unpredictable and uncontrollable. Despite her continuous endeavor to create systems and structures and ceaseless reflections regarding her worldview and her self, she manages to be contented only sporadically and changes her mind continually depending on small things that might have happened. We have no information about the last nine days of her life and what might have tilted her in her efforts. This chapter is about how Katie employed meaning-making in order to stay alive.

Introduction

Katie's diaries are a challenge and an opportunity. Through reading about her reflections, emotions, ambitions and convictions, we can follow her struggle

DOI: 10.4324/9781003125655-10

to make sense of what is happening to and around her. With a turbulent and traumatic childhood, including sexual abuse and neglect, her background lacks safety, stability and predictability. From a home with an alcoholic and abusive father and a mother with schizophrenia, her life course took her through several different foster care homes and the development of anorexia into a life as a young adult in college. In college, the struggles continue around her finances, academic performance and a somewhat unsettled and problematic relationship with both her boyfriend as well as other friends and colleagues, in addition to perceived weight problems. Alcohol and some drugs are not foreign to her. In our approach to Katie's diaries, we are not focusing on possible psychiatric conditions as our main interest is to see how Katie tries to survive through meaning-making. As Park expresses it: "Meaning in life is, arguably, the most important, pressing, and profound concern of human beings, at the core of existence" (Park, 2017, p. 69).

Coming from a Catholic family, faith seems to have some influence on Katie's meaning-making processes in the emotional tumult that characterizes her story. In her efforts to take control over life, she is torn between strong emotions as the meanings that she ascribes to situations and the intentions attributed to different people seem to change constantly. What characterizes Katie through these diaries are the ceaseless attempts to make meaning and take control that she never gave up before she stopped writing in her diary, nine days before she took her life.

Meaning and Meaning-Making

After Viktor Frankl published his book *Man's Search for Meaning* in 1946, the concept has been popular and has attracted a lot of attention that has resulted in different theoretical perspectives on meaning and meaning-making in areas reaching from psychology and neurophysiology in the health sciences to linguistics and semiotics (Bruner, 1990; DeMarinis, 2018; Frankl, 1946/1985; Park & Folkman, 1997; Proulx & Inzlicht, 2012). Frankl made a distinction between meanings in life and the meaning of life. Finding the ultimate meaning of our lives is a life-long quest, whereas meanings in life are everyday events or activities that we find important and that guide us to act in accordance to our value systems (Frankl, 1969/2014). Lack of meaning can evoke strong emotions that even can be fatal: "the acute suffering of someone who lacks meaning in life can lead to stress, ulcers, and even suicide" (Baumeister, 1991, p. 30). During the last few decades, the meaning-making concept has gained renewed attention and further development (DeMarinis, 2018; Park, 2005a, 2005b; Park, 2010; Proulx & Inzlicht, 2012; Seligman, 2011).

Although defining the concept of *meaning* may be difficult, it can, in general, be understood as expectations or schemes of future events that allow us to feel a certain security in believing that we understand our experiences (Proulx & Inzlicht, 2012) and can act accordingly. However, meanings need constant adjustment in our interaction with the socio-cultural environment and give rise to anticipations for further experiences. To make meaning is essential for successful adaptation to shifting environments. Baumeister's definitions are still important as he states that:

> Adaptation involves controlling oneself. This includes regulating one's behavior so as to respond effectively to the environment. Without meaning, behavior is guided by impulse and instinct. Meaning enables people to make decisions based on considering options, consulting values, and referring to long-range plans and hierarchies of goals. . . . Meaning thus liberates the human being from the present situation. It allows behavior to be guided by many factors beyond the immediate environment.
>
> (Baumeister, 1991, p. 18)

Consequently, to be able to make meaning can be described as human beings' lifebuoy in changing environments and, if the meaning-making fails, we become reactive without sufficient stamina to control ourselves and our emotions.

The meaning-making model of Park and Folkman distinguishes between the concepts of global meaning (i.e., fundamental goals, commitments and beliefs about life) and situational meaning (i.e., appraisals of specific events) (Park & Folkman, 1997). Park's elaboration of that model has been useful at the outset for empirical studies (Park, 2005a, 2005b; Park, 2010). According to Hall and Hill (2019), the global meaning system can be understood as a personal worldview outside the immediate awareness of people, but with a powerful impact on thoughts, actions and feelings. Our personal worldview or global meaning system is constructed through both our accumulated personal experiences and our cultural influences, including dominating belief systems (Baumeister, 1991). Within our personal worldview, we find broad conceptions about control, predictability, goals, benevolence or personal vulnerability, among others (Janoff-Bulman, 1997; Mischel & Morf, 2003; Park, 2005a, 2005b; Park, 2010).

As life is rarely a smooth path from birth to death, several things can happen during the life course, for example, assaults, injustices, loss of loved ones, illness, financial constrains or more drastic catastrophes. Encountering such situations, the person must figure out to what extent the situation is threatening and/or controllable, which implications it may have for the future (Park, 2010) and whether the appraised meaning of the situation conflicts with the personal worldview. If a discrepancy is detected, the person might experience the world as incomprehensible and hence unpredictable, which then might be accompanied by a feeling of loss of control and meaninglessness. In case of a discrepancy, the individual must revise either the global meaning system (accommodation) or the appraisal of the situation (assimilation). These processes are both cognitive and emotional (Hunt et al., 2007; Sloan et al., 2007), a process named cognitive-emotional processing by Hayes and colleagues (2007).

Meaning-making can be described as the process of restoring the global meaning system when it has been disrupted or violated (Park, 2005a, 2005b) and is similar to the coping model of (Lazarus & Folkman, 1984). This perspective presupposes that the individual has a relatively stable global meaning system. According to Ahmadi and Ahmadi, one can view the meaning restoration process after a violation of the global meaning system as coping (Ahmadi & Ahmadi, 2018). Park (2013) refers to the products of the meaning-making processes as "meanings made," which can be very personal. The most common product can be described as having "made sense" (Davis et al., 1998), although it seems unclear exactly what people are referring to about the sense they have made as it can include growth, predictability or acceptance. Acceptance means here to achieve a sense of coming to terms with an event or condition and is considered as meaning made (Evers et al., 2001). Other perspectives on meaning made are reattributions and causal understanding (e.g., Janoff-Bulman, 1997; Westphal & Bonanno, 2007), changes in identity (Martin & Tesser, 2006), global beliefs (Park, 2005a, 2005b, 2010) or global goals (Resick et al., 2008). One can also mention the reappraisal of the meaning of a stressor as meaning made (e.g., Resick et al., 2008) as the implications of an event or conditions are reevaluated in a more positive light (Park, 2010). This means that meanings can be made in several personal ways and are considered widely (but not universally) essential for adjusting to stressful events:

> Distress is mediated through discrepancy, and reductions in distress are dependent on reductions in discrepancy. Thus, attempting to make meaning is not necessarily linked with adjustment but may merely signal ongoing discrepancy between an individual's global meaning and an event's appraised meaning. Until meaning-making attempts result in some change or product that reduces the discrepancy between appraised and global meaning, they may be positively related to distress; over time, meanings made (and concomitant decreases in discrepancies) should be related to better adjustment.
> (Park, 2010, p. 261)

In a person's struggle to make meaning, some individuals may get support from their religions, which are comprehensive meaning systems (Hood et al., 2005; Newton & MacIntosh, 2013; Silberman, 2005) offering meaning and hope in a variety of situations (Hall & Hill, 2019). According to Paloutzian (Paloutzian, 2005; Paloutzian & Park, 2005), the meaning system cannot be understood independently of some element of faith, which might contribute to coping in the context of encountering difficult life events (Hall et al., 2018). The question is how Katie worked on her meaning-making processes and the establishment of a global meaning system that could equip her mentally against adversities and disappointments.

Katie and Her Meaning-Making

In a unique way, Katie's diaries allow us to follow her attempts to make meaning of what happens to her and her efforts to get a sense of control and predictability as the basis for a liveable life. On October 17 (year 1), she writes: "I so much want to take control of absolutely everything in my life. It feels like everything is controlling me. It is all so horrible."

In her efforts to take control over life and emotions, she is constantly occupied with meaning-making processes in order to be able to understand the relationship with Mark (boyfriend), sister, fellow students and friends, significant adults and her own past, as well as God. To be able to understand and predict is the presupposition of getting control. When we experience a clash between our global meanings and "reality," and the world seems more unpredictable, feelings like insecurity and anxiety arise. As the global meaning system or personal worldview seems to be central, it is important to look at Katie's worldview against which she interprets all her experiences.

Katie's Worldview

In the global meaning system or personal worldview, we find, as mentioned earlier, three core elements that Park and Kennedy (2017) define as: (1) beliefs about the self and world (e.g., predictability, controllability and the benevolence of humanity), (2) goals (e.g., companionship, self-acceptance, financial security and achievement) and (3) a general sense of meaning or purpose. In Katie's worldview or belief of the world, her relationship with God seems to be significant. According to Hall and Hill (2019), religion can offer meaning and hope in a variety of situations. With her Catholic family background, Katie believes in God and asks for divine help on numerous occasions. The noun *God* is mentioned 195 times in her diaries, and we find appeals to God in both her first and her very last entrance in the diaries:

> God give me strength. Help me today. I feel so unbelievably lonely and battered.
>
> (June year 1)

> Please, dear God, let things pick up in my life beautifully. I want to feel whole inside, instead of being severed in hundreds of little pieces from my own and others' actions.
>
> (June 20, year 2)

Katie asks for help in order to get a feeling of internal coherence and strength, which she seems to lack. In her urge to get control over her own life and emotions, she appeals to the existence of a supreme power which she presumes to be in control. Her faith, which she keeps throughout the diaries, could have been a tool to cope and endow her with some power of resistance as religion "can help to satisfy the urge for control at least through secondary control. . . . Understanding events is an important form of secondary control, and religion typically offers a fairly extensive means of understanding all sorts of events" (Baumeister, 2005, p. 158).

However, even though religion is part of Katie's worldview, she does not use her faith as a tool for understanding events and conditions, which would make her better equipped to cope with everything that she experiences. She probably feels a form of consolation in her belief of a supreme power that she can appeal to and hope for betterment, but it does not seem to help her in her everyday struggle of meaning-making in order to get control, and she must rely on her own abilities:

> I also want to spend time on healing myself, healing my connection with God and changing my life for the better. I do believe in God. I got some incredible strength from God last semester and all year. I don't want to spend my life to try to discover where He comes from or where He is. All I know is that what I can perceive of Him, and the touch of Him is real, and that is what I know. I will still try to discover and make sense of things since that is my nature. But I will focus on what I know to be real for extra help and support.
>
> (June 9, year 2)

Despite her creed, she seems to acknowledge that she needs to rely on her own abilities to make meaning, as well as "real" help and support from this world, rather than divine intervention. Still, throughout the diaries, she appeals to God for fulfillment of a variety of needs as, for example, protection of loved ones, restoration of herself/wholeness/faith in humanity, financial situation, weight and academic performance. In her worldview, God is important but not perfect, as both she accuses God of playing cruel games with her by "bringing and offering things but taking it away" and she admits being afraid of God (June 24, year 1). Her faith does not appear to be a stable meaning system against which she can interpret her everyday struggles. God is significant in her worldview, but Katie does not use her faith as an explanatory model, and her perception of God is changing back and forth from benevolent to cruel. The only stability we find is her belief of the existence of God, which in itself might be consoling, but seems not to be of sufficient constructive help.

In Katie's global meaning system, we also find fundamental values, which she describes as "traditional" and which help her greatly in giving some sense of boundaries, even though other were not established as well (July 7, year 1), as she describes. She seems to see her values as necessary boundaries that function as guidelines for her perceptions and actions. Here she is close to Proulx and Inzlicht (2012) who stated that individuals, in their attempts to adjust their meanings in case of conflict between the global meaning and reality, affirm meanings in other areas than the violated, especially in moral and ethics. Thus, the moral meanings or what Katie calls the "traditional values" determine the boundaries for ongoing coping processes and are simultaneously affirmed further. For example, honesty seems part of Katie's traditional values, and she distances herself from stealing and lying as not being part of her moral make-up (August 17, year 1) despite having done both in the past. She believes that she will manage to avoid lying, while occasional stealing appears to be a must for her despite her values. She describes herself as moralistic (August 20, year 1), but one month later, she sees herself as a moral failure:

> I'm going to punish myself severely for my lack of moral and inability to control my feelings and life. I'm going to purge myself of all of this. I will shed the excess baggage of mortality and lean upon a higher existence— not the one with and out of hell.
>
> (September 28, year 1)

Here, her urge for control seems to lead her thoughts to death as a possible solution where she can free herself of the burden of pursuing bodily and spiritual perfection and live on as a purified spirit, which implies a belief in an afterlife in the Christian sense. Purity and perfection based on her values are significant parts of her global meaning system, and she struggles intensely to obtain both. Repeatedly, she tells her diary (herself) that she must mold herself to total physical perfection, and she both envies and despises others whom she thinks have obtained this goal. But Katie is changing her mind constantly from pursuing control and perfection to distancing herself from the same aspiration: "The world of subtle and extreme attempts toward spiritual, mental, and physical perfection is so mundane and nauseating for me" (August 28, year 1). It would be wrong to accuse her of being ambivalent, as she seems to believe totally in her viewpoint there and then, but then again her conviction may shift: "So I need to be perfect. I have nothing else to really hold on to right now, and I don't feel rooted at all anywhere. So, I want to focus on my grades, work and weight. That's all" (June 18, year 2). In Katie's intense urge for control, she pursues personal perfection on all levels but repeatedly feels that she fails, which causes despair: "I have been quite depressed this weekend. Everything seems so much out of my control" (February 20, year 2). But during the duration of the diaries, Katie never gives up making meaning and trying to get control. This continuous urge for control and the ceaseless efforts to obtain it seem to be the most stable element in Katie's universe. Despite frequently occurring stumbles, she continues to set goals that she works toward.

Katie's Goals

As mentioned earlier, goals are core elements of the global meaning system or personal worldview that describes our motivation for living. According to Park and Kennedy (2017), the global goals can be about, for example, relationships, self-acceptance, financial security or work achievement, which are all highly relevant and significant in Katie's diaries. In addition, the goal of physical perfection stands strong in Katie's universe. The global goals provide the basis for self-esteem, for judging one's own and others' behavior, as well as the incentive to work toward attainment of these goals, which can be quite idealistic: "I want: to do well in school, broaden and learn my mind, good relationships with good people, good relationship with myself, my mind in control, spirit, life, strong in my recovery, free. All because I want to be free, balanced life, starts inside with self" (6 June 14, year 1). Throughout the diary, we follow how Katie pursues her goals in a constant struggle of meaning-making in order to obtain control. Consequently, on March 31, year 2, Katie declares "I'd like this journal to be a goal-oriented journal mostly. Purging also when needed."

In her diaries, we find a lot of reflections on which goals and priorities might be important and how to reach them. Katie is bright and frequently makes a list of her goals and priorities as a tool of gaining control in life. Her lists can be both all-embracing and detailed at the same time:

Goals

> Stick to twelve steps
> Focus: Mark, grades, inner balance, honesty, trueness, realness (not all the time), openness
> Realness—be true to heart and mind, voice it to the world
> Be objective—treat oneself and others fairly
> Body will come all into play naturally, spirit be natural

(July 3, year 1).

Goal Personal

1. Good grades
2. Good workmanship—job
3. Develop exercise ritual
4. Dev. good relationship with self
5. Socialize more (balance)

Goals Make Me Happy Get Control

1. Make all classes/app/work
2. Do all work (catch up to do well)
3. Be mature about relationships & people—got down fighting virtually to zero—work on just becoming close as friends
4. Physical self—develop exercise ritual—lose weight
5. Pay off all bills on time

(October 1, year 1)

From practical to spiritual, all levels seem to be covered in Katie's goals that build on her very high ideals as she aspires to personal perfection, which she sometimes realizes is impossible to achieve. Accordingly, her self-esteem, self-acceptance and belief in her own abilities shift. During a period of 14 days, she swings from not trusting herself (June 8, year 1), self-hatred (June 23) to inner peace and self-control: "I know I can condition myself in any situation to be fully alert and be mentally free. I feel very beautiful and strong right now. I have this inner loving feeling that is so deep and joyful" (June 24). But two days later, Katie again has changed her self-perception: "I know I can't be perfect. So I won't try. It is a shallow empty pursuit is life anyway. There is no sense" (June 26). She not only realizes her own inability to reach perfection but simultaneously perceives life as meaningless or without sense. Her self-perception goes hand in hand with her experience of life as such and changes continuously.

Two days after she has distanced herself from her goal and perceives life as shallow and empty, she is at peace again: "I feel myself changing and maturing so much lately. I feel so much more at peace with myself. I'm so incredibly happy and overwhelmed with this" (June 28). Without a fixed point and some stability and continuity in her global meaning system, Katie is caught up in emotional turbulences while shifting between extreme convictions, and she knows that she must get this stability through control: "I am making a change for the better—organizing my life beautifully where I have control once again academically, personally, spiritually, socially, & intimately & morally. I can't take this sloppy ambivalence I've been living in" (September 30, year 1). As her self-perception and her personal worldview are not stable over time, she becomes vulnerable to others' actions and environmental changes as well as to her own impulsivity and she feels: "severed in hundreds of little pieces from my own and others' actions" (June 20, year 2).

Relatively stable, however, is her "traditional" goal to marry a kind man with good finances and eventually have children. Her dreams about the future include physical, psychological and financial security as well as the opportunity to experience new things:

> I want to marry a family man, good job, and utter loyalty to me. I want to have children and live comfortably and travel a bit. I don't want to be shaken and abused or mistreated at all. But I'm so afraid. My trust is not very good.
>
> (December 1, year 1)

Her goals are clearly expressed, but so are her doubts. Katie struggles to understand and trust herself. Consequently, her unstable self-perception is a weak basis for understanding and trusting other people, which again is an impediment to obtaining control and reaching her fixed goals. During her introspection, Katie realizes that her mistrust of others is rooted in her own struggles to understand and accept herself. Katie is here citing the Chinese philosopher Sun Tzu, who lived over 2,700 years ago: "When you truly know yourself, that is when you can know other people. This is where the heart becomes whole, where the balance with God begins, all in relationship to yourself" (June 24, year 1).

Katie seems to know that the basis for her meaning-making processes and getting control over her own life starts within herself, but she struggles with self-acceptance. The ongoing internal fight is aggravated by her relationships and especially the one with her boyfriend, Mark. Most of the time, she is convinced that she loves and will marry him and, thus, fulfill her goal of a happy marriage, but she is not always sure about Mark's feelings and plans for her, which again results in emotional instability. Most of the time Katie has this clear plan and is convinced that, if she succeeds in becoming perfect, Mark will not look at other girls and only want her, and she will get his utter loyalty and "complete attention" (October 2, year 1). However, it seems that Mark complains about her constant aspiration toward perfection, and she admits that he might be right: "He was right that me constantly trying to be perfect for him ruined some of our relationship. He is entirely right" (November 28, year 1). The self-knowledge she displays here, however, soon gets lost in her all-embracing aspiration for control and perfection, and her struggles continue, although sometimes she actually admits not being fully committed to the goal: "However I do want to be perfect—but then again not really" (November 9, year 1). Mainly she wishes for a perfect relationship with Mark, which she believes can happen only if she is perfect for him. Her entire meaning system and consequently self-perception and acceptance are based on the goal that she must feel beautiful inside and outside.

Her goal for the relationship with Mark is idealistic but not without conditions. She requires (sometimes) that he loves her and behaves toward her the same way that she is feeling and behaving herself:

> If I put time into people, I will not settle for anything less in return. I know I am truly beautiful that way—saying anything less would be a lie. I will search until I find someone with as much trueness and depth as within myself. I do think I've found some of this in Mark. He loves me, I know. When we truly connect with each other, it's all there. But if we do not, I question and search. It is imperative if I am letting someone this close to me, where no one else is even close to this place, that I can depend on them and trust and connect with him freely. He is truly beautiful, but I know he is equally as confused—saying anything else would be a lie. This is reality.
>
> (July 17, year 1)

At this time, she seems to have some self-acceptance and even pride about her own way of being and that this is the measure for how she wants others and especially Mark to behave and feel toward her. But she is not sure about him, still. Interestingly, in Book 4 (February 3, year 2), Katie admits that she has read Mark's diary during last summer but then stopped again in August because she felt awful. She started to read his diary because she wanted to know how he really felt about her. Her concern is that he just wants her for sex, which she consented to because of her aim to be perfect for him despite being very ambivalent about sex. In his diary, she seems to have read that he wanted only to have sex, but *"he was stuck with me"* (March 2, year 2). Her mistrust of Mark that we witness throughout her diaries was, therefore, not only built on her own insecurities but also the result of her breach of confidence during the entirety of her first diary (Book 1). Through prying into his intimate thoughts, she got information resulting in an ever-immanent mistrust, threatening her goal of a perfect marriage and love.

Maybe it is because of her own betrayal that Katie ruminates about Mark reading her diaries. She writes that she knows Mark "must be dying to read my diary. I guess I would be too" (June 28, year 1) or "I'm always so afraid that he would read this. I wonder what Mark would think and how he would react if he read this?" (July 7, year 1), or "I wonder if Mark would? I hope he doesn't. But if he does, I hope he tells me. It would make me feel a lot better" (July 11, year 1). Sometimes she seems to want him to read the diaries: "I want Mark to read some of my journal. I don't know why. I suppose I want him to read and understand at a deeper level even though he really connects with me" (July 1, year 1). In some places, Katie even explains a little about her diary to a potential reader, probably Mark: "Well, I just have to say something important. I have written in this journal in all moods—have had the world in many perspectives, but even though I've been angry at Mark and said I hated him, I never meant it. I have always loved him through everything" (June 24, year 1).

Despite her doubts about Mark's sincerity, she continues her attempts to improve herself. The fight for physical perfection takes a lot of space in Katie's universe, and she has a very tense relationship with her body from the first entry in the diaries: "I really hate my body" (June 8, year 1) to the last: "I'm so sensitive about my body beyond belief" (June 20, year 2). She feels disconnected with her body (June 14, year 1), and considering Katie's past with incest and abuse, her urge for purity and perfection makes sense and maybe especially her never-ending efforts to perfect her body. In her diaries, it seems as if physical perfection is a way of cleansing herself and a way to reach purity, and she describes exercise as her meditation as she then feels connected to the body (June 14, year 1). Most of the time she has a strict regimen with different diets and exercise with very structured plans:

> Food: oatmeal 1/2 cup cooked
>   1 peach
>   8 oz skimmed milk
> Lunch tuna and lettuce
> stay away from sugar
>
> (June 24, year 1)

Katie's diets and exercise plans shift throughout the diaries, while her goal of physical perfection remains stable. Eighteen days before her suicide, she finally seems to feel the way she always wanted and has achieved her most important goal:

> I know I'm beautiful. I thank God above that I am. He was so kind to bestow this to me. But inside I know my heart is beautiful, and I once

again thank God to give me such sincerity. I want to feel beautiful. When I don't feel such a way, I lose grasp as to who I am, that is. I lose grasp as my sense of self and strength and humor.

(June 11, year 2)

She acknowledges that feeling beautiful inside and outside is essential for maintaining a stable self-perception. Her expression is, however, a bit startling. In the first part, she accepts herself as beautiful and thanks God for this. Then she continues with a "but," which indicates that she now expresses something in contrast to the first part. Yet she continues to realize that her inside is also beautiful and again thanks God for this. Katie's self-acceptance would have been perfect, if not for the little word "but" which confuses the harmony. Even at a time when she seems to be at peace with herself, Katie's self-acceptance cracks. As this is a very fundamental element, the following question arises. If Katie struggles with two of the core elements (beliefs about the world and goals) in her global meaning system, which includes her self-perception and self-acceptance, what does this mean for the last element in the meaning system, which is the sense of purpose in life?

Purpose in Life

To feel a purpose in life and that one makes a difference and is significant is one important element in a well-functioning meaning system that guides our experiences and actions: "Because of its essential role in meeting a number of specific demands, including those for coherence, mastery and control, the reduction of uncertainty, identity, existential answer, and behavioral guidance, a well-functioning meaning-system is likely to be necessary for healthy functioning" (Park et al., 2013, p. 158). As we have seen, Katie struggles to obtain control, which seems to overshadow everything else. This struggle seems never-ending because her meaning system is not robust, and she is vulnerable to whatever happens in her life without a stable basis for interpreting experiences.

It also means that her feeling of purpose in life is vague and sometimes completely missing: "I have failed and lived a hollow existence for a few years. I focused so much on the means of my existence to take away the reality of my emotions and existence. I lost my drive, my focus, my purpose in life. This inner spiritual fire, it's mine" (June 14, year 1). Katie expresses that her meaning and purpose in life have been lost because she has focused more on material than on spiritual matters. About six months later, she regrets this once more and is a bit clearer about what she reckons has happened as she blames her loss of purpose to her loss of morals: "My father rest in peace somewhere—wrapped up in the morals I had. They gave me purpose and strength, and then they just got so damn lost" (December 1, year 1). Katie repeatedly stresses her family's traditional values as important guidance in life but, as she frequently has violated these values, she obviously does not perceive them as binding standards anymore and, consequently, they lose their meaning-making potential. Katie states in her diaries that she does not believe in these values anymore and cannot live according to them, but she cannot stop trying to live by them either:

> Such a conflict with myself. Maybe if I analyze my conflict, I'll understand my actions better.
>
> | Mark | close with someone | alone |
> |---|---|---|
> | trust | relationship tension | myself |
> | school | perfect | human |
> | relationships | close with someone | shallow |
> | | | superficial |
> | person | perfect | human |
> | harsh with self | | real with self |
> | self | survivor | victim |
>
> Maybe there are others (June 14, year 1).

Katie seems confused and her attempt to analyze the situation in order to find some direction in life looks equally confused. The desire of being in a close, trusting relationship is prominent in her analysis, as are the self and perfection, while school seems less important. But we probably also see her doubts as "superficial" and "shallow," as well as her internal conflicts. One could probably view Katie's analysis in several ways, but, in general, it looks fragmented and open-ended and quite shaky to lean on in the search for meaning or purpose in life. As with the other two core elements of the global meaning system (global beliefs and goals), we find insufficiencies and instability in her goals and maybe even an absence of purpose in life. Katie's mental make-up does not equip her adequately for her struggles in life. For example, after an unsatisfying meeting with Mark where she worries about his feelings toward his ex-girlfriend, her entire world seems to fall apart, and she cannot see any purpose in living:

> I feel so unable to find solace in anything. I have all these dreams for our future, but they are only dreams as I found out before. There really seems to be nothing for me. I could easily kill myself. No one would notice. Everyone has seemed to get the most out of me they wanted. I feel so used in every way possible. I work so hard with him and everyone, but it doesn't seem to get me anywhere.
>
> (February 20, year 2)

Katie obviously feels that all people take advantage of her without giving anything back. Without the experience of gratitude and love from others, she feels invisible and nobody would even notice her suicide. Her motivation for living and feeling of being significant seem to fade. Eleven days before her suicide, she expresses similar feelings about the future: "I just don't know. I hate the future so much. I'm so overwhelmed. I need to sleep now" (June 18, year 2). Through Katie's diaries, we only have seen in glimpses that she has been contented and maybe even happy, but we have also experienced a very bright person who had an extremely difficult and turbulent background and who, before her death, never gave up trying to obtain control over her own life and making meaning of it.

What Is the Meaning, Katie? Concluding Remarks

In studies of coping and meaning-making, Park et al. (2013) found

> ample evidence for the proposition that meaning systems are essential and that they serve a number of critical functions in meeting specific demands for coherence, mastery and control, the reduction of uncertainty, identity, existential answers, and behavioral guidance. These demands are present in both everyday life and times of crisis.
>
> (p. 160)

With these essential functions of meaning systems in mind, it seems fully understandable that Katie has an extremely hard time finding security and purpose in life, although she sometimes seems contented for short periods. Without a stable purpose in life, Katie becomes vulnerable both to her own impulses and to things that happen in her environment. Nietzsche put it like this: He who has a *why* to live for can bear almost any *how*. Katie really must be praised for her perpetual efforts to create a "why" to live for. She reflects about herself, God and her world, constructs regimens of exercise and diets and aspires to perfection on all levels. We do not know what happened during the last nine days of her life, but we can say that she put in enormous efforts in order to be able to survive. We would like the final words to be Katie's as she captures her struggles and her (almost) never-ending fight to get control and meaning in life:

> Whether it's lying to people, or stealing, or being cruel by hurting my body. Whether it's all the helplessness I had to accept—lack of control which both of these were imperative factors. But the truth lies in the fact that I can attain this peace of mind, by being true, taking responsibility and charge over my behavior, of taking back control, taking it back, acting free in the area of positive respectable construction vs. other methods of approach to me life. . . . I can take control of any situation. I have the hearts and brains to . . . These dots look like tiny footprints.
>
> (June 24, year 1)

References

Ahmadi, F., & Ahmadi, N. (2018). *Meaning-making methods for coping with serious illness*. New York: Routledge.

Baumeister, R. F. (1991). *Meaning of life.* New York: Guilford.
Baumeister, R. F. (2005). *The cultural animal: Human nature, meaning, and social life.* New York: Oxford University Press.
Bruner, J. (1990). *Acts of meaning.* Cambridge, MA: Harvard University Press.
Davis, C. G., Nolen-Hoeksema, S., & Larson, J. (1998). Making sense of loss and benefiting from the experience: Two construals of meaning. *Journal of Personality & Social Psychology, 75,* 561–574.
DeMarinis, V. (2018). Foreword. In F. Ahmadi & N. Ahmadi (Eds.), *Meaning-making methods for coping with serious illness* (pp. x–xvi). New York: Routledge.
Evers, A. W., Kraaimaat, F. W., van Lankveld, W., Jongen, P. J., Jacobs, J. W., & Bijlsma, J. W. (2001). Beyond unfavorable thinking: The illness cognition questionnaire for chronic diseases. *Journal of Consulting & Clinical Psychology, 69,* 1026–1036.
Frankl, V. E. (1946/1985). *Man's search for meaning.* Washington, DC: Washington Square Press.
Frankl, V. E. (1969/2014). *The will to meaning: Foundations and applications of logotherapy.* New York: Plume.
Hall, E. M., & Hill, P. (2019). Meaning-making, suffering, and religion: A worldview conception. *Mental Health, Religion & Culture, 22,* 467–479.
Hall, M. E. L., Shannonhouse, L., Aten, J., McMartin, J., & Silverman, E. J. (2018). Religion-specific resources for meaning-making from suffering: Defining the territory. *Mental Health, Religion & Culture, 21,* 77–92.
Hayes, A. M., Laurenceau, J., Feldman, G., Strauss, J. L., & Cardiacotto, L. (2007). Change is not always linear: The study of nonlinear and discontinuous patterns of change in psychotherapy. *Clinical Psychology Review, 27,* 715–723.
Hood, R. W., Hill, P. C., & Williamson, W. P. (2005). *The psychology of religious fundamentalism.* New York: Guilford.
Hunt, M., Schloss, H., Moonat, S., Poulos, S., & Wieland, J. (2007). Emotional processing versus cognitive restructuring in response to a depressing life event. *Cognitive Therapy & Research, 31,* 833–851.
Janoff-Bulman, R. (1997). The impact of trauma on meaning: From meaningless world to meaningful life. In M. J. Power & C. R. Brewin (Eds.), *The transformation of meaning in psychological therapies: Integrating theory and practice* (pp. 91–106). Hoboken, NJ: Wiley.
Lazarus, R. S., & Folkman, S. (1984). *Stress, appraisal, and coping.* New York: Springer.
Martin, L. L., & Tesser, A. (2006). Extending the goal progress theory of rumination: Goal reevaluation and growth. In L. J. Sanna & E. C. Chang (Eds.), *Judgments over time: The interplay of thoughts, feelings, and behaviors* (pp. 145–162). New York: Oxford University Press.
Mischel, W., & Morf, C. C. (2003). The self as a psycho-social dynamic processing system: A meta-perspective on a century of the self in psychology. In M. R. Leary & J. P. Tangney (Eds.), *Handbook of self and identity* (pp. 15–43). New York: Guilford.
Newton, T., & MacIntosh, D. N. (2013). Unique contributions of religion to meaning. In J. A. Hicks & C. Routledge (Eds.), *The experience of meaning in life: Classical perspectives, emerging themes, and controversies* (pp. 257–270). New York: Springer.
Paloutzian, R. F. (2005). Religious conversion and spiritual transformation: A meaning-system analysis. In R. F. Paloutzian & C. L. Park (Eds.), *Handbook of the psychology of religion and spirituality* (pp. 331–347). New York, NY: The Guilford Press.

Paloutzian, R. F., & Park, C. L. (2005). Integrative themes in the current science of the psychology of religion. In R. F. Paloutzian & C. L. Park (Eds.), *Handbook of the psychology of religion and spirituality* (pp. 3–20). New York: Guilford.

Park, C. L. (2005a). Religion and meaning. In R. F. Paloutzian & C. L. Park (Eds.), *Handbook of the psychology of religion and spirituality* (pp. 295–314). New York: Guilford.

Park, C. L. (2005b). Religion as a meaning-making framework in coping with life stress. *Journal of Social Issues, 61*, 707–729.

Park, C. L. (2010). Making sense of the meaning literature. *Psychological Bulletin, 136*, 257–301.

Park, C. L. (2013). Positive psychology perspectives across the cancer continuum. In B. I. Carr & S. Steel (Eds.), *Psychological aspects of cancer* (pp. 101–117). New York: Springer.

Park, C. L. (2017). Unresolved tensions in the study of meaning in life. *Journal of Constructivist Psychology, 30*(1), 69–73.

Park, C. L., & Folkman, S. (1997). Meaning in the context of stress and coping. *Review of General Psychology, 1*, 115–144.

Park, C. L., Edmondson, D., & Hale-Smith, A. (2013). Why religion? Meaning as motivation. In K. I. Pargament, J. J. Exline, & J. W. Jones (Eds.), *APA handbook of psychology, religion, and spirituality (Vol. 1): Context, theory, and research* (pp. 157–171). Washington, DC: American Psychological Association.

Park, C. L., & Kennedy, M. C. (2017). Meaning violation and restoration following trauma: Conceptual overview and clinical implications. In E. M. Altmaier (Ed.), *Reconstructing meaning after trauma: Theory, research, and practice* (pp. 17–27). Cambridge, MA: Academic Press.

Proulx, T., & Inzlicht, M. (2012). The five "A"s of meaning maintenance: Finding meaning in the theories of sense-making. *Psychological Inquiry, 23*, 317–335.

Resick, P. A., Monson, C. M., & Rizvi, S. L. (2008). Posttraumatic stress disorder. In D. H. Barlow (Ed.), *Clinical handbook of psychological disorders: A step-by-step treatment manual* (pp. 65–122). New York: Guilford.

Seligman, M. E. P. (2011). *Flourish: A visionary new understanding of happiness and well-being*. New York: Free Press.

Silverman, I. (2005). Religion as a meaning system: Implications for the new millennium. *Journal of Social Issues, 61*, 641–663.

Sloan, D. S., Marx, B. P., Epstein, E. M., & Lexington, J. M. (2007). Does altering the writing instructions influence outcome associated with written disclosure? *Behavior Therapy, 38*, 155–168.

Westphal, M., & Bonanno, G. A. (2007). Posttraumatic growth and resilience to trauma: Different sides of the same coin or different coins? *Applied Psychology, 56*, 417–427.

10 A Safe Place for Katie

A Gestalt Therapy Perspective on Her Suicidal Experience

Karolina Krysinska, Jan Roubal and Dave Mann

Gestalt psychotherapy, which was founded by Frederick (Fritz) and Laura Perls in the 1940s, can be characterized as a process-based phenomenological-existential therapy (Yontef, 1993). Its roots and inspirations can be traced back to psychoanalysis, Gestalt psychology, Kurt Goldstein, Kurt Lewin, Wilhelm Reich, Martin Buber and Paul Tillich (Clarkson & Mackewn, 1993). Gestalt psychotherapy has been evolving since its seminal text *Gestalt Therapy: Excitement and Growth in the Human Personality* was published in 1951 (Perls et al., 1951). Three philosophies (field theory, phenomenology and dialogue) are the foundations, or pillars, that define Gestalt psychotherapy (Resnick & Parlett, 1995).

Within Gestalt therapy, there is a lack of consensus over how *field* is defined. The term *field* has been used interchangeably with *situation*, *lifespace* and *lifeworld*. Kurt Lewin, whose work on field theory has been imported into Gestalt therapy (Parlett, 1991), alternated between using each of these terms. Misunderstandings and misconceptions have also resulted from indiscriminate and inaccurate use of the term *field* in Gestalt therapy (Staemmler, 2006). In our view, the major implication of field theory for Gestalt therapy is adoption of a perspective of a continuous, indispensable and indissoluble interaction between a living organism and its environment (Francesetti et al., 2013). From the contextual standpoint, the organism needs to be seen in its environment and can only be understood as a part of its smaller (e.g., couple, family and group) and larger (community, nation and planet) fields (Resnick & Parlett, 1995). Consequently, the Gestalt psychotherapy views the organism as being *of* the field rather than *in* the field.

A Gestalt psychotherapist works with a client using the *phenomenological* method of awareness (Yontef, 1993). This allows the therapist to distinguish ("bracket") between directly experienced feelings, perceptions and actions, on the one hand, and interpretations and pre-existing attitudes, on the other hand. In Gestalt psychotherapy, the former is considered more reliable than the latter, and there is an emphasis on what is "here and now," whilst recognizing the historical ground, both recent and distant, from which this present experience has emerged. Using the phenomenological method, both the client and the therapist are aiming "to describe rather than explain and to start with equal value to all observations" (Resnick & Parlett, 1995, p. 4). In seeking description, the Gestalt therapist adopts a stance of respectful curiosity in an enquiry oriented toward understanding the client's subjective experience of how they reach out to and make sense of their world.

Furthermore, a Gestalt psychotherapist and a client engage in an open *dialogue*. They share their phenomenological perspectives (Yontef, 1993). The "I-Thou" dialogue (Buber, 1958) requires:

- Presence—the therapist makes their experience and phenomenology available to a client in the service of the dialogue
- Inclusion—An existential movement by the therapist toward experiencing both sides of the dialogue (Mann, 2020)
- Commitment to dialogue—the therapist holds an openness to what may emerge in the between of the relationship
- Confirmation—The acknowledgment of the other's whole being (Hycner, 1995).

The therapist's self-disclosure is carefully modulated with the aim of enhancing contact between the client and the therapist, modeling sharing an experience and providing the client an opportunity to be with, see and hear another person. In essence, in adopting a dialogic attitude, the therapist works with neither the I nor the Thou in isolation, but with the between of the relationship, hence the importance of the "-" to illustrate the eternal connection between I and Thou.

Gestalt Therapy's Understanding of Suicide Risk

Gestalt psychotherapists, like their colleagues from other schools of psychotherapy, frequently encounter clients who raise the subject of suicide, but suicide risk assessment has been only sparsely covered in the Gestalt literature (Mann, 2013). As the Gestalt approach is a process-based therapy, no specific theories relate specifically to suicide or self-harm (Mann & Roubal, *submitted*). As with therapeutic work with any clinical presentation, the three pillars of field theory, phenomenology and dialogue form the basis of the relationship when working with suicidal clients.

For epistemological, historical and political reasons, which are outside the scope of this chapter,[1] Gestalt therapists usually are cautious about the concepts of psychopathology and diagnostics, and they do not make a clear-cut distinction between so-called "healthy" and so-called "pathological" experience. Nonetheless, there is a specific psychopathological understanding in Gestalt therapy, which encompasses the suffering of a suicidal client. The word "psychopathology" consists of three roots: *psycho-*, *-patho-* and *-logy*. *Psyche*, meaning soul in Greek, derives from *psychein* (to breathe); *patho*, from the Greek *pathos* (affection, suffering), derives from *paschein* (indeurop.) (to suffer), and *logos* in Greek means discourse. Consequently, staying close to its etymological origin, Gestalt defines that psychopathology is a "discourse on the suffering of the breath, of something elusive, which cannot be confined within a stable object form" (Roubal et al., 2017, p. 2).

Gestalt therapy views psychopathology as emerging at the *contact boundary*, that ever-changing, fluid space "where "I" ends and "other" begins" (Mann, 2020, p. 18), and thus concerns client's interaction with the environment. More specifically, it is not only the client that suffers; the suffering relates to the disrupted relationship between the client and their world. From a phenomenological-field perspective, the client is suffering, the client's world is suffering and the relationship between the client and their world of which the therapist is a part is suffering too. Gestalt therapists work with a matrix of disrupted relationships rather than with an individual in isolation. Consequently, psychopathology is the *pathos* (suffering) of the relationship, of the contact boundary, of the between (where "I" of the client ends and "other" begins). The client is the receptor of this suffering and feels the relational rupture (Mann & Roubal, *submitted*). Moreover, the psychopathology is actualized in the therapeutic relationship, co-created by the client, the therapist and their respective phenomenal fields. The therapist represents here the other who co-creates the relationship "here and now" in which psychopathology emerges. This way we can talk about the client and the therapist "depressing together" (Roubal et al., 2017) or, as in case of suicidality, "suiciding together."

In suicidality or self-harm, the disruption is often due to the hardening and decreased permeability of the contact boundary. In a suicidal client, any combination of moderations ("resistances" or "interruptions") to contact can contribute to this process. Examples are desensitization where clients numb themselves to their environment and deflection where the person turns away from direct contact. In retroflection, the impulse is turned in upon themselves, and Fritz Perls considered the retroflective form of homicide to be suicide (Perls, 1992). Although introjection is generally associated with a permeable contact boundary in which the person absorbs material and messages without discrimination from the environment, this can then lead to a rigid contact boundary if cultural introjects such as "be strong" or those dismissing vulnerability are internalized. In the more communal Eastern cultures, a contact boundary markedly influenced by confluence, where there is little or no differentiation, and other forms of introjection may be at play in instances of altruistic or mass suicide (Colucci & Lester, 2012).

Traditionally, based on psychoanalytic thinking (Yakeley & Burbridge-James, 2018), there is an abundance of theories that relate suicidal or self-harming behaviors to retroflection of impulsive or aggressive behavior. While acknowledging that such retroflection increases risk (Greenberg, 1989; Perls, 1992; Saner, 1989), in the clinical experience of Gestalt psychotherapy, the most effective way of countering suicidality is increasing the client's awareness of their connectedness between them and the world. This includes increasing awareness of supports existing in the client's situation and, consequently, contact with those supports, rather than experiments oriented toward undoing retroflection through catharsis (Mann, 2013). If, as Laura Perls stated, the "unmentionable and inexpressible, are retroflected and turn into feelings of guilt and worthlessness from the torture of which death is the only feasible escape" (Perls, 1992, pp. 8–9), creating a supportive environment facilitative of connection will counter suicidality.

A link between shame and suicide has been hypothesized in Gestalt psychotherapy (Hycner & Jacobs, 1995), with suicide as a most dramatic expression of a desire to hide forever from the sight of others. Consequently, if an experience of powerful shame can trigger suicidal thoughts and intentions, building resilience to shame within a grounded psychotherapy relationship can increase the client's safety and counter their suicidality (Mann & Roubal, *submitted*). Also, the individualistic cultural ground can create fertile ground for the internalization of affects such as shame that can lead to a "rupture in the field of belonging" (Wheeler, 2000), resulting in isolation and a delinking from possible supports. In such a cultural field, therapy itself can be seen as shameful.

In understanding a suicidal client's phenomenology, what is happening in the "here and now" of a Gestalt psychotherapy session is as important as the client's world outside the therapy room (Mann & Roubal, *submitted*; Zeleskov Djoric, 2013). Suicide risk assessment in Gestalt psychotherapy takes this into account in considering four time zones (Yontef, 1993). The *Here and Now* refers to the client's environment at a particular moment in the therapy session, including the ongoing phenomenological exploration about the suicidal thoughts and intentions. The *There and Now* refers to the client's situation or lifespace outside the therapy session, especially the suicidal client's support systems and stressors. The *Here and Then* forms the ground of the psychotherapy relationship and includes relational patterns between the therapist and the client, which may contribute to "depressing" or "suiciding together" (Roubal et al., 2017). Finally, the *There and Then* refers to the client's development, such as attachment style and traumas, which may contribute to current suicidality.

The risk of suicide in the psychotherapy can be tackled on a macro- and micro-level (Howdin & Reeves, 2009). The macro-level refers to risk factors identified through research, the broader landscape of suicide prevention policies and guidelines, organizational risk assessment standards and procedures. This macro-level is immersed in the "prediction/prevention culture," based on the premise that if suicide risk can be recognized and assessed, then intervention is possible and suicide can be prevented. The micro-level deals with the suffering and pain of suicidal individuals and a "struggle to understands and articulate their self-annihilatory thoughts" (Howdin & Reeves, 2009, p. 10). Gestalt psychotherapy does not eschew the macro-level, since epidemiological and suicidology research data, including information pertaining to risk and protective factors, classical diagnostic categories and practical issues such as access to lethal means of suicide, can support the clinical work on the micro-level (Mann & Roubal, *submitted*). However, we need to remain mindful that, "statistics alone can be misleading when such a cold science is applied in isolation to the give and take of human relating" (Mann, 2013, p. 324). The art of good Gestalt psychotherapy lays in maintaining a balance between a thorough risk assessment and planning an appropriate response ("I-it") and a contactful therapeutic process ("I-Thou") (Howdin & Reeves, 2009) or, to put it another way, in assessing the client's need at any given moment for strategy or inclusion and confirmation of their being, and for the therapist to move fluidly as they attune to the presenting need moment to moment.

How Can a Gestalt Psychotherapist Work With a Suicidal Client?

A starting point for formulating treatment plans and strategies for intervention is seeking clarification as to whether a client is experiencing suicidal ideas, whether there is (or has been) suicidal intent and what contributes to movement between ideation and intent. Mann provides examples of questions which help to "flesh out a picture of the client's behavior" (Mann, 2013, p. 325): Have you ever thought of suicide? How often do you think of killing yourself? In what situations, do these thoughts/impulses arise? Do you think about how you might kill yourself? Have you ever moved toward action and, if so, what did you do and what stopped you? Can you describe what happens to you when you think of killing yourself? Are these thoughts with you now?

These questions, which can be labeled as "risk assessment," are asked within the Gestalt process of direct phenomenological exploration and dialogue (Mann, 2013). Yet, here the psychotherapist needs to direct the conversation to areas usually associated with risk, such as isolation, hopelessness, helplessness, shame, guilt and desperation. This direct enquiry invites an explicit dialogue about client's suicidality, thus counteracting anxiety stemming from the "not knowing" (Howdin & Reeves, 2009). As Howdin and Reeves eloquently observed, for a psychotherapist "trying to engage with hints, suggestions and subtleties can typically be more frightening than responding to a more explicit suicidal discourse" (Howdin & Reeves, 2009, p. 11) and for the client, "the terror of suicidality often lies in the unexplored, the 'not asked' and therefore that which is out of awareness. The 'monster' that can be suicide risk can be retransfigured through awareness in the intimacy of the dialogic relationship" (p. 11).

Informed by field theory, the process of risk assessment in Gestalt psychotherapy through phenomenological enquiry includes an exploration of the (dis-)connection between the client and their world. An individualistic cultural bias in which the person is seen as primary to the environmental field may prevent a psychotherapist from exploring the environment's interaction with the client, thus blinding the therapist to the "suffering in the way [client] is reaching out to the world and the way in which [client's] world meets him [sic]" (Mann, 2013, p. 326).

Although there is controversy in the broader field regarding effectiveness of *no-suicide contracts* in psychotherapy (Edwards & Sachmann, 2010; Range, 2005), some Gestalt psychotherapists may ask their clients to agree to a no-suicide contract in order to create more space to explore the suicidal client's ideas and intent (Mann, 2013). Such a contract or agreement may relate to the whole duration of psychotherapy or short-term work and, in some cases, may even need to be renewed every session. If suicidal ideation or intent is present when a client attends therapy, there must also be a pull toward health and life by virtue of the client walking through the door of our therapy room. Without a no-suicide agreement in place, the therapist will at some level (possibly out of awareness) hold back from investing fully, with all their being, in the relationship. Of course, such an agreement offers no guarantees that the client will not desert their relationship with their world, including their relationship with the therapist, but making such a commitment in the face of an opposing polarity highlights a continuum between the polarities of life and death. What is essential in the forming of such an agreement is the attitude of the therapist. This should not be a cold, contractual agreement but rather one fully embracing the principles of dialogue and thereby holding an I-Thou attitude (Buber, 1958; Hycner & Jacobs, 1995; Hycner, 1993). Such a stance demands bold relational swinging between the therapist and the client with presence, openness and inclusion that allows the therapist to sense the others hurt, pain and anguish (Mann & Roubal, *submitted*).

Mann warns of the risk of *pre-configuring the psychotherapy field* around suicide risk (Mann, 2013). This may happen when a new client referral (with good intentions) comes with information highlighting client's risk. As a result of countertransference and the co-created nature of a psychotherapeutic relationship, prior knowledge of a potential threat could actually increase the likelihood of risk by proactively maintaining its presence in the background of the psychotherapeutic work (Blaize, 2003; Mann & Roubal, *submitted*). Information about suicide risk may negatively influence the level of contact between the client and the psychotherapist and limit the phenomenological exploration, thereby leading to further disconnection of the client from their world and available support (Mann, 2013).

The *experimental dimension* is built into the very foundations of Gestalt psychotherapy (Amendt-Lyon, 2003; Roubal, 2009), and carefully graded experimentation may help in the management of self-destructive impulses (Mann, 2013). An experiment is a therapeutic intervention, which emerges from the relational ground between the therapist and the client, where a new experience is created in an effort to help the client enhance their awareness and get in touch with their unseen potential (Mackewn, 1999). As the client is invited to experiment with the unfamiliar, the founders of Gestalt therapy described experimentation as the creation of a "safe emergency" (Perls et al., 1951, p. 65). A new experience for the suicidal or self-harming person may mean constructively directing their aggressive impulses outwardly rather than turning them destructively in upon themselves. Nonetheless, there are misunderstandings and simplistic ideas about using experiment to undo retroflection in relation to suicide risk which ignore the complex background narrative to a client's suicidality (Mann, 2013).

Such experimentation often revolves around cathartic expression of anger or rage that can become circular, leading to an addictive pattern of repetition compulsion. While it can be argued that cathartic expression may challenge introjected beliefs that support retroflection, neurological research shows that repeated expression of anger or rage strengthens neural pathways that lead to aggressive behavior (Petzold, 2006; Staemmler, 2009). It then becomes clear that repeated cathartic expression can heighten the risk of suicide as those neural pathways that lead to aggressive behaviors are reinforced in a person with a tendency toward turning them upon themselves. Experimentation with the suicidal client needs to begin with a focus on building supports, building ground to challenge sedimented beliefs and increasing contact with the person's environment in the "here and now" of the therapy room. The simplest of interventions can form the building blocks to increase the client's ability to make contact and build support. Inviting the person to experiment with making different forms of eye contact and noticing what sensations surface as they do so, experimenting with breathing in the present environment and engaging in the exercise alongside the person, are just two examples of unremarkable experiments that can be the first steps to remarkable change.

Mann stresses the need to "explore what has been effective to date for the client and how those strategies can be adapted safely to enable the client to hold themselves safely until such time when sufficient support has formed to move towards lasting change" (Mann, 2013, pp. 331–332). In some cases, these strategies may seem counterintuitive and be perceived as signs of disintegration, for example, delusional ideas, hallucinatory experiences, obsessive-compulsiveness or bizarre behaviors. Yet, these experiences are not necessarily life-threatening states in themselves and may hold a supportive function as "glue" for a particular client (Stratford & Brallier, 1979). Interventions, which loosen the structure and allow the client new experiences and possibilities, can be anxiety-provoking and are likened to a "solvent for the old 'stuck' patterns" (ibid; p. 93). On the other hand, interventions focusing on the familiar, organizing client's energy and decreasing the stimuli refer to what feels comfortable, stabilize and "reglue." In crisis situations, including a suicidal crisis, the task is holding rather than challenge, "glue" rather than "solvent."

Three Strategies of Working With Suicidal Clients

Mann and Roubal (*submitted*) suggest that it can be helpful for Gestalt therapists to consider the three stages of pre-suicidal syndrome: contemplation, ambivalence and decision making in their work with suicidal clients (Pöldinger, 1968; Rau et al., 2013). Strategies for the therapeutic work and challenges faced by the therapist differ in each of the three phases. In the stage of *contemplation* (or crying for help), the client experiences suicidal thoughts but is able to control their behavior. Here, the therapist works "as usual" using the phenomenological enquiry to explore thoughts of suicide, as one of the many phenomena appearing in the client's life and brought into therapy. The challenge for the therapist is not to be afraid to explore the phenomenon of suicidal thoughts in the context of client's life situation and to search together for a meaningful understanding of the situation and not problem solving.

In the stage of *ambivalence* (or balancing on the edge), the client's suicidal impulses become more apparent and frightening. For instance, a client may experience a bodily felt impulse to jump from a window or under a truck. The client's ability to distance themselves from these impulses and to control their actions becomes limited. They find themselves balancing on the edge between life and death, and the therapist works with them facilitating communication of these competing pulls. The challenge for the therapist here is not to prefer one of these polarities; to allow the client to experience support in their existential struggle and get relief from the unbearable tension and ambivalence. If the therapist holds onto or identifies only with the "life" polarity, the danger is that only the opposing "death" polarity becomes available for the client. Paradoxically, the more the therapist persuades the client to stay alive, the more the client may emphasize the death polarity as s/he does not feel seen and accepted with it.

In the stage of ambivalence, the therapist can provide practical support. The more the client is losing control over the suicidal impulses, the more the therapist needs to take responsibility for securing the situation. For instance, with the client's agreement, the therapist may contact the client's family or a psychiatrist to discuss an option of medication. The possibilities for managing the crisis may also include hospitalization.

In the stage of *decision-making* (or final decision), the client experiences calm and relief, which can erroneously be understood by the therapist as improvement. Such relief can manifest when the unbearable tension between life and death is finally resolved, and the client has decided to die. At this stage, clients no longer have reason to seek psychotherapy, and they may be brought to the therapist by family members. The therapist's challenge here is to accept the responsibility and make decisions for the client, which frequently lead to hospitalization. This situation is unusual for therapists working in private practice and may seriously challenge their ethical values. Taking responsibility for the client needs to be combined with respect, as it may prove to be key in restoring the therapeutic relationship when the suicidal crisis subsides.

Our Work With Katie

To illustrate the Gestalt therapy approach, we introduce basic guidelines for our work in the hypothetical situation when Katie comes to therapy with us after she finished writing her diary (nine days before her death). What can we do? In our work, we start from the "here and now" situation, and we follow the natural flow of the dialogue. In this dialogue, we are present genuinely as one human being meeting another human being. We do not follow a general prepared in advance procedure. The therapy is an emergent process cultivated by our practice and informed by our knowledge. At the same time, however, our work is channeled by guidelines that serve us as a supportive "third party" (Francesetti et al., 2013), guidelines that are grounded in the theoretical concepts of Gestalt therapy work with suicidal clients and that are adjusted for this individual client. We are prepared to walk a narrow ridge (Buber, 1958) between, on the one side a possible need for techniques, risk assessment and strategies, and on the other side the call for dialogic human encounter. Now, Katie is knocking at the door, and we let her in.

Maintaining an I-Thou Attitude

Building an inclusive trustful relational ground with Katie is crucial for us. Our intention is to create such a place where Katie would feel respected and accepted, confirmed for all she is and can be, with all her emotional states and thoughts about herself, no matter how confused or contradictory they might appear. In equalizing the relationship, we need to hold a dialogic attitude with Katie from the beginning, with the possibility of I-Thou moments emerging from the ground of such an attitude of mutuality later in the therapy. We accept Katie as she is and work with what is. This is our basic attitude and we believe that Katie has the capacity to feel our care and internalize it even if that capacity is deeply buried beneath layers of conflicting messages from her relational ground. This approach seems specifically important when we realize how unstable and insecure the ground was for Katie in her childhood. In very practical terms to help Katie to feel being accepted, we follow a simple general rule for our interventions: listening and noticing are more important than talking. We notice how Katie may deflect or resist any feedback that we may offer that conflicts with her self-image, and how she moves away from direct contact whether that is through the use of language or bodily, for example, a retroflective armoring herself bodily against anything that may be ego-dystonic. We may also need to model direct relating, and this may involve self-disclosure. If suicide is in the picture, we consider it part of building a relational bridge to share something of our reaction to that directly.

Phenomenological Exploration

We are interested in the context of her current life situation as a whole and how that is shaping our meeting in the present. We explore this with Katie, using our natural curiosity for keeping our outlook fresh, to discover the uniqueness of her story and herself as a person. As far as possible, we bracket any material that will preconfigure our meeting with Katie, so that we can be touched by the "virgin experience" (Husserl, 1931) to gain a flavor of the world as she experiences it. This approach includes offering to Katie the possibility to speak openly about her suicidal thoughts and tendencies. We carefully explore her experience of being stuck: "I feel like I'm losing touch with everything, that I'm slipping away without choice—or everything else is slipping away" (June 18, year 2). In the dialogue, we explore the two foci of Katie's act of intentionality: *what* she reaches out to in her world and *how* she reaches out to it. In doing so, we seek a description of her phenomenal world.

Although we explore what is experienced, we also need to consider that which is not experienced, as the two are intimately connected (Roberts, 1999).

Through adopting a phenomenological approach and bracketing our experience, we are able to "study of the *advent* of being to consciousness, instead of presuming its possibility as given in advance" (Merleau-Ponty, 1962, p. 61). Our dialogical stance involves inclusion, when we enter Katie's self-annihilatory world through phenomenological exploration. This can be extremely challenging, even engulfing and overwhelming. The practice of phenomenological enquiry requires developing good awareness of our own personal history, beliefs and attitudes in relation to suicide, which can be supported by supervision and personal therapy (Howdin & Reeves, 2009).

Structure Providing Safety

There are, however, some issues where we actively take a lead. We open the issue of suicide and discuss Katie's experiences connected with it. As discussed, we ensure that a no-suicide agreement is in place and reinforce this agreement and our reasons for making it. We encourage Katie to share her inner states with us, so that she can experience that she is not alone in it anymore. We encourage her to share with us more explicitly what she is only vaguely suggesting: "I wish I could just melt away right now" (June 1, year 2). We also actively offer an external support in the form of medication and hospitalization to her, which she, however, refuses: "I will not end up in the hospital again" (May 30, year 2). Importantly, we explain why we are offering these supports and explore alternatives alongside seeking description regarding her resistance to hospitalization.

We discuss Katie's plans for the next days, and we make an agreement with her about our future collaboration. We set concrete dates for our meetings that, over an emergency period, might be as frequently as daily. This may be supplemented with other contact, such as via telephone, email or text messaging. We also need to be careful not to parallel a process of isolation by managing the situation alone. If other professionals have been involved, communication with them is indicated at times of crisis. Building awareness of resources in the local community, such as those in the voluntary sector that are likely to include telephone helplines, can help further in helping Katie through periods of crisis. The therapist needs to model a healthy process by using their own support systems, including clinical supervision, and informal supports. By doing so, seeking support becomes a more figural element in the field between Katie and her therapist.

Glue Rather Than Solvent

Our general strategy is to support integration and grounding. Therefore, we validate Katie's habitual patterns as a source of self-support for the moment (her faith in God, her focus on her body and her focus on the partner relationship). Although we are aware of the limiting aspect of these fixed patterns, we would not push for change. Katie herself indicates in her diary that there is too much change for her. We would not focus on exploring the limitations of fixed patterns. We would rather appreciate their stabilizing function for the moment. Any experimentation that may emerge with Katie would focus on increasing her awareness of supportive elements in her life, building ground for her to stabilize upon. As fragmentation is present, we would avoid high-graded experimentation that invited a process of further splitting such as two-chair work. Fritz Perls (1992) might have said, "disintegrate to integrate," but he also invited us to see resistances as assistances, and at this point with Katie, the emphasis would need to be on the latter.

Balancing

In the following sessions, we continue our work on the collaborative phenomenological exploration of Katie's experience. We legitimatize her tendency to death. "Yes, Katie, I hear that there appears a wish to die in you. I hear it and I take you seriously. I can really understand that such a wish appears in your very difficult situation, and I feel sad that you are in this situation." In respecting this tendency as Katie's experiential reality, we do not aim to change it but confirm her experience and practice inclusion. We see it as a radical expression of her need to "take a vacation for herself" (May 30, year 2) and to "free herself" (May 30, year 2). At the same time, we see the situation in its wholeness. We see that Katie comes to therapy and is willing to be engaged in the dialogue with us, and that contradicts, at least to some extent, her tendency toward death through suicide. In noticing this, we also validate her tendency to life. We believe that the therapist's inner stance is crucial here: we respect both the contradictory tendencies and accept them as a whole and as polarities characterizing Katie's lived experience "here and now."

We are careful not to favor any of the polarities, as this could raise the risk of a suicide. If we favor the tendency to life, Katie would likely balance it by favoring the tendency to death. Moreover, if we try to manipulate her to life, she would feel missed in her tendency to death and abandoned in her suffering, which again would raise the risk of suicide. Keeping such a stance is not easy for us, and therefore we use the principle of the "paradoxical theory of change" (Beisser, 1970; Roubal & Francesetti, *submitted*) as the supportive theoretical third party: the change comes when accepting what is not when trying to arrange what is not. "Many people, including myself, always want to do things differently, or make a change. . . . However, the point is that no one makes a plan that makes things more attainable at all" (June 2, year 2). From the perspective of the paradoxical theory of change, we can connect to Katie's position, while keeping hope at the same time. We aim to raise awareness of a connection between the polarities that underpin the poles of death and life, respectively, those of despair/depression and hope, as a continuum exists between them. By raising awareness of movement over time through simple enquiry, "Did you feel as low as you are describing this morning (or yesterday)?" we introduce the possibility of movement. Even if, as may be likely, that movement is toward the suicide (death) polarity of the continuum, it implicitly highlights that a continuum exists, rather than a black-and-white choice, and that movement is possible.

Broadening

In general, there is a specific kind of field dynamics of the suicidal situation: the tendency toward narrowing (Shneidman, 1996). This tendency appears as limited scale of options on different levels (cognitive, emotional, behavioral and relational). While appreciating Katie's perception, it is neither helpful nor therapeutic to become confluent with such narrowing dynamics. Our intention is to support broadening, broadening on different levels, making the implicit explicit. Therefore, in dialogue with Katie, we search for different kinds of emotions involved, for different resources of inner and outer support available (physiological and environmental), for similar life situations in the past where she has successfully creatively adjusted, for different kinds of body experiences and for different kinds of relating to others. We actively create the sense of future in the between of our dialogue with Katie. In the language we use, we consciously and repeatedly refer to our future collaboration with Katie, and we negotiate long-term psychotherapy goals with her.

Working With Our Own Experience

We pay attention to what is happening to us in Katie's presence. We become aware of the sense of urgency ("I need to do something to prevent her killing herself," "This is not a usual psychotherapy situation, it is really critical, I must not make a mistake"), and we actively dissolve it. We pay attention to ground ourselves well (body, breathing and theoretical third party) before intervening. We actively slow down our own speed, and we regulate the intensity of our experiences in order to listen to the softer nuances of what is happening to us in our relationship with Katie and her field. We listen to what we might term our counter-transferential reactions to Katie, which help us identify any emerging and enduring relational themes (Jacobs, 2017; Mann, 2020). We gradually increase our presence in the service of our dialogue with Katie, our intention being to increase our visibility as we sit alongside a fellow human being who is suffering. We attempt to attune to any sense of her feeling abandoned that could destroy the fragile sense of hope emerging. We also become aware of our own tendency to dichotomize (Either—Or), and we actively transform it to seeing both polarities as a dynamic whole (And—And) connected by a continuum.

Working With Borderlining Tendencies[2] and Post-Traumatic Experiences

This last point would already be a step to future therapeutic strategy when Katie's suicidal experience withdraws to the background. Then, we would work with her borderlining behaviors and post-traumatic experiences. We would stress mainly the relational stability and predictability of the psychotherapy relationship, acceptance and respect, combined with a clear and reliable setting of our collaboration. We would support Katie in her growth by letting ourselves be guided by a metaphor: Katie grows like a tree which started its life in a very difficult and poor land and has survived by her unique way of creative adjustments. The way Katie functions now is the result of such adjustments. We respect and appreciate them, despite how dysfunctional they might look now. We see them as a shape of a tree which grows in a very inhospitable place, a shape which might seem strange, but which, however, enabled her to survive.

Conclusions

Approaching the client from a free and grounded dialogical position (Roubal & Francesetti, *submitted*) enables a Gestalt therapist to immerse through the phenomenological enquiry into the suicidal experience and to discover the need expressed indirectly through the suicidal thoughts in relation to the person's phenomenological field. There is a movement from "I want to finish my life" to "I want to finish my life as it is now," and finally to "I so much long for . . . in my life" (Mann & Roubal, *submitted*). There is an inherent hope in the situation, in the between of the relationship. For the therapist, the hope is in the fact that the client attended and is present. For the client, the therapist's accepting and containing presence can be an embodied hope that someone still has the desire to understand. The client has already taken a calculated risk and has begun to experiment by virtue of stepping into our therapy room. This reality reveals the extreme difficulty of the client's situation but, alongside this seemingly unbearable struggle, lies a yearning for help that has led the client to therapy.

Notes

1. For an in-depth discussion of the Gestalt therapy approach to psychopathology, see Francesetti and colleagues (2013).
2. We use the term "borderlining" in preference to "borderline" in order to demonstrate the fluidity of our approach to diagnostic terms. The use of verbs rather than nouns fits better with Gestalt therapy's theory of self-as-process rather than seeing self as fixed.

References

Amendt-Lyon, N. (2003). Toward a Gestalt therapeutic concept for promoting creative process. In M. Spagnuolo Lobb & N. Amendt-Lyon (Eds.), *Creative license: The art of Gestalt therapy* (pp. 5–20). New York: Springer-Verlag.

Beisser, A. (1970). The paradoxical theory of change. In J. Fagan & I. Shepherd (Eds.), *Gestalt therapy now* (pp. 77–80). New York: Harper Colophon Books.

Blaize, J. (2003). An individualistic or field-oriented point of view? *International Gestalt Journal*, 26(1), 21–25.

Buber, M. (1958). *I and Thou* (2nd ed.). Edinburgh, Scotland: T & T Clark.

Clarkson, P., & Mackewn, J. (1993). *Fritz Perls*. London, UK: Sage.

Colucci, E., & Lester, D. (2012). *Suicide and culture: Understanding the context*. Cambridge, MA: Högrefe Publishing.

Edwards, S. J., & Sachmann, M. D. (2010). No-suicide contracts, no-suicide agreements, and no-suicide assurances. *Crisis, 31*(6), 290–302.

Francesetti, G., Gecele, M., & Roubal, J. (2013). Gestalt therapy approach to psychopathology. In G. Francesetti, M. Gecele, & J. Roubal (Eds.), *Gestalt therapy in clinical practice: From psychopathology to the aesthetics of contact* (pp. 53–100). Siracusa: Istituto di Gestalt HCC Italy.

Greenberg, E. (1989). Healing the borderline. *The Gestalt Journal, 12*(2), 11–56.

Howdin, J., & Reeves, A. (2009). In the fragility of contact: Working with suicide risk in the dialogic relationship. *British Gestalt Journal, 18*(1), 10.

Husserl, E. (1931). *Ideas: General introduction to pure phenomenology* (Vol. 1). New York: Macmillan.

Hycner, R. (1993). *Between person and person: Toward a dialogical psychotherapy*. Highland, NY: Gestalt Journal Press.

Hycner, R., & Jacobs, L. (1995). *The healing relationship in Gestalt therapy: A dialogic/self psychology approach*. Highland, NY: Gestalt Journal Press.

Jacobs, L. (2017). Hopes, fears and enduring relational themes. *British Gestalt Journal, 26*(1), 7–16.

Mackewn, J. (1999). *Developing Gestalt counselling*. London, UK: Sage.

Mann, D. (2013). Assessing suicidal risk. In G. Francesetti, M. Gecele, & J. Roubal (Eds.), *Gestalt therapy in clinical practice: From psychopathology to the aesthetics of contact* (pp. 324–337). Siracusa, Italy: Istituto di Gestalt HCC Italy.

Mann, D. (2020). *Gestalt therapy: 100 Key points and techniques* (2nd ed.). London, UK: Routledge.

Mann, D., & Roubal, J. (submitted). Gestalt therapy approach to suicide and self-injury. In G. Bohall, M. J. Bautista-Bohall, & S. Musson (Eds.), *Dangerous behaviors in clinical and forensic psychology*. New York: Springer.

Merleau-Ponty, M. (1962). *Phenomenology of perception*. Translated from French by C. Smith. London, UK: Routledge & Kegan Paul Ltd.

Parlett, M. (1991). Reflections on field theory. *British Gestalt Journal, 1*(2), 69–81.

Perls, F. (1992). *Gestalt therapy verbatim*. Highland, NY: Gestalt Journal Press.

Perls, F., Hefferline, R., & Goodman, P. (1951). *Gestalt therapy: Excitement and growth in the human personality*. London, UK: Souvenir Press.

Perls, L. (1992). *Living at the boundary*. Highland, NY: Gestalt Journal Press.

Petzold, H. G. (2006). Aggressionsnarrative, Ideologie und Friedensarbeit: Integrative Perspektiven. In Staemmler, F-M. & Staemmler, B. (Eds.), *Aggression, time, and understanding*. Ego, Anger & Attachment. Santa Cruz, CA: Gestalt Press.

Pöldinger, W. (1968). *Die Abschätzung der Suizidalität*. Bern, Switzerland: Huber.

Range, L. M. (2005). No-suicide contracts. Assessment, treatment, and prevention of suicidal behavior. In R. I. Yufit & D. Lester (Eds.), *Assessment, treatment, and prevention of suicidal behaviour* (pp. 181–203). Hoboken, NJ: John Wiley & Sons.

Rau, T., Plener, P., Kliemann, A., Fegert, J. M., & Allroggen, M. (2013). Suicidality among medical students: A practical guide for staff members in medical schools. *GMS Zeitschrift für Medizinische Ausbildung, 30*(4), Document 48.

Resnick, R., & Parlett, M. (1995). Gestalt therapy: Principles, prisms and perspectives. *British Gestalt Journal, 4*(1), 3–13.

Roberts, A. (1999). Digging up the bodies. *British Gestalt Journal, 8*(2), 134–137.

Roubal, J. (2009). Experiment: A creative phenomenon of the field. *Gestalt Review*, *13*(3), 263–276.

Roubal, J., & Francesetti, G. (submitted). Field theory in contemporary Gestalt therapy: Part two: Paradoxical theory of change reconsidered. *Gestalt Review* (Unpublished).

Roubal, J., Francesetti, G., & Gecele, M. (2017). Aesthetic diagnosis in Gestalt therapy. *Behavioral Sciences*, *7*(4), #70.

Saner, R. (1989). Culture bias of Gestalt therapy made in the USA. *Gestalt Journal*, *12*(2), 57–72.

Shneidman, E. S. (1996). *The suicidal mind*. Oxford, UK: Oxford University Press.

Staemmler, F-M. (2006). A Babylonian confusion? On the uses and meanings of the term "field". *British Gestalt Journal*, *15*(2), 64–83.

Staemmler, F-M. (2009). *Aggression, time and understanding*. Cambridge, MA: Gestalt Press.

Stratford, C. D., & Brallier, L. W. (1979). Gestalt therapy with profoundly disturbed persons. *The Gestalt Journal*, *2*, 90–103.

Wheeler, G. (2000). *Beyond individualism: Towards a new understanding of self, relationship & experience*. Hillsdale, NJ: The Analytic Press.

Yakeley, J., & Burbridge-James, W. (2018). Psychodynamic approaches to suicide and self-harm. *BJPsych Advances*, *24*(1), 37–45.

Yontef, G. (1993). *Awareness, dialogue & process: Essays on Gestalt therapy*. New York: Gestalt Journal Press.

Zeleskov Djoric, J. (2013). Assessing suicidal risk (Comment). In G. Francesetti, M. Gecele, & J. Roubal (Eds.), *Gestalt therapy in clinical practice: From psychopathology to the aesthetics of contact* (pp. 337–339). Siracusa, Italy: Istituto di Gestalt HCC Italy.

11 Writing to Remain

Two Diaries From Young Women Who Wrote to Survive

Linda Collins

KATIE: Only these pages can carry the weight, nothing else. Only these wonderful pages—they will not hurt me at all—not like people.

VICTORIA: I think [writing] calms me down when my thoughts get out of control. But on the other hand, it can also fuel them. Words, I mean.

Many young people write secret diaries, a rite of passage documenting crushes and the self-absorption of adolescent angst that is cringe-making for one's older self to look back on. However, unlike the Katie of *Katie's Diary: Unlocking the mystery of a suicide* (Lester, 2004), and my own daughter, Victoria McLeod (2014), most do not end up killing themselves. Victoria took her life aged 17 in 2014, a decade after the publication of the first Katie book. As with 20-year-old Katie, Victoria wrote extensive diaries leading up to her death. For both of them, their writing went beyond the usual self-conscious outpourings. Their personal diary keeping is articulate, self-reflective and deeply moving in a way that most youthful documentation is not.

These are not coming-of-age stories where the writer learns valuable lessons in their fumbling toward maturity. Their writing is not the stuff of popular fiction with storylines in which the protagonist's entries about awakening sexuality are discovered, and betrayal leads to emotional growth. In real life, there was no intervention that saved Katie or Victoria. Katie has a poem titled, *Marilyn Read my Diary*, which refers to a person in her life: "I am so hurt . . ./. . . violated inside," and so it seems that someone did read her intimate thoughts but did not act to get help for Katie. Victoria, meanwhile, wrote alone, her thoughts discovered only after her death. However, their diaries do have, in common with all young people, a longing for acceptance, love and a sense of purpose and direction in the life ahead of them.

As the author of a memoir about Victoria, *Loss Adjustment* (Collins, 2019, 2020), and as her Mom, I wanted to look at the questions: Why do their words linger in our hearts so, and their messages continue to resonate?

Their Stories Today

As with Katie, Victoria's diaries have been shared with researchers, including journalist Lucy Clark in *Beautiful Creatures* (Clark, 2016) and Jesse Bering,

DOI: 10.4324/9781003125655-12

in *Suicidal: Why we Kill Ourselves* (Bering, 2018). The young women's diaries give researchers the opportunity to learn more about the suicidal mind and to develop or enhance psychological approaches, counseling strategies and suicide prevention. Yet, Katie and Victoria have a command of language and an eloquence that make their writing much more than research material. A reviewer of Bering's book, Brett Swanson, wrote in *The New Yorker* that Victoria was "a winsome narrative persona" (Swanson, 2019). Swanson hailed her as a writer in her own right with an important narrative to tell, declaring: "In her diary, Vic was at work on a profoundly important story, one that was asking all the right questions."

Bering, for his part, says in his book,

> I felt like I'd come to know Vic through her crystalline words. . . . Vic had managed to stir in me something rather surprising, what I suspect are dormant parental emotions. I found myself wanting to reach out through space and time and put my own clumsy gay wing around her, to help usher her through this thorny psychological world and search, side by side, for beauty in the absurd.

I have wondered about the ethics of making public extracts from a dead person's private diary. While "Katie" is a *nom-de-plume*, Victoria McLeod is my daughter's real name. Literature scholar Eilene Hoft-March (Hoft-March, 2012) notes: "Writing about the dead—indeed, writing in anticipation of the deaths of others—raises ethical problems: what relationship to the other is appropriate? What way of speaking or writing honors rather than obscures, betrays, or exploits the other once she can no longer speak for herself?"

However, I believe both Katie and Victoria speak for themselves through their diaries in writing intended to be read. Through a combination of luck in being found after their physical presence ended, their voices have been recognized and amplified. Today, they inspire, move and inform researchers and general readers alike.

One example that shows me that Victoria wanted this is that she mentions wanting to help others like her. In an entry one month before her death, she asks for her college fund to "be given to charity. One that raises awareness about social anxiety. . . . So that teachers don't always assume that the kid at the back of class who never raises their hand isn't just 'shy', when they are really paralyzed with fear and hopelessness that they believe no one could ever understand." It is a powerful voicing of the anguish of what social anxiety can do to a person. I think Victoria knew that her expressive writing skills were such that she would touch people deeply in her description and move them to take action.

Katie, early in a section covering the last five weeks of her life, clearly indicates that hers is a testimony that others might witness, when she writes: "What I really hate is my body . . . if I get rid of all this disgusting excess weight. . . . I have to say just for the record that I am not going to try to kill myself by doing this—only perhaps the old Katie, so a new isolated individual one could rise up and emerge." Katie adds: "Maybe I will be listened to now—taken more seriously." It's not clear whether she means that losing weight will result in this, or whether it will be due to the transformation into a new individual. I think she is floating ideas about what might happen should she change in some way, but, currently, the diary is the one safe "person" she can tell.

This process of telling allows Katie to reach for more self-realization. Several hours later, Katie writes a new entry in which, after several sentences, she reveals that she might be pregnant. This momentous sentence is not addressed much further, and the rest of the entry is about wanting to exercise to lose weight and about her relationship with her boyfriend, Mark. The sentence about pregnancy casts the earlier remarks, about getting rid of weight and allowing a "new isolated individual to rise up," in a new light.

As a reader, I feel her worry and fear. By now expressing her words here, I am trying to honor her attempt to make sense of her confusion about possibly having another individual growing within her. I think that this highlights how, if only she had a person in authority to confide in rather than an imagined reader, perhaps she could have been helped. In this manner, her process of telling and trying to find a way forward alone are a call to action.

Women Who Would Not Be Silenced

Who were these young women, beyond their diaries? What remains of them?

It was only after I read Katie's diary entries that I read about her life. I realized that the term *suicide* can reduce a person to being a victim. Katie, in reality, was an incredibly strong person to have endured an abusive childhood and to try with all her heart to forge a life despite that. From a very young age, she was sexually abused by her father who died when she was 11 years old. Not long afterward, her mother was diagnosed as a schizophrenic and put in a mental institution. Katie and her sister were fostered out. There was no fairytale ending. She writes, "People used to tell me I was always wrong (foster parents). They were all so abusive to me."

On the other hand, Victoria, to my knowledge and to my husband Malcolm's knowledge, had a safe and happy childhood. In fact, she writes, "I have had nothing bad happen to me except my own doing." Malcolm has two sisters who admire him very much and has a strong family background, as do I. Victoria was an only child. Katie had a younger sister.

I regard Victoria as a strong young woman too, like Katie. Victoria suffered in the modern world's exam-based, outcome-focused school system. My "illogical soothsayer," as she once described herself, did not have the mind for mathematics, statistics and scientific analysis. Nor, although unforgettably beautiful, did she have many friends who liked her for who she was inside. Victoria lacked self-esteem and was ostracized by the "cool kids." School was a living hell, and yet she did not disclose this to me, her mother. I think she did not want to feel that she had let me down. I admire her immense bravery in that decision, even as it ended in tragedy.

The extract in *Katie's Diary* cover the last year of Katie's life, ending just before she turned 21, although her poetry goes back earlier than that, and some wording implies that she was writing diaries then, too. After her death, her writing came into the hands of her sister, who happened to know suicide researcher David Lester (her teacher and advisor) and passed them on to him.

With Victoria, the journal of her last four months, when she had just turned 17, was only uncovered seven months after her death, as the result of a criminal investigation. In Singapore, abetting a minor in suicide is a crime with the punishment being either the death penalty or life imprisonment, or up to 20 years' jail and a fine. A few hours after Victoria died, police took her effects including her laptop computer for their inquiry. Months later, an officer gave it back, saying that there was nothing of interest inside. As I write in *Loss Adjustment*, "How can he be so sure? Victoria used to type on it, night and day. I am very interested in what it might contain." We got an IT person to gain access to her laptop, and "Suddenly, we hear Victoria's voice, in written form . . . She has written a journal of many entries explaining things to us.'"

An Act of Explanation

Katie's early upbringing was traumatic, yet, in her diary's intense last month, there is an attempt to put that behind her. In this, there is a performative aspect to her writing, and also Victoria's. Both write as if a part of them has committed to death, so that their entries have a sense of explaining themselves posthumously.

But their diary writing also seems to postpone the inevitable. With great intensity, they tried to make sense of their lives, but there was always an undercurrent, of being dragged to the edge of a waterfall. The young women fight against it. Oh, how they explain themselves, their lives and their feelings about others! They examine the mundane and the profound. They articulate the unspeakable. It is particularly touching how they reach out to people important in their lives—family, or in Katie's case, substitute family.

In her last year of diarying, Katie rarely mentions her mother or father directly; but there is an adult who may be a foster parent or significant figure, Mrs. Walch, whom she does refer to at least twice fondly as 'Mama' Walch. There is a sense that Katie wants this person to know she mattered in a maternal sense. There are indirect references to parents, such as this positive entry, which reads as if Katie wants it as a testament to who she became in a moral sense, despite the immorality of her father's abuse: "I've made amends with mom and dad and (sister), for the most parts [sic] my parents."

Victoria says of her parents: "(They) had a crackdown about my education . . . Mum overreacted and said . . . that life isn't some TV-happy set-up and things can't be perfect. She went on complaining about her life and all she has to do." (In light of Victoria's perfectionism, it does not seem unreasonable for me to have said that.) Victoria later says quite casually: "They don't know that I won't be here by the end of the year. It'll kill them. But I have to stop caring."

The "It'll kill them" has an unreality to it as if Victoria knew she was being flippant, that she could not imagine us taking our own lives in the manner she would go on to do. This in turn suggests that she did not really accept how final death was. Somehow, her death would not be the end of our relationship. With the discovery of her journal, this has been very much the case.

While Katie was an articulate writer—what reader could not fail to be struck by the profundity of "I want to experience solitude, not alienation, nor isolation"—she did not seem to write for a specific, intended audience. The only indication of one is that, near the end, she says she hopes her boyfriend Mark does not read her diary, implying that she thought it was possible that he would read it. Katie's entries, all handwritten, are more that of using the diary as an ally: "I intend to make this book my best friend and only confidante."

Victoria, meanwhile, addressed her entries, mostly typed into a journal on her laptop computer, to an unknown "Lorraine." I had thought that this may have been a substitute for my own name, Linda. However, I have since learnt that Lorraine was the middle name of a girl, a fellow student named Mary, for whom she had romantic feelings that were not reciprocated.

The writing does seem intended specifically for someone who is well-read, who expects self-reflection and personal growth and who is aware of fictional convention and the need to hold the reader's attention. It is focused and interrogative. Lester (2004) writes about transference, and I wonder if Victoria was also writing to an ideal listener—Mary?—as opposed to her real-life school counselor who did not give her the help she needed. If indeed Victoria's writing was intended to be read by Mary one day, it forges a connection of hope, that life turned out okay for her friend, even if not for her.

When the 'I' Becomes Another Person

KATIE (from a poem, *Marilyn Read my Diary*): "I ask myself over and over/ where is life going to lead me now/I'm so scared not knowing where to go/or who to turn to."

VICTORIA (from a poem, *Winter Mind*): "You want to be alone, but you crave company./But in your heart you know that no one wants to be dragged/ Into your toxic, morose-ridden domain."

Katie and Victoria used a personal confessional tone in a stream-of-consciousness style in their diaries. They show frequent use of the personal pronoun "I." But Victoria, close to the end of her life, increasingly began using the second person "you" instead.

Katie uses very many first-person pronouns. The few uses of the second person that do occur are interesting. "You" first occurs when Katie refers to God, "Thank you, God" and then, in a letter to Joyce, the woman who slept with boyfriend Mark—"sweet Mark"—she declares, "You have hurt me very deeply." Later, in a passage where she says she wants to change her behavior to have a better life, she addresses herself as if to another person: "Be happy, laugh and be free, Katie; I give you permission."

Victoria initially uses a plethora of "I" pronouns. However, this pattern changes in the last five weeks or so, from February 28 to March 30. The February 28 entry's first paragraph starts by omitting the "I" pronoun altogether. "Was last very happy Feb13 . . . Thought about death." It also uses passive construction: "Ineptitude stemmed from recent lingering despondency." This is the first entry in the diary to stop using the "I" this way and to use extensive passive construction.

From this entry onward, there is a marked decrease of the first-person pronoun compared to before. There are many more "you's" and third-person references to parents, other people and Victoria's friend Mary. She also writes a poem about herself in the third person:

She prayed and prayed,
The covers wrapped around her,
Listening to the clock tick away her time,
Until the day she left the bed,
And left herself behind.

Why would Victoria write about herself in the third person? Was she performing for future readers, distancing herself from her present reality to make it easier to bear? Fantasizing about her last day and the relief she thought it would bring?

Indeed, both Katie and Victoria wrote poetry. Poetry conventionally does not comprise grammatically correct full sentences but fragments of expression. Furthermore, the spaces between lines and verses, and indeed the entire page itself, carry their own relationship to the text in aspects including pause, hesitation and negative space. Both wrote free verse, although Victoria's is laid out more conventionally. Katie makes interesting use of space, with lines displayed to echo context, such as lines referencing falling:

To what depth you ask?
  to the depths of the inner soul.
    —answer precisely?
      correctly? Perfectly?

There is also use of enjambment to create interesting emphasis, such as "The feeling of writing helps lose/the anxiety of existing" so that "lose" and "existing" carry extra weight. In tone, there is much anger as Katie uses poetry to express her feelings about being abused. In a poem, *A hand of 5 finger penis's*, she writes: "Old man—this dirty man is stabled to death/She is free by her own hands b/c she killed the hands that hurt her."

On the other hand, in a moving poem titled Mother, Katie experiences a yearning for maternal love: "Alone again/but now with the realization of/

goodbye upon my lips and the knowledge/of never feeling her moist skin/and her tears upon my lips. Never /again to rid her of the fears I chose/to battle. The scent I miss so/much of her inward spirit and/scent of tears./To miss the sight of the sun /upon her red hair. Her pale/and rosy skin./Her green eyes—gray eyes./To miss her arms of safety /Her caress. Her kisses. /Her love. If this is what /growing up, to leave all this /is all about. I don't want to /grow up."

Victoria also shows a yearning for maternal comfort, but, in her poetry, the roles are reversed, it is the mother—"she"—who needs comforting, and Victoria does not feel that she is truly seen: "*She looked into that girl's eyes whose shoulder/Her head lay against; a dream-girl she used/As her deploy from the mundane reality of/Love, marriage and detriment—that stretches/Into a flat field,/And ends without a view.*" It is sad to think that Victoria saw my life so bleakly, but she is right about being my "dream-girl," I was so proud of her. I did not see her mental pain.

The cognitive behavior commentary in the book *Katie's Diary* notes that suicide always involves loss. Perhaps for Victoria and Katie, this involved the loss of the idealized mother figure.

Writing to Postpone Suicide

Using verse gives a distance for a writer from a reader, allowing freedom to be bolder in thought and also to find refuge in metaphor and ambiguity. These qualities that the form allows perhaps also allowed Victoria and Katie to more fully acknowledge their wish to die—and write against it.

Toward the end of their poetry, both Victoria and Katie reference similar images of being caught in the strands of a web. Katie:

> I am the maiden trapped in the
> dungeon of cobwebs—it was me all alone now free
> here—Inside and outside of me—I rise
> with the heavens and lay down with
> the cuddling winds—no one can take
> this away from me I gave it to myself
> I am all my own

Victoria

> *I am almost peaceful.*
> *There is a strange acceptance about expiry,*
> *Finality.*
> *Closure.*
> *Nothing more can taint your head.*
> *No more voices can eat away*
> *The gossamer strands of thought*
> *. . . The wind comes.*
> *You blow away.*

Was the act of writing expressively their way of staying alive? The remarkable fact is that both stopped writing within 9 and 14 days, respectively, of their deaths.

The poets Sylvia Plath and Ann Sexton wrote feverishly in the last months of their lives, notes David Lester in *Katie's Diary* (Lester, 2004). He wonders if this was a safety valve, and perhaps the act of writing postponed the suicide, as it helped give them intellectual control over their behavior and also distanced them from trauma. Sexton was a favorite poet of Victoria, about whom she wrote: "I listen to sad descants and instrumentals. I read Ann Sexton, a poet whose words uncover beautiful and terrible reality."

Indeed, Katie writes early in her last month's diarying in a more positive tone, and she lists ways she can make her life better. Katie lost the weight that she wanted to, she gets good grades, she stays away from Mark and she grows psychologically and spiritually. She even says: "Objective realistic thinking is not bad at all."

In early March, five weeks before she died, Victoria, too, was more positive than she had been: "Was very happy last Friday. Not really sure why. Must have been transient joy from the prospect of no further assignments, besides exams. Got to the point where when I got home, I started dancing, stayed up late spontaneously decorating my room. It's full of happy posters."

Several times in their last months, both women say they aren't going to kill themselves—highlighting another contradiction: such statements fail to address the fact of their past history of suicidal behavior. And for Victoria, two weeks later, her thoughts have turned resolutely toward death, with her writing: "We are each given a life. We're supposed to live it. I don't. It's as simple as that."

However, while Victoria's writing shows an intense self-reflection in which she builds on the knowledge that is revealed for internal change, and an interrogation of why she wants to kill herself, and the consequences, Katie's writing seems to focus on external change as a way to evolve internally, such as in believing that, if she is thinner, life will be better. However, understandably, it all gets too hard. Lester notes that Katie's entries have no rational evaluation, monitoring of conflicting ideas, no challenging and no correction. They are the same from the entry a year previously. Whereas with Victoria, she is alert to a reader's potential queries and addresses them.

In her last entry, Victoria says:

> I guess I'm nothing more than another suicidal white girl. Just another first-world brat succumbing to society's perfect illusions. The only person anyone can blame for where they are and where they're at, are themselves. It doesn't matter how badly anyone treated you. In the end, the only person who can save you, is yourself.

The tragedy is that despite this coolly-expressed evaluation, Victoria's conclusion was not accurate.

A counselor to whom I showed Victoria's journals agreed, saying: "Importantly, in her journal Victoria is very rational and sane. It is her understanding of life—she is very true to her values, which would lead perhaps to her thinking that her life is not worth living—though this was the wrong conclusion to make."

I think Katie also seems rigorously true to her values, too much so. Perhaps with the right, qualified third-party intervention, both women could have been saved. Both showed striking insights into their weaknesses but not their strengths. It is a lesson that readers could take note of. By raising others up to see and value their strengths, can we avoid the outcomes of Victoria and Katie? Can the need of Katie and Victoria to remain alive in the world through their writing, be turned into a positive force for change to help others stay?

Fixing the Problems of Others

I believe that their writing can be healing and redemptive for others. After all, they were such empathic people, and this is reflected in the personalities on and off the page. Both Katie and Victoria wanted to study psychology. Katie talks about wanting to get an MA in psychology; Victoria wanted to be a psychologist or counselor but was frustrated in this, noting that she did not have the ability with statistics to qualify for the necessary study.

There is a sense that both women felt that they were responsible for other people's feelings, that they both wanted to help others who were struggling as a direct response to their own needs and lack of support. Like the perfectionists they both were, they shared a desire to "fix" things in others—even as they could not "fix" themselves. Katie's boyfriend Mark appears in her diary appears to be quite needy and also self-harms and threatens to kill himself. In fact, Katie says: "I want to put my focus on building him up inside . . . I'm very good with people this way."

Victoria, in the very third entry in her four-month diary, writes, "When people think of social anxiety, they associate it with shyness. That just pisses me off when people think that. I need to get inside the head of every person who has it." It was only in the last five weeks of her journals that, suddenly, there were no entries about wanting to help other people. I imagine any energy that Victoria had left, after fighting the urge to die for so long, went into trying to stay alive.

One wonders, then, what collapsed, or was lost? In *Katie's Diary*, the commentary on cognitive behavior notes that Katie displayed a lack of ego and points out that ego strength is a protective factor against suicide. The commentary notes that traumatic disruptions can handicap a person's ability to develop mechanisms or ego functions that help one cope. Relating this function of ego, or the *adult*, to Victoria, it allows for the possibility of reflection, looking back at previous entries and observing change and any progress and new knowledge acquired. Was there a traumatic event that put a halt to that? Mary's rejection of her love, perhaps? And in Katie's case, was there something that occurred in her relationship with Mark? Something that could not be fixed, no matter how much Katie and Victoria wanted it to be fixed?

Whatever the case, until they stopped writing, or perhaps, chose not to give voice on the page to their hopes and fears. They very much wanted to be heard in a world where they felt silenced and ignored. The publishing of their writing now is too late for them. But it is not too late at all to recognize their collective sense of agency and to use it for good. Here are some issues they were telling us about.

Pressure Over Exams and Body Image

Victoria writes: "People don't want to hang around people who don't make them happy." Katie writes: 'I need to be perfect."

Both women are super-stressed—and surely, aware of this even as they wrote—in comparing themselves unfavorably with others. (In Katie's case, there may well have been abuse-induced self-loathing over her body.) Katie writes. "I hate the fact that Claudia is so smaller and thinner than me." Victoria says: "We saw (Alice) . . . one of those chicks that look like they have it all. Blonde. Lithe. Head-Girl. Top grades. Popular. The whole jealously wrapped-up package. I mean she was *exercising*, for heaven's sake."

However, one thing that Victoria does do, that Katie does not, is interrogate her viewpoint: "Maybe I should start comparing them allegorically to filing cabinets. Each file section is a subdivision of life. Academics. Family ties. Extra-curricular activities. Social stature. Looks. Boyfriends/girlfriends. Socioeconomic state. Mental health. Physical form . . . I gave up on trying to be an Alice long ago."

Both were especially worried about doing well in exams.

KATIE: "Please, dear God, let me get an A on that test today."
VICTORIA: "I know that when I see those grades bold and black on a piece of
 paper—I will either jump for joy, or jump off the top floor of this condo."

However, Katie was scoring respectable B passes, and the previous semester had "made Honors—or whatever the school may call it." Yet, in her very last entry—on a day she was clearly emotionally fragile, admitting that she had "cried like a baby"—she puts pressure on herself. She tells of taking notes for her final examination, and pleads for an A, saying: "It would mean so very much to me. It would lift my spirits higher. It truly would. And please let everything work out wonderfully the rest of the summer and let me accomplish a lot of good things for myself and be healthy and disciplined." As for Victoria, she catastrophically escalates exam failure: "If I fail these exams, I know that . . . I can kiss university goodbye. I can kiss my life goodbye."

Counselor Patricia Evans tells me that Vic was an overachiever but focused on avoiding failure rather than achieving a good outcome. "This means your emotional life is constrained and success is more a relief than joy. You are in a state of perpetual relief. Vic, in her journals, tried to make light of this aspect. Suicide, though, was a permanent solution to a temporary problem—in this case, exam results. Teenagers stake their identity on outcomes. that people judge their worthiness based on them, when they know this is not necessarily really the case."

Pressures from society's messaging on body image can be seen in Katie's obsession with diet and exercising. *Katie's Diary* notes that at around 11 or 12 years of age, Katie developed anorexia. This coincides with just after her abusive father died. Was there a sense that she wanted that abused body to die and that she absorbed a message that she could transform that body to something more socially "acceptable," a skinny one? Indeed, it is a source of shame. As Katie writes: "I love all these fashions with the hair and clothes. But oh, how I would love to fit in them all . . . I would so love to break 130 lbs. even." "Am I really that fat? . . . I am so sick of these comments. I want to be proud of my body, not shameful about it."

In her commentary in *Katie's Diary* (Why did you kill yourself, Katie? Questions and reflections on a young woman's suicide), Silvia Canetto (2004) notes aspects such as cognitive distortions, problem-solving deficits, overgeneralization, and dysfunctional attitudes such as social oversensitivity and a perfectionist streak. Canetto observes that, ironically, society makes such thinking almost conventional for young women, such as worry about weight.

Victoria's journal does not mention dieting or any focus on calories. However, when she was 14, her diaries then contained many such references. Vic became depressed and began to purge herself after consuming food. Unlike Katie, I feel she did not want to leave her happy childhood. Growing up frightened her. She was not prepared for the complexity of adulthood. By 14, her social anxiety was already crippling. In her final journal, although Victoria does not mention dieting, she berates herself for not exercising enough: "I hate my Health class . . . there's always the terrifying possibility that we could have a Prac class, where I get to show my un-sportiness and unpopularity." By then, she may have realized that being slimmer did not make her the right "fit" to be accepted by her peers. This must have been devastating. Instead of fixating on the externalities of diet and exercise, Victoria turned the focus inward and expressed her anguish by cutting herself with a knife.

In the journal of her last four months, Victoria explains why she self-harms: "The pain distracts you and is a form of release. The endorphins momentarily fix your problems. Seeing the crimson makes it seem like the cut wasn't a worthless scratch. That it wasn't for nothing. But in the end, you're always left with scars you have to hide."

Ironically, this passage occurs in a section where Victoria discusses seeing her school counselor who wants to know why she self-harms. She writes: "I tried to use the comparison of it being a coping mechanism like how anyone would turn to drinking or cigarettes when they experience emotional distress. . . . The pain itself is the escape. It's like a device that converts mental pain into physical pain. The pain distracts you. It can either give you a break, or make you feel something."

I say *ironically* because, if true, then the counselor did not inform us. Victoria explains to her journal how she explained self-harming to the counselor and, at the same time, also posthumously wants us to know that she did seek help in her struggle to deal with society's expectations.

So Very Needy

Society's expectations and the pressure this puts on young people are an external issue affecting interiority. But what of inherent factors? Perhaps Katie and Victoria were always going to be vulnerable to external pressures. The chapter in *Katie's Dairy* on cognitive function notes that beliefs formed early in life can be easily activated. Those beliefs may have predisposed Katie (and Victoria) to emotional and behavioral responses, such as being quick to become defensive about perceived slights.

An example of how Victoria quickly accelerates situations emotionally is when she writes about Mary: "I wish I could talk wholeheartedly to M. I know now that she'll understand. She's gone through it too. She is the most alike person to me that I have ever met. We have a code for when we want to talk about these sorts of things. . . . If we say '125' we'll talk on the phone about the serious stuff because we can both relate to it. I think we need this support. It's like a breath of fresh air when you realize that someone *gets* what you're saying. Cathartic."

However, Victoria was heavily invested emotionally in this relationship to the point where her feelings became attachment and dependence. She writes the next day: "I've kind of been expecting Mary to come online and talk and now I'm worried that being honest has made things awkward. Oh, and the fact that it's after three (in the afternoon) and I'm still wearing pyjamas . . . Pathetic, just pathetic." In fact, she was so invested in the relationship that she was worried that, if she revealed too much, she would scare Mary off. She was not as honest as she could have been. She tells her journal that she regrets that she had not told Mary she was suicidal, "but if I mentioned suicide, she might not want to have anything to do with me. I'd be a toxic sort of person."

A few days later, Victoria does seem to have revealed something to Mary, as there is an almost euphoric entry: "I'll never forget (unsuccessfully) constructing a fort out of your bed sheets at four in the morning. . . . I won't forget tearing our walls down and talking about all the things we were so afraid to talk about, in said gym in the middle of the night. I don't know about you, but I think those nights will always be some of the most emancipating times of my life . . . Seriously, I never imagined I would say any of those things to anyone, let alone someone who *got it* . . . you make me feel like I'm not alone . . . thank you for being my fabulous person! . . . I love you, darling."

Betrayals, Secrets and Lies

Yet their care was not reciprocated. Victoria expressed to Mary she was suicidal, yet Mary does not appear to have done anything to save her. Victoria portrays her yearning for help as a failure, even as she appears not to see the shortcomings of Mary, saying in one of her last diary entries: "I'm tired of this. I'm tired of being needy—always needing someone to come and save me."

Betrayal or distancing by friends became a catastrophic event for Katie and Victoria. Mark slept with another woman, for example. He never seems to realize how fragile Katie is or seek responsible help for her. In her last entry, Katie is concerned for him, although she must have been in terrible mental pain: "Please, dear God, let Mark come to good grounds with himself," even as she indirectly writes of her need for herself: "Please don't let him fall for any other girl."

Victoria wanted to take her friendship with Mary deeper, perhaps to reveal her romantic feelings. But it seems that Mary did not really reciprocate these feelings. Worse, Mary did not act on Victoria's cries for help. Six weeks before Victoria took her life, there is a diary entry where my daughter states that she discussed with Mary that she was suicidal. The entry, strange, when one considers the importance of this revelation, is mostly about her relief that Mary knows and about how it is strange how parents never really know their children: "how a parent can have no idea that their son or daughter wanted to kill themselves. . . . That's perhaps why we don't want them to know. We know that they won't get it."

Why didn't Mary ask Victoria to seek help? Why did they just console each other with the thought that parents "don't get it"? Because, if someone had told me, her mother, that Victoria was suicidal, I would have acted on it, asked her about it and, even if she denied it, sought professional help. There was a chance to save Victoria. Yet Mary for whatever reason kept this a secret. If only an adult had been told.

I wonder why Victoria did not reflect on this, and wonder, if Mary was truly a friend, surely she would not want her best friend to kill herself? Why did she not wonder why Mary doesn't encourage her to seek help? I suspect Victoria knew deep down that Mary was the wrong person to confide in, if she was to overcome her suicidal thoughts. Perhaps staking everything on having Mary as a confidante was her way of sabotaging herself.

Katie, too, was attached to Mark and berated herself over perceived failings in their interactions. Unlike Victoria with Mary, she does not appear to have revealed to him the extent of her suicidal thoughts: "I just spoke with Mark. I felt like I lied to him. Maybe it's because I am not out of the dark waters yet, ice waters, ice sky. I'm feeling really scared." An important difference between Victoria/Mary and Katie/Mark is that he was supportive and reciprocated her feelings. She writes: "I know he cares about me."

However, unlike Victoria with Mary, Katie was riven with doubt even as she wrote that Mark had a brief relationship with another young woman, Joyce. This made Katie angry: "Maybe now I will express my ruthless hatred for Joyce. . . . I can't afford to let anyone close to me again to hurt me. . . . Her selfishness has . . . made me think that what I have is not real with Mark—that he doesn't love me." Feelings surface of anxiety and neediness surface: "I feel like I am stuck in a very bad pattern. It frightens me. Mark is right about my dependence . . . It is so hard to fall in love with him, make myself vulnerable, and make him responsible for my heart . . . He never asked for me to give up my dreams and self, and I must remember that." Perhaps the betrayal by Mark, and Katie's rage and acknowledgment of her neediness, activated her lack of self-worth at a deep, dysfunctional level?

Words Become Silence

Poet Lee Li-Young (Ingersoll, 2006) is quoted as saying in *Breaking the Alabaster Jar*, "I think we use language to inflect silence so we can hear it better. ... Inflected silence could be explained by the way everything seems quieter after you hear a bell ring. It's almost as if we're using language, but the real subject is silence."

Importantly, as I have noted, the act of diarying seems to postpone suicide, or at least, give purpose to Katie and Victoria. Both stopped writing shortly before their deaths: They wrote and wrote, until they became silent. Then they died. Why? We will never know, but perhaps they had mentally "checked out," and there was no longer a need to write in order to live.

Both left no known explicit suicide note, although they had earlier written of the need to write such a letter. This absence is strange considering their lengthy, detailed diary entries. And yet it ties in with the days of silence once the entries stopped. In her essay, Silvia Canetto (2004) wonders if it is because all Katie's energy went into surviving first and then the suicide; or perhaps she was ashamed because she had a major emotional downfall when she had been so positive before.

And yet, as I say, both wrote so copiously in their diaries. Victoria's diaries are particularly extensive. Writing and the process of reflection on the writing were a source for both to self-diagnose, gain control over their lives and find ways to live. They were especially a way of putting their suicide ideation on the page, to externalize it. In some ways, this increased self-knowledge and containment, or expression of psychological despair, may have helped prolong their lives. But, for both, there were also downsides. The constant rumination may have led them deeper into self-recrimination and suicidal ideation; and the sheer process of writing such long entries was time-consuming and added to their social isolation.

However, once they felt they were ready to die, that it was time, the decision to go was resolute and absolute. Therefore, there was no need to document further struggle, there was no struggle to document and no need to try and preserve one's physical existence through writing.

A Fatal Falling Away

Katie's last entry, that of June 20, displays a falling away of grammar and structure, ending,

> Please let us unleash, and a spiritual and emotional relationship emerge. Now focused. Please help me through this and next week especially. Things are so hard right now
>
> I must write
>
> Completed two weeks

14 days

PS Please make my package get here within two weeks, tomorrow.

(Katie was found dead on June 29, nine days after this entry.)

Victoria first shows fragmented writing in the entry of February 28th when she begins to omit the first-person pronoun but, for a while thereafter, she resumes her more controlled style, with full and correct grammatical structure. She ends with her usual sign-off of *Love always, Vicky*. However, unusually there is one last line that now reads as a self-epitaph: "God knows that I've failed. But he knows that I've tried."

Victoria did not make any more entries in her laptop computer. However, I later found two handwritten entries in a notebook written in the last weekend of her life. They are on opposite pages to each other, showing first the resistance to death and then the decision to go.

Middle Page, Left-Hand Side (Neat Writing, Readable)

> I want to find a place where no-one can find me. I want to go back to the fire exit. I felt alone, but now I want to be alone. A place where I can properly be alone with my thoughts. Is it really so morbid to want to be dead? I want to leave. But I am not on the brink. If I were, I would be on the top floor by now. I'm waiting for that moment to come. I'll know when it does. And it will come eventually.

Opposite, Right-Hand Page (Disjointed, Initially Readable, Becoming Emphatic Scrawl)

> I want to be dead. I want to be dead maybe the reason why I haven't mentioned it is because I don't want to stop feeling like I have access to this option. I just want to fucking be dead is that too much to ask??? Please tell me that

The first entry is measured and coherent in structure. In the second, Victoria's writing becomes fragmented, as if she cannot function cognitively anymore, and it ends in mid-thought.

In the end, writing could not postpone their suicides forever. Katie and Victoria held it together for as long as they could, until they could no longer do so. In this aspect, their writing, in its increased fragmentation, reflects that inner turmoil. It loses structure, sentences are incomplete and thoughts ill-formed.

Remaining in a New Form

These are indeed insightful windows to the suicidal young person. In his *New Yorker* review, Barret Swanson writes that Vic's journal is an "extraordinary" portrait of cognitive unraveling, adding: "While scrutinizing the diary of an adolescent may seem like a dubious scientific enterprise, Bering shows how the evolution of Vic's dejected bulletins accords with the social psychologist Roy Baumeister's 'Suicide as Escape from Self,' a six-stage theory demonstrating how a person might descend into the pit of self-extinction."

While there are some significant contextual differences between the diaries, there are also many similarities, such as a writerly tone of expression, and thematic matter of anger at self and society, comparison with peers, catastrophizing of relationship difficulties, psychological existential pain, extensive ruminating on suicide, partners who are needy and self-harming and extreme feelings of isolation and alienation. Both could not cope with the intrapsychic pain of life's demands, and suicide was an escape from that intolerable suffering.

Katie tried to overcome the handicap of her dysfunctional family by doing well at school. Grades mattered a great deal to her. Victoria kept silent about her struggles with schoolwork, out of pride, I suspect, and passing exams assumed a disproportionate importance in her life. Both women were caught up in contemporary social and economic hierarchies that value academic success and well-paid occupations. Their strengths, of kindness, sensitivity, responsibility for those in need, generosity of spirit and a flair for the written word were not valued.

Low status in a hierarchy produces the stress and anxiety that trigger immune system-damaging cortisol to be released in the body. Whether this is a factor cannot be deduced now. Whatever the underlying contributors to their suicides, Katie and Victoria had tried their best to fit in, but their social hierarchies wrote them off. They could not see a place for themselves.

It is significant that both women's manner of death had strong associations with the school system. Katie killed herself in her student room. Victoria took her life the first day of a new school term, when she was due to get exam results. One cannot help but wonder if they were sending one final, angry message to the systems that failed them. Both also draw the reader—and reviewers such as Swanson—to connect powerfully with their likeable personalities amid their vulnerabilities and perceived failings, putting a human face to suicide in testimonies opening up further conversations and narratives.

If only some authority figure had read their writing, to recognize incoherence and what that signaled about the disintegrating mind! The fragmentation that fell away to silence contains a valuable message, a call to action to all who work with young people, to use this methodology more and to find ways to help the suicidal feel comfortable with sharing their diaries with adults.

While they may have physically departed, these women's words have their own life as readers continue to encounter them and make meaning for their own lives and those of others.

References

Bering, J. (2018). *Suicidal: Why we kill ourselves*. Chicago: University of Chicago Press.

Canetto, S. S. (2004). Why did you kill yourself, Katie? Questions and reflections on a young woman's suicide. In D. Lester (Ed.), *Katie's diary: Unlocking the mystery of a suicide* (pp. 41–54). New York: Brunner-Routledge.

Clark, L. (2016). *Beautiful creatures*. Sydney, AU: Penguin Random House Australia.

Collins, L. (2019/2020). *Loss adjustment*. Singapore: Ethos Books; Wellington: Awa Press.

Hoft-March, E. (2012). Being at a loss: Death, mourning, and ethics in Cixous's Benjamin à Montaigne. *Women in French Studies, 20*, 47–58.

Ingersoll, E. G. (Ed.). (2006). *Breaking the alabaster jar: Conversations with Li-Young Lee*. Rochester, NY: BOA Editions.

Lester, D. (Ed.). (2004). *Katie's diary: Unlocking the mystery of a suicide*. New York: Brunner-Routledge.

McLeod, V. (2014). *Journal* (Unpublished).

Swanson, B. (2019, January). The two faces of suicide: A new book stresses the biological causes of self-destruction, but what about the social ones? *The New Yorker*. www.newyorker.com/books/under-review/the-two-faces-of-suicide

12 Why Are We so Bad at Preventing Suicide?

Donna Holland Barnes

I am a survivor of the suicide loss of my son who died in 1990 (Barnes et al., 2007). Having worked in the field ever since my loss, my perspective on whether or not we can prevent suicide has evolved. This evolution was in part driven by my interactions with other loss survivors who lost loved ones to suicide and has been reinforced in my reading of Katie's diary. In this chapter, I will address several issues outlined in more detail in the following text.

First is the question of whether or not suicide can be a rational decision? Was Katie's decision to die by suicide driven by rational or irrational thought processes? Throughout her diary, she certainly seemed ambivalent, as if she had the desire to both live and die. What triggered her desire to die in her? Was this driven by distorted thinking? What ultimately drove Katie's desire to die by suicide is unable to be answered given her not being here to tell us and because we know nothing of her thought processes in the nine days prior to her death after she finished her last diary entry.

Another consideration that I will discuss in relation to the diary is whether or not it is the society's responsibility to act immediately when the idea of suicide is raised by an individual. For example, should the suicidal individual be hospitalized voluntarily or involuntarily? Should lethal means for suicide be taken away from them (such as firearms and medications)? Should they immediately be given medication to treat some disorder? Where do we draw the line on what is deemed "normal" versus "abnormal." For example, do we assign therapy and medication when a common stressor, such as the death of a loved one, financial instability, job loss or a divorce occurs?[1] Socially deviant behavior and conflicts that are primarily between the individual and society are not mental disorders unless the deviance or conflict results from a dysfunction in the individual (American Psychiatric Association, 2013). According to Szasz (1986), "helping an individual who is suicidal depends on many things, such as their spirit, who they are surrounded by, their community, their connectedness with others, their finances and more importantly . . . are they interested in working with someone at staying alive?" It is irresponsible to apply the same treatment to all suicidal people. It should also be noted that adults have freedom of choice and may not be treated against their will.

Finally, why has it been so difficult to prevent suicide? As we are moving into a new decade, it is worrying that the suicide rate has increased over 30% since the 1990s and is steadily rising year after year. Do we know what we are doing? Reading Katie's diary, it is obvious that, at times, she wanted to live. Like most people, she had, at times, a will to live. However, there are times when our coping mechanisms break down. This breakdown can happen at any time depending on the conditions and circumstances. Take, for example, the case of Anne Sexton, the Pulitzer Prize winner for poetry in 1967. She knew her coping mechanisms could breakdown at any moment, and she carried a bottle of barbiturates in her purse so that she would be prepared when the impulse hit. She had thoughts of suicide since her early 20s and finally died by suicide at the age of 46 despite years of treatment with a psychiatrist (Middlebrook, 1991).

Rational Suicide Versus Irrational Suicide

Rational suicide is perhaps best defined as a well-thought-out decision to die by a person who is in a state of mind capable of decision making (e.g., not in a psychotic episode).[2] For example, Emanuel (2014) published an article, when he was in his 60s, that he did not want to live past 75 years of age. He presented a lengthy thesis as to why, and it was a well-thought-out decision. However, he decided not to die by suicide through an active attempt but rather by ceasing to take any medications and by doing nothing to prolong his life.

In older adults, there is a phenomenon that suggests the presence of "silent" suicidal attitudes (Gramaglia et al., 2019). Approximately 55% of late-life suicides have a severe physical illness (Conwell & Thompson, 2008; Zeppegno et al., 2005), and there is a high risk of unrecognized and untreated psychiatric illnesses, mainly depression, among these older adults (Simon, 1989; Zeppegno et al., 2019). Physical illnesses often result in functional disabilities and loss of dignity and pleasure with life, coupled with loss of self-esteem. In some cases, thoughts of suicide can simply be due to loss of financial stability. The way I interpret Emanuel's decision, mentioned earlier, stems from not wanting to get to that point of losing dignity, self-esteem and purposefulness. Szasz (1986) argued that, under no circumstances, should a society be in control of whether or not someone decides to take their own life. The majority of mental health professionals assume that they have a responsibility to keep people alive, even when they want to die; but Szasz argued that individuals should be able to take their own life under their own terms. Szasz would respect Emanuel's right to his decision.

In reading Katie's diary, it seems obvious that she really wanted to live. However, there are times when our ability to cope cannot manage the stress one is under, and suicide becomes a means of escape. Although our coping skills may come back at some point, when someone is in the midst of suffering, that is not always readily apparent. Are we able to save a life in such a situation? I am doubtful for a number of reasons. First, we never know when someone will reach their breaking point, where the desire to die outweighs the desire to live. Second, we cannot read minds! Even experts in the field of suicide prevention are incapable of predicting when a person will die by suicide. We know that roughly 40,000 people out of the population of 330 million residents of the United States will die by suicide in 2021, but we cannot reliably or usefully identify which 40,000 individuals.

Generally, when the desire to die outweighs the desire to live, it is because of a loss or perceived failure, frustration, low integration, diminished hope, guilt or an imbalance among social conditions (Peck, 1989). Therefore, in order to prevent suicide as an option, we need to take many things into consideration, including their social network and who they are surrounded by, their spirit, their cognitive ability, their willingness to work things out in a positive manner, their culture, their connectedness, their impulsivity and their fearlessness, just to name some of the factors that should be taken into consideration. Therapists or psychiatrists look at only a few factors, such as mental illness, previous attempts or a family history of suicidal behavior.

Suicide used to be viewed as a criminal behavior (and still is in some countries). It is still viewed by many as deviant behavior and the result of mental illness. In other words, it is an act that society frowns upon, and there is stigma attached to suicidal behavior. Robins (1981) examined 134 suicides and decided that 98% of them had a diagnosable psychiatric illness. The remaining 2% did not have enough information for Robins to make a decision. Therefore, for Robins, there is no rational suicide. In contrast, Lester (2003, 2014) has argued that suicide can be a rational decision. Lester presented the case of Marin Manley (1953–2013) who created a website prior to his suicide in which he argued forcefully for the rationality of his decision. Indeed, countries and American states, in setting up procedures for assisted suicide, thereby have acknowledged that rational suicide is possible.

Some argue that, if there are loved ones who will suffer from the loss, or if there are situations that would be left unsolved or impaired because of the suicide (causing emotional, physical, or financial harm), then the suicide has not been well thought out and probably is not rational. Those who lose loved ones to suicide do experience mental pain, but it may be argued that it is cruel to expect others to live, even though suffering immense pain themselves, in order to spare the survivor's mental pain.

Was Katie's mental capacity impaired causing her to make this decision? Shneidman (1985) wrote: "(O)ne should never commit suicide while disturbed. Suicide is not rational if the thought of aggressive suicide ideations is coupled with frustration, failure, self-pity, and despair or when you have experienced something traumatic or life changing." Shneidman continued: "Never kill yourself when you are suicidal." In other words, it takes a mind capable of scanning a range of options to make a rational decision to die by suicide.

Jamison (1999), a psychiatrist who wrote a memoir about her own depression and suicidal behavior, noted that, when she got into a deep state of suicidal ideation, *"Nothing alive and warm could make its way in through my carapace."* Jamison believed that those in her life would be better off without her. She felt she had nothing left to give. That mental state is as crippling as any incurable and painful physical disease that would warrant killing oneself and, perhaps, makes the decision to die by suicide irrational. On the other hand, if the physical pain of a terminal illness is considered to be sufficient justification for assisted suicide, the perhaps severe mental pain should be considered sufficient justification also.

Sylvia Plath and Ernest Hemingway

Let me examine the suicides of two famous individuals. Sylvia Plath was a poet credited with advancing confessional poetry. She thought about and attempted suicide several times in her 30 years of life, but at the same time clung to the thought of staying alive. At the time of her death (February 11, 1963), she was in treatment, talked with those who were in her space about her feelings of despair and had a two-year-old and a nine-month-old to care for. According to reports, she not only left behind two infants who were in the next room, but also left a note to remind her to call her doctor. Her kitchen looked as though she was in the middle of preparing food, and she showed no signs of planning on ending her life such as making plans for someone to care for her children or leaving a suicide note. However, in her moment of vulnerability and impulsiveness, she did take the time to seal her children's rooms with cloth and tape. Plath's suicide could be attributed to mental illness because of her clinical depression from which she suffered for most of her adult life. Clinical depression causes one to be in constant despair, while not getting much enjoyment out of life. Unfortunately, this is what most mental health professionals assume is the reason for an individual's thoughts of suicide, believing that a prescription of anti-depressants is generally the solution for preventing suicide. Plath's suicide was not well thought out, especially because she left behind small children and, therefore, may not be a rational suicide.

Ernest Hemingway died by suicide, as did his father, sister and brother. By age 60, Hemingway's mental and physical health had declined. He was in and out of hospitals several times for various reasons in his last years due to a diagnosis of hemochromatosis which is an excessive accumulation of iron in the body's tissue. This causes rapid deterioration of mental and physical health. After spending two months in a psychiatric hospital and administered electro-convulsive shock treatments for his suicidal behavior and paranoia, he went into the basement of his home, retrieved his favorite double barrel shotgun, went upstairs to the kitchen and shot himself. Since electro-convulsive shock impairs memory in most patients (almost always short-term memory and frequently long-term memory), this loss of memory would have been devastating for a writer who used his own experiences as the basis for his fiction.

Hemingway's mental state contributed to his inability to think clearly and write. Writing may have been what he lived for, and personal ineptitude was setting in. Did he have the ability to reason? A suicide is rational when the individual has the ability to reason with a realistic world view and is not causing harm to anyone (Gramaglia et al., 2019). Before his two-month psychiatric hospital stay, his wife caught him trying to shoot himself in their kitchen and quickly got him admitted. Hemingway had no desire to continue living with his physical and mental ill-health. He had no desire to get weaker and weaker. He had no further interest in watching himself deteriorate. Perhaps, therefore, his suicide was rational?

According to Szasz, you should never help people using force. Szasz argued that people should be able to decide whether or not their life has any value. This statement has merit in Hemingway's case but not in Plath's. She was only 30, very talented and, if given proper treatment in time, she may have been saved. However, we never know when the presence of fearlessness, access to means, personal vulnerability and impulsiveness will line up, and that is what keeps us from saving lives.

Occasional suicides do leave suicide notes, or in the case of Martin Manley mentioned earlier, complete websites, but Kate did not do so. Her diary reveals her thought, conflicts and emotions but does not detail her reasoning, especially in those nine days prior to her suicide. We are unable, therefore, to decide about the rationality of her decision.

Is Suicide Ever Acceptable?

Lester (2003) has discussed what might make a death, even a suicide, an appropriate or acceptable death. Weisman and Hackett (1961) suggested that an appropriate death must reduce the conflict in your life, be compatible with your conscience, maintain important relationships in your life and you must sincerely desire the death. Richard Kalish (unpublished) felt a death was appropriate if your biological death (your body ceases to function), your psychological death (you mind ceases to function) and your social death (your loved react to you as if you were dead) all occur at the same time.

Some existentialists argue that your death is appropriate only if you play a role in it. Other commentators argue that an appropriate death maintains your physical integrity or that your manner of dying is consistent with your manner of living. Finally, there appear to be some occasions in your life when death seems to be fitting. Perhaps you have achieved all of your goals or that more living would simply be a repetition of what has transpired before. Lester (2003) argued that some suicides could meet one or more of these criteria.

Alvarez (1971) asked the question, "Why do these things happen? Is there a way such waste can be explained since it can hardly ever be justified?" Who decides a suicide is never justified? But what if the person does not like it here on earth? What about being sick and tired of being sick and tired? What about exhaustion so intense that no one can penetrate your shields, your walls, your strong sense of determination to end it all?

Whether suicide can be the result of a rational decision or not, is suicide acceptable at some point? Szasz asserts that people should be able to take their life under their own terms, and therefore, do we have the right to say that a loved one does not have the right to die? Who is selfish, the person who wants to die or the person who wants you to live even when you are miserable? Hemingway's wife stopped him the first time that he tried to die by suicide and prolonged his life for a few months. Was that the correct decision?

It is hard for me to believe that there is something wrong with your thinking if you chose to die, no matter your age. Society has conditioned us to think that living is the choice we have to make, and that suicide is a socially incorrect behavior. You just don't do it! It is not a logical decision when you leave loved ones behind or when you leave financial burdens to someone else. But when you have the ability to reason, have a realistic world view and adequate information on avoiding harm and achieving goals, do what you know and do what you feel. Szasz (1986) says under no circumstances should a society stop anyone from ending their life. I have run support groups for many years and occasionally will ask the survivors of a loss what right do they have to feel their loved one should have not ended their internal pain? What right do we have as a society to insist that one live with their pain? Who is the selfish one, the person who took their life or the family they left behind who insist that you live through your pain?

Could Katie's Suicide Have Been Prevented?

Plath and Hemingway are two extremes. What about the gray areas? What was the situation for Katie? From her diary, it may seem that she was suffering from a major depressive disorder and an eating disorder, and she had symptoms consistent with borderline personality disorder and possibly post-traumatic stress disorder. With all this possible suffering, her pain became unbearable. Katie did not write in her diary the last nine days. Had she given up trying to make something out of her feelings? Was she tired of trying to make things right in her life?

Could Katie have escaped from her painful mental state? Would therapy have helped her? If therapies help suicidal patients, why do we have such increasing rates of suicide every year? Why do we have suicides occurring even in psychiatric hospitals? Are there some people who have decided that life is not for them? Perhaps they no longer want to continue on medications all their life, or perhaps they are exhausted from their negative emotions.

Not everyone has access to psychiatric treatment or psychotherapy. Resources are limited. It is often difficult to find a mental health unit or professional in order to make an appointment. Many people do not have medical insurance or sufficient money that would cover the cost of treatment. An initial psychiatric evaluation today can cost $500, and medications are an additional expense. In addition, many psychotherapists and counselors do not have experience with suicidal individuals and would not accept them as patients. Others do not have the requisite skills, and sometimes the client and therapist simply do not make a good fit.

Katie certainly had her strong moments of positive thinking and moments of making sound decisions to move forward and rid her life of negative and toxic people. When reading her diary, there are times that you would think she is going to make it, that she is going to be okay. Would good psychotherapy have saved her such as Firestone (2004) indicated. Firestone suggested the types of treatments available for Katie, including establishing support and outlining protective factors and risk factors so that Katie would have a complete understanding of her support system. After all, Katie mentioned that she did not know to whom she could turn to when in need of support. Assessment and treatment for suicidal patients is always considered a necessary component in keeping one alive.

In addition, we never know when that impulse is going to come over a person about whom we may be worried. Suicidal people encounter crises, and there is often no-one to turn to. There are suicide hotlines in many countries, including the United States, but often people in crisis do not call such services, and the help that these services provide is very limited (often to restricted to *active listening* [client-centered therapy]).

For example, a 19-year-old male was committed to a psychiatric hospital that I worked at several years ago. After his 72-hour hold, he laughed and joked with the nurses as he was being released. He went home with his parents, got the keys to his car and drove it into a tree and died instantly. We can desire to prevent suicide, to understand suicide and to work on research that will help build tools for physicians, ER departments and first responders to use, but we rarely are present to catch an individual in that vulnerable, impulsive and fearless state when suicide occurs.

Discussion

My son was, I thought, a well-balanced young man. I learned from him. My family thought well of him. That he took his own life was an enigma to my family. They did not and would not believe it. I viewed his drowning as a suicide because he left a note. I saw his decision as a conscious and rational thought that his life was not worth the pain and suffering that comes with it. Like most young 20-year-old college students, he wanted a promising future, but obstacles kept getting in the way.

It appears from Katie's last entries that she had all the intellectual skills to keep moving forward and to concentrate on the things she had to live for—that quality of life we all yearn for. But not everyone can sustain the pursuit of happiness. Katie stopped writing toward the end of her life. Perhaps she was no longer interested in prolonging her life by working at making the changes she needed in her outlook on life. If she did not have the mental capacity to make those changes, what was there to live for?

It has been argued that Sylvia Plath wanted to be saved. She waited until 6:00 AM in the morning, knowing her au pair would show up at 9. It seems she may have had hopes of continuing to get her poetry published. She had two young children whom she cherished. But no one got to her in time. Her body was still warm when found, and it happened that the au pair could not get into the house when she first arrived. The neighbor upstairs, who may have had a key, overslept and could not hear the pounding by the au pair on Sylvia's door.

There were maintenance people following up on a problem in the building who finally let the au pair in two hours later. Perhaps Plath was ambivalent to the end? Perhaps she locked her door because she did not want to be saved? Perhaps she left a note for her doctor because she expected to be saved? Perhaps she just felt she needed to do *something*, anything to shake things up?

Was Katie ambivalent? It seems unlikely, although we do not know what she was thinking in her last nine days. She stopped writing in her diary, but what was in her mind? However, had her boyfriend not become concerned about her, Katie would not have been discovered for several days and her isolating herself from others who might intervene suggests that she was not ambivalent.

Notes

1. One of the editors had a close friend who was prescribed an anti-depressant after his wife died from cancer. The anti-depressant failed to stop his grief.
2. Lester (2003) has provided a series of issues to address, questions to ask oneself and actions that are required to make a rational decision to die by suicide.

References

Alvarez, A. (1971). *A savage God*. New York: Norton.
American Psychiatric Association (APA). (2013). *Diagnostic and statistical manual of mental disorders* (5th ed.). Washington, DC: American Psychiatric Association.
Barnes, D. H., Lawal-Solarin, F. W., & Lester, D. (2007). Letters from a suicide. *Death Studies, 31*, 671–678.
Conwell, Y., & Thompson, C. (2008). Suicidal behavior in elders. *Psychiatric Clinics of North America, 31*, 333–356.
Emanuel, E. (2014, October). Why I hope to die at 75. *The Atlantic*. www.theatlantic.com/magazine/archive/2014/10/why-i-hope-to-die-at-75/379329/
Firestone, L. (2004). Separation theory and voice therapy methodology applied to the treatment of Katie. In D. Lester (Ed.), *Katie's diary* (pp. 161–186). New York: Brunner-Routledge.
Gramaglia, C., Calati, R., & Zeppegno, P. (2019). Rational suicide in late life: A systematic review of the literature. *Medicina, 55*(10), #656.
Jamison, K. R. (1999). *Night falls fast: Understanding suicide*. New York: Vintage Books.
Lester, D. (2003). *Fixin' to die*. Amityville, NY: Baywood.
Lester, D. (2014). *Rational suicide*. Hauppauge, NY: Nova.
Middlebrook, D. (1991). *Anne Sexton*. Boston, MA: Houghton Mifflin.
Peck, D. (1989). Evaluation of a suicide diary. *Omega, 19*, 293–230.
Robins, E. (1981). *The final months*. New York: Oxford University Press.
Shneidman, E. S. (1985). *Definition of suicide*. New York: Wiley.
Simon, R. (1989). Silent suicide in the elderly. *Bulletin of the American Academy of Psychiatry & the Law, 17*, 83–95.
Szasz, T. (1986). The case against suicide prevention. *American Psychologist, 41*, 806–812.
Weisman, A., & Hackett, T. P. (1961). Predilection to death. *Psychosomatic Medicine, 23*, 232–256.

Zeppegno, P., Gramaglia, S., di Marco., S., Guerrierco, C., Consol., C., Loreti, L., Martelli, M., Marangon, D., Carli, V., & Sarchiapone, M. (2019). Intimate partner homicide-suicide. *Current Psychiatry Reports, 21,* 13.

Zeppegno, P., Manzetti, E., Valsesia, R., Siliquini, R., Ammirata, G., DeDonatis, O., Usai., C., & Torre, E. (2005). Differences in suicide behavior in the elderly. *International Journal of Geriatric Psychiatry, 20,* 769–775.

Conclusions

13 From the Ashes of Suicide
A Life Repurposed

Katie's Sister

A quarter-century has passed since suicide ripped my sister from this world and turned my life upside down. Despite the time that has passed, it was only until about a year ago when another encounter with suicide made it undeniable that there were still so many emotions left unresolved. It was not until the commitment was made to writing this chapter that I was forced to exam the totality of my sister's suicide. The following pages are an intimate story of loss, hope and gratitude.

It was close to the end of the college semester when a roommate and I decided that it was best to move off of campus and move in with her parents. Rooming with two other women, nothing was sacred, and we never knew what we would encounter on our return. After the move, most days were spent studying on campus or meeting up with friends. Minimizing the time spent at my new residence was to avoid feeling like an imposition since I was staying there rent free. However, the one night I remained home would alter the course of my life in ways never imagined.

On the one evening I agreed to stay in, I did so at the request of my friend who needed support in dealing with the drama of her recent breakup. In the middle of all her woeful utterances, the phone rang. Wide eyed and believing it was him calling to apologize, she promptly answered. After hearing the caller's introduction, a puzzled expression came over her face. Removing the phone from her ear and placing it against her chest, she repeated the message on the other line, "Will you accept a collect call"? In that moment I felt the imposition that I had been avoiding was now unavoidable. I took the phone in time to hear the operator repeat her question, and I begrudgingly accepted the cost of the call. I immediately took an angered tone and berated my sister for her complete lack of consideration. When the opportunity was afforded her to speak, my sister's tone was unmistakable. Brokenness echoed in her voice, and she was quick to try and end the call. All efforts to undo my reprehensible reception failed, and no matter how hard I tried, there was no mending what I had done. In that one instance, I had severed any possibility of uncovering why she sounded so dispirited. I could only promise that we would reconnect soon and to see her when the semester ended. Little did I know that it would be the last time we would ever speak? Even more disheartening was the later realization that I had lost the one opportunity to change the course of what was to come.

Summer finally arrived and I had returned to the place I had stayed prior to leaving for college. Taking the place of my studies was a mundane workday schedule. Looking back on what could only be described as my darkest day, prognostication could not have prepared me for the events which would unfold. Everything about this day was contradictory to my ordinary days. My brightly colored workday ensembles were replaced by the only black piece of attire I owned. Eerily, it was as if I was unknowingly preparing for what was going to greet me that evening. Driving home that day, the traffic was exceptionally heavy. I passed the time listening to the radio and of all things a Christian station. The faith that was very much a part of my life growing up had been abandoned many years before. Recalling the previous couple of days, it seemed the familiar was drawing me back, and there was a feeling of hope.

Walking in the door, the sad and dismal mood of the room was hard to ignore. It was immediately obvious that something traumatic had taken place, and what self-control existed would be lost with the first spoken word. The silence was finally broken by the request I take a seat. Circumspect in her responses, my roommate tried to push through the details. With each word more difficult than the last, it became obvious that caution was being exercised so not to exacerbate my already anxious state.

It is strange how the mind can take flight with the anticipation of bad news. When the news of my sister's passing was finally delivered, it was as if the world ceased to exist in that one moment. A lifetime of memories began flooding my mind, and as each memory followed another, an inescapable presentiment emerged. The feeling of dread was inescapable and the manner of her death could not be any clearer. The final detail of her death only needed confirmation. With the validation of suicide came an unearthing of emotions so debilitating that, for a moment, it was as if I was a spectator to someone else's tragedy. The few memories that remain afterward are of the moments when the finality of the situation was inescapable.

At my request, I alone was to be the first and only one to enter her dormitory room. The investigator working the case was apprehensive but relinquished his control. Unbeknownst to him, my request was based on some outlandish belief, as I envisioned with certainty that her spirit was awaiting my arrival. The idea that she would just abandon me was simply preposterous. The reality of the situation sunk in as I stood in complete silence awaiting to hear an angelic voice telling me there was no need to worry. When there was no voice, increased desperation opened way for compromise, and I waited for another sign—any sign. The silence remained unbroken and the room remained painfully still. The minutes that passed became agonizing and a loneliness came over me. It was at that moment that I realized my sister was gone and there was never to be another form of communication between us. Standing alone in that dreadful place, I felt a prisoner to the torment of our last conversation as it was all that played in my head. Guilt and regret quickly replaced whatever hope remained.

The immediate aftermath of my sister's suicide left me constantly preoccupied with the details of her death as it replayed in my mind every second of every day. Most agonizing was the knowledge that she clearly intended to die and with a ferocity so intense that she overcame any primordial instinct to intervene. The most tormenting of facts was that she was not suspended during her hanging. It was so unimaginable that, many times, I found myself pursuing the belief that she was murdered just to avoid the reality of the situation. It was far more acceptable to think that she had been murdered because it meant that it was not her choice to leave me. It did not help that the police and autopsy reports conflicted on many key facts and that her death was called a suicide even before an investigation was ever requested. Again, all distractions to avoid the painful truth.

To think she was alone, enduring a pain so intense and deep that death seemed the only cure, made my sister's suicide even more difficult to accept. Even when it came time to view her body, my mind struggled to grasp what I was seeing. A scarf placed around her neck to hide the ligature marks, and the heavy makeup to obscure the marks left by the petechial hemorrhaging, only intensified the grief and disbelief. It was everything she was not. It was only when I focused on the distinct characteristic shape of her fingertips and felt the cold of her hands did it become reality who was before me.

From the very beginning, it was hard to tell others of the manner of her death. I could feel the stigma in every word spoken—or avoided, and this was even more evident when I attempted to seek counseling. On the recommendation of a long-time friend, I made an appointment with a faith-based practice that was run by a husband-and-wife team. The session began as any normal counseling session but quickly became nothing short of an exorcism. After telling my story, the couple insisted I pray. Their reasoning? Somewhere in my family lineage there had been a hex placed on my family, and that I needed to plea to God to remove the evil entity before it could take me as well. In a very vulnerable state, I could do nothing else but comply. I sat in a dimly lit room and recited exactly what they said. For what seemed like an eternity, I asked God to lift my curse and to save me from this demonic force. What followed was what I now understand was the development of PTSD. Immediately after leaving the so-called counseling session, a foreboding panic set in while I was driving home. Nights became filled with anxiety as I became petrified of the dark, and I could no longer safely drive at night. There was a constant fear that there was a dark entity that was hunting whatever was left of my former self.

Long before ever considering turning over my sister's journals to David Lester, I had to overcome the mistrust that had developed from what was painfully learned as society's view on suicide. Returning to college was difficult following the death of my sister, but it was a necessary escape from what had become my new norm. At the age of 19, I alone shouldered the aftermath of my sister's suicide. Helplessness consumed me as I realized that I would never muster up the courage to read a single page of the journals. Beyond the unanswered questions was a feeling that there had to be something more—it was inconceivable to think that this would be the end to my sister's story.

It was as if fate intervened when our two paths crossed. I met Dr. David Lester while attending Stockton University, although it did not have that title at the time.[1] When I signed up for his class, I was not aware that his field of expertise was in suicide. It was only after sitting through his lectures that it became evident. As he spoke about suicide, there was an essence of familiarity and openness about him that was in stark contrast to what I had experienced. There was an easiness to his approachability and a humbleness to him that seemed to dispel the wall I had erected. There was finally someone trustworthy and open-minded who deserved to know my sister's story. He would become my sister's voice and the keeper of her memory. Giving him the journals gave me hope that, from my tragedy, something consequential could transpire.

Never did I imagine that David would ask my permission to use my sister's journals to write the first book. When he presented the idea, there was first disbelief followed by immense contemplation. Truth be told, not knowing the other individual authors bought about feelings of apprehension. The most difficult aspect was that I was consenting to allow complete strangers access to the most private of my sister's matters and treat them, and her, only as a subject to be studied. It became a leap of faith, believing that, no matter its contents, there was something within those pages that could be of some importance in understanding what could have driven her, and others like her, to overcome the strongest of human instincts and die by suicide.

Since the journals were turned over sight unseen, there was a fear that the character of my sister would be overshadowed by her vulnerabilities and never would anyone be given the opportunity to know, in entirety, just who she was in life. Despite her troubles, she had an altruistic nature about her, and she loved with all she had. At a very young age, she was propelled into the role of caretaker, and she did so with a dedication that was far beyond her years. In the absence of any meaningful parental archetype, she summoned the courage that would sustain us, even if it was at the expense of her own childhood. Beyond the normal sibling relationship, our relationship was forged out of the necessity to comfort and protect each other as we attempted to survive in an often-volatile home. We made a pact early on to never leave each other because, in this world, all we had were each other. In losing her, I lost the most familiar part of myself.

The days, weeks and years to follow were filled with constant reminders of the loss. Birthdays were especially hard. Every birthday became a ritual, where we would reconnect no matter where we were, and this always gave me a sense of being grounded. After her death, I spent these days overwhelmed by sorrow. For years, each birthday would be spent watching the *Little Mermaid* just to still feel some connection to her. Her loss was felt with every empty seat, be it my graduation, wedding or the birth of my children. To this day, a glimpse of a childhood photo can send me into tears.

There was no single motivation that empowered the turning over of the journals. It was a complicated network of emotions, beliefs and an indescribable need for hope. Some might question my decision regarding handing over my sister's most intimate of thoughts. I must admit that I too had questioned my own actions, but I knew that handing over her journals gave her the opportunity—in death—to do what she never had the courage to do in life. While the torments and struggles of her time on earth remain, her writings are a testament to her struggles and, for the first time, she was free to be who she was without any confines.

To have relinquished my sister's journals was one of the most difficult decisions of my young life. The initial decision to turn over the journals was almost out of necessity. Immediately after learning of my sister's death, the cascade of traumatic experiences left me incapable of reading a single page. The impression left by the manner of her death, and the fear of what those pages contained, left me paralyzed and unable to mentally take on the possibility that, in some way, I was directly responsible for what my sister had done. It was not that I was not familiar with her torments. At the time of my sister's death, I had been searching for some normalcy. The greater part of my life had been tending to and then avoiding my sister's demons. Our relationship toward the end became strained because I had grown tired of the emotional rollercoaster. Many days were spent unnecessarily troubled by and for her. It was also incredibly difficult to handle the constant dredging up of old traumas and the constant feeling of stagnation with her. It became too much of a burden to carry. I understand now just how troubled my sister was, but unfortunately at that time I lacked the ability to sustain her.

After her death, there was a constant debilitating realization that my sister would be erased from time. Regardless of her faults, she was still an incredible person who shouldered the problems of the world and had enormous potential to make this world a better place. She was so young and would never have the opportunity to make her mark. It was beyond painful to think that her life had not mattered, that for all that she had been through, she would never have the opportunity to take her traumas and transform them into something worthwhile. It was inconceivable that all that would remain of her was a monologue of suffering hidden among pages never to be felt or understood by another. To give her life renewed purpose, meant that I had to share the part of her that still remained.

The day came when David's book finally arrived. Holding it in my hands, there was an enormous sense of gratitude and fulfillment. There had been so much leading up to this point that, when it came to reading it, it was far too much to tackle. Over the next several years, many attempts were made, but there was always some reason to avoid reading the book. It was not until the prospect of a second book that I was finally compelled to read the first. In a single evening, I read it in its entirety. It was not what I envisioned, but it was exactly what I needed.

Reconnecting with David came when another encounter with suicide left me remembering a time when our paths first crossed. The loss was that of a fellow firefighter I had known my entire career. Following the news of my comrade's suicide, days were spent in avoidance of the emotions that kept trying to creep to the surface. Avoidance was masked by purpose, and time was spent designing a helmet decal to be worn as tribute to her memory. After her funeral, there were no more distractions, and I was forced to look at just how similar my sister's life was to that of my sister-in-service. It was nothing short of reliving the moment when I lost my own sister, and the familiar heartbreak I felt for my comrade's brother was hard to escape.

When the prospect of a second book was presented, I could not but feel validation regarding my decision to relinquish my sister's journals. This time, however, an opportunity was presented to me to write a chapter. The idea took me by storm, and I eagerly accepted the gracious offer. With this opportunity, I was immediately filled with a sense of hope that I may, in some capacity, find closure. Motivated by sheer determination, I embarked on a quest that has taken me full circle and has given me the insight and perspective that I had not previously been able to see.

Before a single word could be written, one final piece to this story needed to be completed. Even before the news of my sister's death made it to me, the person my sister often referred to as Mama Z, took it upon herself to dictate the place of my sister's burial and purchased what I later learned was a double stacked plot. Immediately upon my sister's burial, my attempt to design and place a headstone met with intense resistance. This really should not have come as a big surprise, given that Z attempted to dictate who could attend my sister's funeral. There were years spent attempting to purchase the plot but never was it allowed. With each attempt Z, had the audacity to defend her choice with the ludicrous stance that our biological mother did not have any rights to be buried with my sister. Then the news came like a final blow. The one individual who made coping with my sister's death impossible had done the unthinkable. It was finally clear why this woman had avoided my every effort at placing a headstone on her grave. Buried on top of my sister was now this very woman, Z. Just as it played out with my sister's burial, not a single attempt was made to consult me, the next of kin, so that I may exercise my familial rights as to the circumstances of my sister's final resting place. It was difficult not to feel violated and angry, because to me it was nothing short of feeling robbed of my sister for what would be a second time.

That is where perspective overtook the need for closure. After consulting legal counsel and getting affirmation that the courts would find in my favor, I was preparing for a merciless battle until I found out that, a year after the woman's death, her own daughter was reported to have died by suicide. Then there was the knowledge that for the two remaining family members, neither were capable of handling the distresses of a legal battle. The husband of this individual Z was elderly and frail. The surviving son, who falls on the Autism Spectrum, would ultimately have to be tasked with the legal matters. Given that my youngest son is autistic, I could not but feel sympathetic to what he would have to endure. I could not in good conscience drag the one innocent person through such an ordeal. Instead, the hatred that consumed me was replaced by pity. Finding perspective made it possible to see that the greatest tribute to my sister was not etched on some headstone, but in the form of sharing the essence that *was* her. To carry her memory, no matter how painful, was my tribute to her. That is not to say I will not place a headstone on her grave. It just means it will be inscribed for two.

In deciding to forgive, I was finally able to forgive myself and to let go of the years of baggage. The need to know why my sister took her own life now seems far less important. In all reality, the absence of any suicide note and the lack of journal entries in the days before her death make it impossible to know with any certainty why she decided to die by suicide. What needed my focus were the things I could control, and I needed to relinquish what I could not. Understanding that, with suicide, comes the sovereignty of choice, I have been able to find resolve. I could not control my sister's decision, but I could control how her decision would continue to affect me.

After all these years, there still exist many reminders of how my sister's suicide impacted me. Stemming from the day I stood inside my sister's dorm room, I feel immense resentment at seeing roadside memorials because it serves as a constant reminder of death's finality. It has made normal childhood behavior unacceptable as my boys are forbidden to ever speak to one another with hurtful words. I remind them often in times of animosity that we never know when there will be a time that we are unable to right our actions. Examining the toll of my sister's suicide has become a bittersweet reality but a reality no less. My encounter with suicide early in life has prepared me to understand, intimately, the very nature of suicide and the importance of ongoing change in the stigma surrounding suicide. It has given me a sense of fearlessness, because running into a burning building pales in comparison to the fear stemming from my sister's tragic death. Deciding to become a firefighter, paramedic and registered nurse came from the desire to do something more than simply exist. It became a matter of living my life to the fullest when my sister was no longer able to.

What I have learned firsthand, and from the countless suicides I have encountered in my profession, is that inherent in suicide are complexities and inimitabilities that are as unique as the human fingerprint. No single case is exactly alike any other. However, facing every survivor are stigmas that make any chance at recovery that more difficult. Even with the countless deaths encountered as a first responder, dealing with the loved ones in the immediate aftermath of a suicide is different and difficult. Early on in my career, I can recall being told by a fellow firefighter to never disclose the manner of my sister's death. Never was an explanation given, but from the very beginning, we are trained by our predecessors and our unique culture to shove the traumas we encounter deep down to the deepest and darkest of places. Vulnerability is not permitted, and so many suffer in silence. What I have seen within my own profession is merely a symptom of a greater problem. Our culture, as a whole, views mental illness as a defect, and our responses to suicide illustrate this.

The designation of suicide as an intentional act gives the impression of choice. Assigning suicide an element of choice seems to give way to the assumption of weakness or mental illness. It is considered a crime and a sin. It is as if suicide does not deserve the same level of devotion or compassion as disease related or accidental deaths. Judgment is passed, and the outcome is the stigma that the survivors endure. Even if some understanding exists, reassurance and comfort are often avoided. There is no reassuring the survivors that the death was painless or that the person did not suffer. After all, it was pain and suffering that drove their action. Fault can only be attributed to the deceased and not some random act of fate or accident. What my sister's suicide has taught me is that the stigma around suicide can have devastating effects and, in all the years since her death, there has been only minimal change in this stigma.

In the end, my sister's journals serve to give an intimate look at the life of someone who ultimately dies by suicide. It is just one story, but it is my hope that it serves to benefit in some way the understanding of suicide. Turning over the journals was a personal decision and one that ultimately changed my life. The purpose that I have found in all of this was not only the ability to honor my sister's memory with a life repurposed, but it has also allowed me to honor her altruistic character by giving of myself so that others may somehow benefit.

Note

1. It was called Richard Stockton State College.

14 What Happened During Katie's Last Few Days

Mark's Account[1]

This may sound a bit odd (and I'm writing this off the top of my head), but the single biggest factor that I always think about that summer was where I was living, and how that impacted Katie and me. I'd just recently moved back to my parents' house in x. I hadn't slept there since x, when I moved back my senior year so that I could sneak out and see my high school girlfriend. Before that I'd lived at my grandparents' house (also in x) during my sophomore and junior years of high school and during college when I wasn't living on campus. My grandparents' house was where I lived when I wanted things to be "better." There were more rules that I had to follow, but it was a peaceful and clean (and large) place, and we also felt more "free" there, too. Katie and I had spent pretty much the entire previous summer there. My grandmother had given her the north-west bedroom, "Katie's room." We also spent our spring breaks, winter breaks and many weekends there since about February of x.

At some point during the end of the spring semester, my car broke down, and I had to get rid of it. I was living off of my paychecks from working at a food store on Rt x as well as a tutoring job I had that semester. But I had no money saved, and I couldn't find a ride to work, so I quit the food store job. As soon as school ended, I moved back into my parent's house. They lived near the downtown part of x where all the jobs were, so I remember spending more than a month walking to almost every store looking for work.

When my car broke down, I knew it was going to be a real problem. I'd driven Katie and me everywhere for a year and a half and, without a car, I felt stranded and immediately feared how it would affect us. I didn't want to ask my grandparents for money again since my grandfather had paid for my housing during the Spring semester. Otherwise, I was already about $12,000 in debt from three years of tuition and housing, and I didn't know what to do. I also figured I couldn't live at their house, since they lived on the other side of town. I didn't think I'd be able to walk to work from there.

I know this is a bit rambling; I'm just trying to explain why I made the very, very bad decision to move back to my parent's house. At my grandparents' house, there was plenty of room for Katie, and I hoped that she felt at home there (and so did my grandparents). But at my parent's house, there was no

DOI: 10.4324/9781003125655-16

room for us. I didn't even have a room; I had to sleep in the semi-furnished basement on a cot with three continually vomiting cats. Katie took everything very personally, and I feared even then that she felt I was purposely moving to a place where she couldn't be with me. She would sometimes read personal attacks into the most random things that I'd do. She ended up staying over twice and slept on the couch, but it was nothing like my grandparents' house. I explained multiple times that it was the only way I could find work. My parents had never given me a dime for school and, when I asked for money for a used car, they said they didn't have any. I think that Katie understood intellectually, but emotionally she may have felt I was trying to push her away, since my grandparents' beautiful house had become our sanctuary.

I remember floating the idea that she could still live at their house while I stayed at my parents, so I could find work. At first, she loved the idea but, once she realized that she wouldn't be able to find work from up there either, she feared feeling trapped, as well as a burden on my grandparents. She ended up pre-emptively enrolling in a few summer classes. I never even asked my grandparents, and Katie basically took the decision out of my hands.

Moving to my parents' house was a terrible decision. I ended up fighting with my dad several times about borrowing his car to see Katie. Only twice in a month and a half did he let me borrow it, since his car was quite old, and the college was a good 90-minute roundtrip. He didn't seem to care that I couldn't see Katie. Ironically, when September eventually came, my grandparents bought me a used car so that I could commute to the college and get a new job. Would they have bought me that car in May had I asked? Possibly, but I didn't want to burden them in May. And I never thought Katie was going to kill herself or that our situation would deteriorate so incredibly quickly when I didn't have a car for a few months.

She was clearly very worried about the impending summer as the semester came to a close. Every change in schedule was a huge and pivotal event for her. But I was way more worried than usual as well (mostly because of the car), and so we were both on edge. We were also often filled with "big" (and unrealistic) plans, like "I'll find a job immediately, and within two weeks I'll have enough money for a used car, and I'll be able to come up and see you every day by June 1." On the positive side, Katie seemed very determined to take summer classes. Katie was always very studious, loved to learn and cared about her grades a lot. So, she seemed happy about the summer classes, but I sensed she was very sad about not being at my grandparents' house. She had her own room there and I felt terrible about (only temporarily!) taking that away from her.

For the first few weeks, I was in a terrible mood as I applied to job after job and found nothing. I continually fought with my parents about seeing Katie, and I had endless allergy fits in the non-air-conditioned basement. Katie began sending me cards—Hallmark cards and things like that. She'd never really done that before. She'd always given me the occasional card, and she'd always underlined the words and sentences that she found most meaningful. But we usually wrote each other lots of letters. I'd stopped writing her letters, too, which I always felt bad about. Now her letters had stopped for over a month, and it was card after card. She sent me at least a dozen. I'll admit that I barely read them. She told me later that the cards were just saying more clearly what she was feeling, but I didn't fully understand that. She'd always had such a way with words. It just seemed odd and distant to me.

She came to visit in early June and slept over a few days, and I came up twice to visit her at the college, but I always had to leave that night to return the car. I noticed she'd really redecorated her room, but this was nothing new, as she loved to decorate, and redecorate, to catch her current moods. I loved her so much and still thought we'd be married someday. I honestly didn't feel anything was that different between us, until the final weekend when she came up to stay for four days.

I think it was eight days before she killed herself when she came over to my parents' house. I think she stayed for four days. It may have been five, but I think the plan was for her to stay for five, but she only stayed for four. Immediately something felt very off. My parents, my 10-year-old brother, and Katie and I went out to dinner, and it wasn't fun like it normally was. I remember Katie cutting me out of conversation the entire dinner, as if she was mad at me. She was excellent at "snubbing" people and becoming the center of attention, while simultaneously ignoring whoever she wanted to annoy. At first, I didn't care because I loved it when she did that to my parents. But I felt it very odd that she was choosing now to do it to me. It didn't make much sense. At one point, she gave me the dirtiest look and rolled her eyes like I was a disgusting idiot. That was the most eye contact she made with me the whole dinner. I almost always knew why she was mad at me, but this time I didn't get it. Admittedly, I may have been in quite a crappy mood already too. I was more depressed than I'd been in probably a year.

That night I remember feeling kind of empty and also really tired, and sad that we couldn't sleep together. I think I passed out on the cot and she watched television with my Mom upstairs before they let her sleep on the couch.

There were obviously so many things going through her head, probably many about me. She seemed mad at me, but I couldn't tell if it was about my grandparents' house, the summer plans, my lack of a car, my lack of job, etc. We did talk about it, but I really don't remember what we said, just that I was still left wondering. Our nerves were on edge the whole time. I thought it might be because of where we were, because my parents' house was always edgy, smoky, chaotic and cramped, while my grandparents' house was basically the opposite. We did stop by to say hi to my grandparents and Katie seemed like her old self again, briefly. We went swimming and I don't remember much else.

When we got back, I took another nap, and I woke to Katie laughing with my brother in the basement. My brother loved Katie so much, and I was very happy to see them having fun, although I remember thinking that she seemed happy with everyone but me, which was very unusual. I almost always was the one who could make her smile or laugh or loosen up. And if we weren't happy, she'd be very emotional and upset with me. But either way, we'd be connecting. But now I was experiencing a new, rigid distancing in a way that I don't think it had ever been before, at least not for any kind of prolonged period.

The second night was the first chance that we got to be alone downstairs. Finally, I felt like we were starting to connect, because we were finally alone to talk for a while. She'd gotten skinnier than I'd ever seen her. Maybe once before she'd been almost as thin. She wasn't unhealthy looking at all. But she'd always been a bit curvy, and she'd clearly lost several pounds that she'd had for at least a year. She looked healthy, and she looked as pretty as ever, but warning bells went off in my head.

I'd never seen her with anorexia, just bulimia. I'm not sure what I would've done if I'd ever seen her looking anorexic. The bulimia was horrible enough, but physically she would usually just gain a few pounds. And when I'd catch her purging, I'd spend the next several weeks encouraging her to keep her food down, telling her she was beautiful, etc. So seeing her suddenly thin was scary to me. She'd told me frightening stories of her bulimia in the past. There was an anorexic woman who'd occasionally come into the food store where I worked. She looked so ill, and Katie had become obsessed with her. One time, Katie had me follow her around the store for 15 minutes. She'd want to shop at night around 11 PM when the woman was usually there. She'd always say, "Look how beautiful and angelic she is," while I just saw a hideously malnourished woman who looked twice her age and was obviously torturing herself.

I made the quick decision not to specifically mention her weight. I told her that she looked beautiful, but I always told her that. I have a feeling she got very upset about this. In fact, I'm certain she probably spent weeks thinking about how I'd react to her "new" body. But that's in hindsight. At the moment, I thought I'd just downplay it, and act as if she was as pretty as she'd ever been, no less pretty, but not more pretty, either. As we started to kiss, she told me she'd bought something, and she took out some really attractive red lingerie. Of course, I wanted to see her in it, but I just wanted us be natural at the moment. I don't remember exactly what happened, I'm pretty sure she put it on and she looked great. But all I remember is that, when we had sex, she wasn't wearing it. And I think that really, really upset her, too. I think she felt rejected again, like I didn't want to see her in the lingerie she'd just bought. Of course, I loved seeing her in it. I guess I felt I didn't want her to feel she had to dress up or something along that line. She'd so often felt that she "had" to do things to keep my interest.

The next afternoon we got into another argument. She said something very nonchalantly about hurting herself while we were watching television. I was getting really exasperated about her negativity. She made some other comment, and I got mad and threw the television remote at her. She acted shocked and so upset. I said something like, "Fine, you do it, then," and she sat there looking so angry. We started to really argue. I don't remember specifically what we said, but I know I was upset about my inability to connect with her. I felt she was being so negative and standoffish and pretty unbearable to be around. I remember grabbing her arms when she got up to walk out, blocking the door and shaking her and saying, "What's wrong with you?" over and over again. In my mind, I couldn't get through to her, and I was getting physically aggressive with her because everything else had failed. I was at my wits end.

She started saying that no one appreciated her, especially not me. I kept telling her that wasn't true. She declared that she was leaving. The sun had started to go down, and she ran away. I quickly made up a story to my dad that we wanted to borrow the car for a few minutes, got the keys and went out looking for her. I ended up yelling her name for over an hour while driving around about 16 blocks of the house. I couldn't find her. This was before cell phones. I thought she might throw herself in front of a car. I was so worried. I parked the car and ran around for another 30 minutes, silently looking for her.

I drove into the next town of x to look for her. After almost two hours I decided to head home and, as I drove up x road, about two blocks from my house, I found her walking right in the center of the road. She was lit up by the street lights, and she was kind of waving her arms about, doing a very purposeful walk. I remember she swung her head, and I saw her hair move, and I thought, "Wow, she looks so free." She looked like she was savoring being let outdoors for the first time in ages. When she saw me, she ran, and I had to chase her on foot and plead with her to come back home.

There's honestly not a lot more to tell. We kind of made up, but I forget what else we did that night, and the next day I dropped her off at her room at the college. I do remember barely saying a word on the drive up. We were both mentally and emotionally exhausted. I walked her to her room and just said, "Bye," in a hurt (and probably annoyed) kind of way. I remember trying to say it firmly so that she knew I was unhappy but not in a permanent way. I never thought it would be the last time I saw her. I was just tired of the struggle at that moment. She said "Goodbye," sounding angry and closed the door.

I do remember struggling not to call her that night. I was trying to remain firm because I was quite mad at her being so aggressively distant with me. The next three days I called her non-stop. She didn't have her own phone, so I'd call the one in the hallway. The day after I dropped her off, I called at least a dozen times. I couldn't get hold of her. No one would answer. I hadn't gone a day without talking to her for almost 500 days, so there was no way I could sleep that night. The second day I called her endlessly, at least for an hour in a row, until someone picked up the phone and dropped it between my calls. It had a busy signal for the final day and a half.

On that second day, I had to go for baseball umpire training. It was the only work I could find. I was taking a three-hour class, but all I could think about was her. It was in my old middle school. During a break, I started opening all the lockers in the hall. The first 6 or 7 opened. I was surprised they were all unlocked for some reason. I decided I'd open 3 more. The third would determine if Katie was ok or not. The first two opened like the other 6 or 7 had. Then I said this is it and tried to open the third one. It was locked. I nearly freaked out. I felt it was a sign that she might be dead.

The third night, I stole my Dad's car after he fell asleep. Her door was locked, so I broke through the window of her room and I found her hanging. And I guess that's the ending of our story. What a terrible month.

We both tried to help each other so much. We DID help each other so much. She was wonderful most of the time, although very troubled and sometimes tortured. But she was an incredible person. She simultaneously helped me more than anyone ever has when she was alive and also hurt me more than anyone ever has when she killed herself.

Note

1. The following is a lightly edited version of what Mark (a pseudonym, of course, as is the name *Katie*) wrote for us. Throughout the account, you will see "x" in places where references have been removed to protect confidentiality. Each of us is, of course, embedded in interpersonal relationships, and our significant others are often struggling with personal issues too. A thorough analysis of the decisions made by an individual must take into account these relationships as well as the internal dynamics of that person.

15 Why Did Katie Die by Suicide?

David Lester and John F. Gunn III

> It is our task now to present the conclusions that we can draw from the interesting chapters written by the contributors to this book. That is not an easy task. Before doing this, we want to summarize what can be learned about Katie from the 2004 book on her life and death
>
> (Lester, 2004)

Katie's Diary: 2004

The commentaries began with a moving letter to Katie by Silvia Canetto (2004). The diary is in five separate books, and Canetto characterized the books as: (i) self-doubt followed by self-awareness, (ii) rage and dreams of a better life, (iii) hate, hurt and longing for psychological space, (iv) dreams under threat and (v) some dreams are fulfilled, but she is isolated. What impressed Canetto was the Katie seemed more positive and upbeat toward the end of the diary. Canetto was expecting to read of an event that may have triggered Katie's suicide, but none was evident. The diary ended nine days before Katie's death. Did anything happen in those nine days that would have helped us understand Katie's decision? In the present book, Mark's account of those final nine days is of particular relevance.

Pennebaker has devised a computer program that analyzes the content of a written text, and James Pennebaker and Lori Stone (2004) put the five books of Katie's diary through that program. They noticed several trends. For example, there was a decline in the use of personal pronouns (I, me) over the five books, a decline in death words, an increase in religious words, and, noteworthy given Canetto's subjective impression, a decline in words concerned with negative emotions and an increase in words concerned with positive emotions.

Pennebaker and Stone look at differences between the five books of Katie's diary. Stimulated by their chapter, Lester (2014) looked at change over the 13 months of the diary and by day over the eight entries in the last month of the diary. By month, the use of pronouns declined, as did words concerned with anger, causation, the past, sex and death. There was also a trend toward more positive emotions, and all of these trends were found over the last month of the diary as well.

Thomas Ellis is a cognitive therapist, and he looked at Katie's diary from that perspective. Ellis (2004) found evidence of the typical thought processes believed to be present in the minds of suicides: dichotomous thinking (thinking in terms of absolutes, black and white), cognitive rigidity, hopelessness (one of the major predictors of suicidal behavior), deficient problem solving, perfectionism and dysfunctional attitudes. Ellis provided examples of these concepts using passages from the diary.

Antoon Leenaars (2004) has studied suicide notes in a series of research papers, and he has identified eight major themes that can be found in suicide notes. All of these themes were evident in Katie's diary: unbearable psychological pain, cognitive constriction, indirect expressions (such as ambivalence and unconscious implications), an inability to adjust, poor ego strength, disturbed interpersonal relationships, expressions of rejection and aggression and a desire to escape.

David Lester (2004) took Mary Pipher's (1994) book on adolescent girls in distress, entitled *Reviving Ophelia*, and showed how Katie fitted the profile described by Pipher which is similar to that experienced by Ophelia in William Shakespeare's play *Hamlet*. Lester also noted the presence of rumination in Katie's diary, a thought process which is common in depressed women. Lester noted that presence of strong resentment by Katie felt toward those on whom she could have turned to for help, which he had identified in his doctoral dissertation in 1968 as characterizing those who had thought about or attempted suicide. The resentment prevents these individuals from seeking help from friends in times of crisis.

Katie refers to God in her diary, and Robert Fournier (2004) explored Katie's life from a psycho-religious perspective. For Katie, God was a potential source of nurturance and her ultimate source of salvation. James Hollis (2004) looked at Katie's diary from a Jungian perspective, while Lisa Firestone (2004) suggests how psychotherapy might have helped Katie through her present life situation.

In the final chapter, David Lester asked the question of whether writing the diary harmed or helped Katie. Several famous poets have died by suicide, including Sylvia Plath and Anne Sexton. In their discussion of Sylvia Plath's suicide, Silverman and Will (1988) argued that writing her poetry, which was highly biographical on occasions, harmed Plath because it encouraged rumination. In contrast, Lester and Terry (1992) argued that, not only did writing the poems help Plath and Sexton express their thoughts and feelings, but also the crafting of the poems that is necessary for poets helped them gain cognitive distance from feelings and, therefore, cope with the thoughts and feelings. Lester and Terry suggested that writing the personal poems may have prolonged the lives of both Plath and Sexton. In a similar way, perhaps writing the diary helped Katie live longer.

Once, when Lester was teaching a television course on deviant behavior, he received a series of letters from an anonymous viewer who was in psychological distress. In her final letter, she wrote:

> Incidentally, Professor, writing this out helps. I become no less sick, but less desperate. It provides not only mental catharsis but distraction as I wonder just what you will think if and as you read these. Would you stop me if you could? Or would you just coldly observe knowing there is nothing that can do more than delay the eventual outcome? Or, just toss these into the wastebasket?

Perhaps writing a diary also helps the writer survive?

New Insights Into Katie's Death by Suicide

As the review of the previous book (Lester, 2004) mentioned earlier shows, the first series of chapters on the diary of Katie were insightful glimpses into the death of this young woman. Therefore, a reader would be forgiven for thinking, what more could there be to say about this diary? Luckily, the contributors to this new look have provided new insights, and they come from different backgrounds to the original contributors. Their backgrounds influence the lens with which they examine the diaries. We are very pleased with the contributions to this book and hope you, the reader, are as well.

In Chapter 4, Gunn examines Katie's diary through a bioecological lens, highlighting the complexity of suicide and various spheres of influence acting upon a person. As the figure on page [36] illustrates, Katie's diary reveals a number of potential contributing factors to her death by suicide. At the macro-level, societal/cultural ideals of body image and ideas surrounding female purity seem to creep into her writings. At the micro-level, exposure to interpersonal conflict, constant comparison to her peer group and stress felt over her relationship with Mark may all have contributed to her distress. Then at the individual-level, Katie expresses feeling a burden on others, having low opinions of her body, feeling lonely and trapped by her circumstances. All of these factors are then set within the historic backdrop of the abuse and trauma that was forced upon her as a child.

In Chapter 5, Lester examines the IPTS in relation to the diary, a relatively novel theory of suicide that was not established at the time that the previous book on Katie's diary was written. His review of the diary found relatively robust support for the IPTS based on Katie's writings. Throughout her diary, Katie spoke of loneliness and feeling as if she did not belong as well as feeling as if she were a burden on those around her. Additionally, she was exposed to a number of painful and provocative experiences that increased what the IPTS labels the acquired capability for suicide. Katie experienced abuse at the hands of her father and suffered from anorexia and binging behaviors.

Another novel theory that was not present at the time of the first examination of Katie's diary was the 3ST of suicide, which was examined within the context of Katie's diary in Chapter 6 by Klonsky and Cetnarowski. After reviewing the theory, Klonsky and Cetnarowski highlight the ways in which the 3ST can shed light on Katie's suicide. Throughout the diary, Katie frequently references her pain ("I'm in a lot of pain" or "I'm really hurting") and her hopelessness ("I do not have any control whatsoever in my life at all."), two key concepts of the theory. Additionally, they provide examples of Katie's desire for and struggles with a sense of connectedness ("I need some real and good friends, really bad" and "[Joyce] hurt me so badly").

In Chapter 7, Zortea and O'Connor take another prominent theory of suicide, the IMV model and apply it to the diary. In this chapter, they highlight how the writings in the diary may apply to the pre-motivational, motivational and volitional phases of the model. Katie's life history (abuse) and environment (stress) coupled with biological vulnerabilities (such as anxiety, or epigenetic processes) may have pushed her into the motivational phase, thereby experiencing the development of suicidal thoughts driven by a sense of defeat, humiliation and entrapment. These exposures when combined in the volitional phase with moderators (such as access to a means for suicide or acquired capability) can help to shed light on the transition from thought to behavior, and in Katie's case, death.

In Chapter 8, Shustov, Tuchina and Borodkina examine how Katie's building of implicit life plans may have contributed to her ultimate death by suicide. They highlight how Katie's suicidal desire may have been driven by her intensive future thinking that was skewed pessimistically. Even when Katie attempted to project positive thinking into the future, the authors note that they were often overgeneral (such as simply becoming happy and healthy) and that Katie's decision to no longer write explicitly about her suicidal desire later in the diary may be masking the implicit suicidal desire that threatened to surface.

Knizek and Hjelmeland, in Chapter 9, examine Katie's diary from a meaning-making lens. Examining the diary reveals difficulty in finding security (not unsurprising given her past trauma/abuse) and a purpose in life—with only short periods where she writes of feeling content. The authors also highlight the enormous efforts Katie took to survive despite her distress, making efforts to find purpose and meaning despite everything.

In Chapter 10, Krysinska, Roubal and Mann discuss Katie's writings from a Gestalt Therapy perspective. Here they highlight how a Gestalt therapist might work with Katie to support her and bolster her resources (cognitive, emotional, behavioral and relational) as well as how they, as Gestalt psychotherapists, have dealt with clients in distress.

Chapters 4–10 examine Katie's diary in novel ways or through novel theoretical/therapeutic lenses compared to those in the previous book edited by Lester (2004). However, similarly to the earlier book, each of these chapters is contributed by researchers and clinicians in the field. The present book, however, deviates from this pattern in two chapters by bringing in those who have experienced the loss through suicide of a significant other, thereby providing their unique perspectives into Katie's life. Collins (Chapter 11) provides us a unique glimpse of Katie's suicide by comparing and contrasting her diary with that of her daughter, Victoria, who also died by suicide. Collins points out that there are some differences between the diaries—but many similarities as well. Both Katie and Victoria had similar expressions in their writings, compared themselves to their peers, felt anger direct at themselves and society, catastrophized their relationship difficulties, experienced existential pain, ruminating on suicide and felt isolated and alienated, to name but a few. Barnes (Chapter 12), a suicide loss survivor of her son's death, discussed Katie's diary in the context of suicide prevention and seeks to answer the question "why are we so bad at preventing suicide?" Barnes highlights concepts of ambivalence, rational suicide and discusses whether or not suicide can be acceptable.

Finally, wrapping up this book are two chapters (Chapters 13 and 14) written by two people who are frequently mentioned in the diary. Katie's sister (Chapter 13) and Katie's boyfriend (Mark, Chapter 14) provide us with details about the circumstances leading up to her death, filling in the gaps in the nine days between her last diary entry and her death. Katie's sister provides us with a unique insight into the experiences of a survivor of suicide loss and the impact and emotional toll of being informed of her sister's death. She also touches on the difficulty in sharing the details of her sister's death with others and journey to come to grips with it, and her ultimate decision to give the diaries to David Lester, prompting the publication of the first book and, subsequently, this one. Mark's account provides us with more of the details leading up to Katie's death. Mark's account highlights things that are often taken for granted in understanding the stressors faced by those who die by suicide, difficulties in where to stay, in transportation and in dealing with school tuition and housing costs. His account also highlights how these factors, the day-to-day struggles, created distance between the two (which as discussed in previous chapters, may have contributed to Katie's sense of disconnection) and the conflict that occurred tied to difficulties in living circumstances and in miscommunications.

Conclusions

There are great difficulties in trying to understand suicide. The research level uses large sample sizes of suicidal individuals, most often focuses on those who have suicidal ideation or who have attempted suicide (and survived the attempt) and uses relatively simple psychological inventories (or scales). For example, as noted in Chapter 5, Joiner's Interpersonal Theory of Suicide proposes three constructs to explain suicide: thwarted belonging, perceived burdensomeness and the acquired capability for self-harm. Katie showed clear evidence of the presence of all three constructs. But does this result help us to truly understand Katie's suicide? We think not. It is too simple. There must be many people who have conflict in their relationships with others, who sometimes feel that they are a burden to others and who have had physiologically painful experience in the past. Hardly any of them die by suicide. A satisfactory explanation of suicide at the general level is unsatisfactory at the individual level.

To understand, not why people in general die by suicide, but why *Katie* died by suicide requires a very different approach. Perhaps only a more qualitative analysis provides an answer as to why *Katie* died by suicide. Others recently have drawn attention to the context-specific nature of suicide (Hjelmeland & Knizek, 2016; White et al., 2016), and this contextualized understanding of Katie's suicide is provided here by Shustov and his colleagues, by Knizek and Hjelmeland and by Krysinska and her colleagues in Chapters 8, 9, and 10. But this raises another problem.

Many years ago, one of the editors of the present book (David Lester) felt so dissatisfied with his understanding of suicide, even after reading every scholarly paper written on suicide from 1897 to 1997, and after conducting dozens of research studies himself, decided that, if he could understand the suicide of just one person, he could continue being an academic scholar. He started with two biographies, on Ernest Hemingway and on Marylin Monroe. He wrote essays on them and felt that he did see why their lives ended with their deaths by suicide. Being an obsessive-compulsive, Lester eventually read over 100 biographies and wrote essays on them, essays which have now been used for research studies (for example, Lester & Gunn, 2021).

However, this raises yet an additional problem. Even if you fully understand why, say, Sylvia Plath (the American poet) died by suicide, that does not help you understand why Primo Levi (a Holocaust survivor) or Sigmund Freud (the founder of psychoanalysis) died by suicide. Each of us, obviously, is truly unique. We are, therefore, confronted with a dilemma. If we try to understand one particular suicide, we may be no more able to understand a suicide by someone else. But if we find ways of understanding suicide in general, proposing and testing theories of suicide, then we distance ourselves from the individual. At present, the field has prioritized generalized knowledge, using quantitative methods and datasets, so much so that the scholarly journals rarely publish qualitative research (Hjelmeland, 2016). We think this is an error as prioritizing one form of knowledge inevitably leads to deficits in another. By focusing solely on general knowledge, we skim only the surface.

We hope that, in this book, we have gone beyond the surface and helped you understand Katie's suicide. We do not presume to know why *all people* die by suicide, but we do hope that, in putting together this book, we have helped you, the reader, to understand why Katie died by suicide. We have tried to give you examples of both quantitative and qualitative approaches and, perhaps combined, they help resolve the dilemma of understanding suicide and will help you understand if someone close to you dies by suicide.

References

Canetto, S. S. (2004). Why did you kill yourself Katie? In D. Lester (Ed.), *Katie's diary: Unlocking the mystery of suicide* (pp. 41–54). New York: Brunner-Routledge.

Ellis, T. (2004). Thought of Katie: A cognitive perspective. In D. Lester (Ed.), *Katie's diary: Unlocking the mystery of suicide* (pp. 81–96). New York: Brunner-Routledge.

Firestone, L. (2004). Separation theory and voice therapy methodology applied to the treatment of Katie. In D. Lester (Ed.), *Katie's diary: Unlocking the mystery of suicide* (pp. 161–186). New York: Brunner-Routledge.

Fournier, R. R. (2004). A psychospiritual approach for understanding heart and soul: Katie's yearning for well-being amidst chaos and confusion. In D. Lester (Ed.), *Katie's diary: Unlocking the mystery of suicide* (pp. 123–150). New York: Brunner-Routledge.

Hjelmeland, H. (2016). A critical look at current suicide research. In J. White, I. Marsh, M. J. Kral, & J. Morris (Eds.), *Critical suicidology: Transforming suicide research and prevention for the 21st century* (pp. 31–55). Vancouver, Canada: UBC Press.

Hjelmeland, H., & Knizek, B. L. (2016). Qualitative evidence in suicide: Findings from qualitative psychological autopsy studies. In K. Olson, R. A. Young, & I. Z. Schultz (Eds.), *Handbook of qualitative health research for evidence-based practice* (pp. 355–371). New York: Springer Science + Business Media.

Hollis, J. (2004). Not waving but drowning: A Jungian perspective on Katie. In D. Lester (Ed.), *Katie's diary: Unlocking the mystery of suicide* (pp. 151–159). New York: Brunner-Routledge.

Leenaars, A. A. (2004). Katie: A protocol analysis of her diary. In D. Lester (Ed.), *Katie's diary: Unlocking the mystery of suicide* (pp. 97–108). New York: Brunner-Routledge.

Lester, D. (Ed.). (2004). *Katie's diary: Unlocking the mystery of suicide*. New York: Brunner-Routledge.

Lester, D. (2014). *The "I" of the storm*. Berlin, Germany: De Gruyter.

Lester, D., & Gunn, J. F. (2021). Is perceived burdensomeness present in the lives of famous suicides? *Death Studies*, in press.

Lester, D., & Terry, R. (1992). The use of poetry therapy. *The Arts in Psychotherapy*, *19*, 47–52.

Pennebaker, J. W., & Stone, L. D. (2004). What was she trying to say? A linguistic analysis of Katie's diaries. In D. Lester (Ed.), *Katie's diary: Unlocking the mystery of suicide* (pp. 55–79). New York: Brunner-Routledge.

Pipher, M. (1994). *Reviving Ophelia*. New York: G. P. Putnam.

Silverman, M. A., & Wills, N. P. (1988). Sylvia Plath and the failure of emotional self-repair through poetry. *Psychoanalytic Quarterly*, *55*, 99–129.

White, J., Kral, M., Marsh, I., & Morris, J. (2016). Introduction: Rethinking suicide. In J. White, M. Kral, I. Marsh, & J. Morris (Eds.), *Critical suicidology: Transforming suicide research and prevention for the 21st century* (pp. 1–11). Vancouver, Canada: UBC Press.

Name Index

Addis, D. R. 90
Agibalova, T. V. 92
Ahmadi, F. 96, 106, 107
Ahmadi, N. 96, 106, 107
Akan, M. 91
Aleman, A. 70
Allan, S. 63, 65, 70
Allroggen, M. 122
Altmaier, E. M. 108
Alvarez, A. 145, 148
Amendt-Lyon, N. 114, 121
Ammirata, G. 149
Aten, J. 107
Awenat, Y. 70

Bagge, C. L. 60, 70
Baiocco, R. 91
Bar, M. 78, 90
Bargh, J. A. 92
Barlow, D. H. 108
Barnes, D. H. 2, 6, 149, 148, 171
Barnhofer, T. 72
Baumeister, R. F. 39, 73, 87, 90, 194, 95, 97, 107
Bautista-Bohall, M. J. 122
Beck, A. T. 65, 70, 72, 73, 90, 91
Beckman, A. 42, 90
Beek, W. van. 73, 89, 90
Beekman, A.T.F. 90
Beisser, A. 119, 121
Benoit, R. G. 91
Bering, J. 125, 139
Berkman, L. F. 42
Berne, E. 74, 90
Berntsen, D. 91
Bijlsma, J. W. 107
Birgegard, A. 42
Blagov, P. 76, 91
Blaize, J. 114, 121

Bloom, J. D. 91
Bodell, L. 49
Bohall, G. 122
Bonanno, G. A. 96, 108
Borod, J. C. 90
Borodkina, A. U. 170
Bostwick, J. M. 73, 90
Bowlby, J. 61, 70
Braithwaite, S. R. 50, 72
Brallier, L.W. 115, 123
Brausch, A. M. 38, 42
Brewin, C. R. 107
Bronfenbrenner, U. 35, 42
Brown, G. K. 91
Brown, T. I. 73, 90
Bruner, J. 94, 107
Bruno, A. 42
Buber, M. 110, 114, 116, 121
Buchman-Schmitt, J. M. 49
Buka, S. L 42
Bulik, C. M. 42
Burbridge-James, W. 111, 123

Calati, R. 148
Canetto, S. 48, 49, 134, 137, 139, 140, 167, 172
Cardiacotto, L. 107
Carli, V. 149
Carr, B. I. 108
Celebre, L. 42
Cetnarowski, O. F. 170
Chang, E. C. 107
Chang, S. S. 60, 70
Chu, C. 43, 49
Clark, A. 70
Clark, L. 124, 140
Clarkson, P. 109, 121
Class, Q. A. 91
Cleare, S. 60, 70, 71

Cole, S. 73, 74, 87, 90
Collins, L. 124, 140, 171
Colucci, E. 111, 122
Conner, K. R. 90
Conner, M. 91
Consol, C. 149
Conway, C. 86, 91
Conway, M. A. 74, 79, 90
Conwell, Y. 90, 142, 148
Costa, M. 42
Crane, C. 72
Cukrowicz, K. C. 50, 72
Cunningham, A. 91

D'Alessio, M. 91
Damon, W. 42
D'Argembeau, A. 74, 76, 81, 86, 89, 90
Davidson, K. 91
Davidson, L. 42
Davis, C. G. 96, 107
DeDonatis, O. 149
DeMarinis, V. 94, 107
Dempsey, R. 71
Devine, P. 71
Dickson, A. 72
Diekstra, R. F. W. 46, 49
di Marco, S. 149
D'Onofrio, B. M. 91
Drye, R. C. 87, 90
Duberstein, P. R. 90
Dunn, G. 70
Durkheim, E. 1, 6, 43, 49

Edmondson, D. 108
Edwards, S. J. 113, 122
Ellis, T. E. 63, 66, 70, 168, 173
Emanuel, E. 142, 148
Epstein E. M. 108
Erlangsen, A. 71
Eschle, S. 71
Evers, A. W. 96, 107
Exline, J. J. 108

Fagan, J. 119, 121
Farberow, N. L. 2, 6
Fegert, J. M. 122
Feldman, G. 107
Ferguson, M. J. 90
Fink, E. 48, 49
Firestone, L. 147, 148, 168, 173
Folkman, S. 94, 95, 96, 107, 108
Fournier, R. R. 168, 173
Francesetti, G. 109, 116, 119, 121, 122, 123

Frankl, V. E. 93, 94, 107
Franus, N. 90
Fraser, L. 71
Friedman, S. L. 90
Frisina, P. G. 89, 90
Fukukura, J. 74, 90

Gagnon, S. A. 90
Gamble, B. 80, 90
Garlow, S. J. 37, 42
Garrison, B. 70, 72
Gecele, M. 122, 123
Gerrans, P. 74, 90
Geske, J. R. 90
Gilbert, P. 63, 65, 70
Glenn, C. R. 70
Goetz, R. R. 91
Gollwitzer, P. 91
Gooding, P. A. 42, 67, 70, 71
Goodman, P. 122
Gordon, J. 71
Gotz, M. 71
Goulding, M. E. 90
Goulding, R. L. 90
Gramaglia, C. 142, 144, 148, 149
Gray, C. M. 72
Greenberg, E. 111, 122
Grof, S. 73, 90
Guerrierco, C. 149
Gunn, J. F. 2, 6, 43, 49, 169, 172, 173
Gunnell, D. 70
Gurrieri, G. 38, 42, 91
Gutierrez, P. M. 38, 42

Haas, A. P. 42
Hackett, T. P. 145, 148
Hagan, C. R. 49
Haines, J. 49
Haith, M. M. 78, 90
Hale-Smith, A. 108
Halifax, J. 73, 90
Hall, E. M. 95, 96, 97, 107
Hall, M. E. L. 96, 97
Hammer, P. 42
Havelka, J. 91
Hawton, K. 67, 70, 71
Hayes, A. M. 95, 107
Hefferline, R. 122
Heisel, M. J. 90
Helzer, E. G. 90
Hendin, H. 2, 42
Hicks, J. A. 107
Hill, P. 95, 96, 97, 107
Hillman, J. 73, 90

Hirsch, J. K. 79, 86, 90
Hjelmeland, H. 43, 49, 170, 172, 173
Hoft-March, E. 125, 140
Hollis, J. 168, 173
Hom, M. A. 49
Hood, R. W. 96, 107
Howdin, J. 112, 113, 118, 122
Huang, J. Y. 92
Hunt, M. 95, 107
Hunter, S. C. 71
Husserl, E. 117, 122
Hycner, R. 110, 112, 114, 122

Ingersoll, E.G. 137, 140
Ingvar, D. H. 73, 90
Inzlicht, M. 96, 98, 108
Irish, M. 89, 90

Jacobs, J. W. 107
Jacobs, L. 112, 114, 120, 122
Jager-Hyman, S. 86, 91
Jamison, K. R. 143, 148
Janoff-Bulman, R. 95, 96, 107
Jeronimus, B. F. 61, 70
Johnson, J. 71
Joiner, T. E. 2, 6, 43, 49, 50, 57, 58, 65, 67, 70, 72
Jokinen, J. 92
Jones, J. W. 108
Jones, S. 71
Jongen, P. J. 107
Justice, L. 90

Kelly, G. A. 47, 49
Kennedy, M. C. 96, 99, 108
Kerkhof, A.J.F.M. 90
Kholmogorova, A. B. 92
Kim, A. S. N. 91
King, M. 71
Kirtley, O. J. 57, 58, 60, 65, 67, 68, 69, 70, 71
Klein, S. B. 89, 91
Kliemann, A. 122
Klonsky, E. D. 51, 56, 57, 70, 170
Knizek, B. L. 43, 49, 170, 172, 173
Kofsky Scholnick, E. 90
Kovacs, M. 70, 72
Kraaimaat, F. W. 107
Kral, M. 173
Krysinska, K. 170, 172
Kuja-Halkola, R. 91
Kvavilashvili, L. 73, 74, 87, 90
Kyle, S. D. 71

Ladd, C. O. 71
Laghi, F. 86, 91
Lardi, C. 90
Larson, J. 107
Larsson, H. 91
Laurenceau, J. 107
Lawal-Solarin, F. W. 6, 148
Lazarus, R. S. 96, 107
Leary, M. R. 107
Lee, H.-J. 70
Lee, S. 91
Leenaars, A. A. 168, 173
Lepore, S. J. 90
Lerner, R. M. 42
Lester, D. 1, 2, 3, 4, 6, 47, 48, 49, 50, 58, 68, 69, 70, 90, 91, 111, 122, 124, 128, 131, 140, 143, 145, 148, 167, 168, 169, 170, 172, 173
Lexington, J. M. 108
Lichtenstein, P. 91
Lim, M. 74, 91
Littlewood, D. L. 67, 71
Loreti, L. 149
Luoma, J. B. 74, 91
Lutz, P.-E. 58, 71

Mace, J. H. 90
MacHale, S. 71
MacIntosh, D. N. 96, 107
Mackewn, J. 109, 114, 121, 122
Mackie, R. 71
MacLeod, A. K. 73, 79, 86, 91
Mann, D. 110, 111, 112, 113, 114, 115, 120, 122, 170
Mann, J. J. 58, 72
Manzetti, E. 149
Mar, R. A 91
Maranges, H. M. 90
Marangon, D. 149
Marsh, I. 35, 42
Martelli, M. 149
Martin, C. E. 91
Martin, L. L 96, 107
Marx, B. P. 108
Masterton, G. 71
Mathy, A. 76, 89, 90
Mattei, S. 91
May, A. M. 51, 56, 57, 70
McKean, A. J. 90
McLean, K. 77, 92
McLeod, V. 124, 140
McMartin, J. 107
Mechawar, N. 71

Name Index 177

Mento, C. 38, 42
Merleau-Ponty, M. 118, 122
Middlebrook, D. 142, 148
Mischel, W. 95, 107
Molnar, B. E. 40, 42
Monson, C. M. 108
Moonat, S. 107
Moore, J. D. 42
Moreau, D. 90
Morf, C. C. 95, 107
Morris, J. 173
Morris, P. A. 35, 42
Muscatello, M. R. A. 42, 122
Musson, S. 122

Naroll, R. 43, 50
Neiderkrotenthaler, T. 42
Nemeroff, C. B. 42
Newton, T. 96, 107
Nock, M. K. 57, 71
Nolen-Hoeksema, S. 107
Nordström, P. 91
Norman, P. 91

O'Connor, R. C. 57, 59, 60, 65, 67, 68, 69, 70, 71, 72, 73, 86, 91, 170
Olson, K. 173
O'Reilly, L. M. 74, 87, 91
Ormel, J. 70
Osborn, D. 71
Owen, R. 67, 71

Pabbati, C. 90
Paloutzian, R. F. 96, 107, 108
Panagioti, M. 71
Pargament, K. I. 108
Park, C. L. 94, 95, 96, 97, 99, 104, 106, 107, 108
Park, J. I. 91
Parlett, M. 109, 110, 122
Pearson, J. L. 91
Peck, D. 143, 148
Pennebaker, J. 48, 50, 77, 84, 85, 86, 87, 91, 167, 173
Penninx, B. W. J. H. 70
Perls, F. 109, 111, 114, 119, 122
Perls, L. 112, 122
Petzold, H. G. 115, 122
Piolino, P. 89, 90
Pipher, M. 168, 173
Pirkis, J. 71
Pisetsky, E. M. 42
Pitman, A. 69, 71

Plant, A. 71
Platt, S. 60, 71
Plener, P. 122
Plotsky, P. M. 71
Pöldinger, W. 115, 122
Portzky, G. 57, 65, 71
Poulos, S. 107
Power, M. J. 107
Pratt, D. 70
Prestwich, A. 78, 91
Proulx, T. 94, 98, 108

Range, L. M. 113, 122
Rasmussen, S. 67, 71, 113, 122
Rathbone, C. J. 73, 91
Rau, T. 115, 122
Reeves, A. 112, 113, 118, 122
Resick, P. A. 96, 108
Resnick, R. 109, 110, 122
Rholes, W. S. 61, 71
Rickert, M. E. 91
Riese, H. 70
Rizvi, S. L. 108
Rizzo, A. 42
Robb, K. A. 72
Roberts, A. 117, 122
Robins, E. 143, 148
Roepke, A. M. 89, 91
Rosenberg, J. 42
Roubal, J. 110, 111, 112, 114, 115, 119, 121, 122, 123, 170
Routledge, C. 107
Runfola, C. D. 42
Russell, K. 67, 71
Ryan, C. 70

Sachmann, M. D. 113, 122
Saffer, B. Y. 70
Salgado, S. 91
Sánchez, M. M. 61, 62, 71
Sander, D. 74, 90
Saner, R. 111, 123
Sanna, L. J. 107
Sarchiapone, M. 149
Saunders, K. E. A. 70
Schacter, D. L. 74, 91, 92
Schloss, H. 107
Schmidt, U. 91
Schmutte, T. 37, 42
Schultz, I. Z. 173
Selby, E. A. 50, 72
Seligman, M. E. P. 89, 91, 94, 108
Shannonhouse, L. 107

Shaw, J. 70
Sheeran, P. 91
Shepherd, I. 121
Shneidman, E. S. 2, 6, 120, 123, 143, 148
Shustov, D. I. 74, 75, 91, 92, 170, 172
Silberman, I. 96, 108
Siliquini, R. 149
Silverman, E. J. 107
Silverman, M. A. 168, 173
Silvestri, M. C. 42
Simon, R. 142, 148
Simpson, J. A. 61, 62, 71
Singer, J. A. 76, 91
Sjåstad, H. 90
Sloan, D. S. 95, 108
Smith, A. 49
Smith, M. 70
Smyth, R. 91
Spagnuolo Lobb, M. 121
Spreng R. N. 74, 91, 92
Staemmler, B. 122
Staemmler, F-M. 109, 115, 122, 123
Stanford, E. J. 87, 91
Stanley, I. H. 49
Steel, S. 108
Steer, R. A. 70, 72
Stefansson, J. 74, 92
Stone, L. D. 48, 50, 77, 84, 85, 86, 87, 91, 167, 173
Stratford, C. D. 115, 123
Strauss, J. L. 107
Stuckler, D. 70
Stuss, D. T. 92
Swanson, B. 125, 138, 140
Szasz, T. 141, 142, 146, 148
Szpunar, K. K. 74, 78, 86, 91, 92

Tan, J. 6
Tangney, J. P. 107
Tarrier, N. 42, 70, 71
Tata, P. 91
Taylor, P. J. 38, 42, 67, 71
Terry, R. 168, 173
Tesser, A. 96, 107
Thompson, C. 142, 148
Thompson, S. 91
Thorne, A. 77, 92
Thornton, L. M. 42
Till, B. 39, 42
Tippett, L. J. 90

Torre, E. 149
Tran, U. S. 42
Trexler, L. 90
Tuchina, O. D. 74, 75, 88, 91, 92, 170
Tucker, R. P. 49
Tulving, E. 89, 92
Turecki, G. 71, 89, 92
Tyrer, P. 91

Ulph, F. 70
Usai, C. 149

Valsesia, R. 149
van der Linden, M. 90
Van Heeringen, K. 58, 72
van Lankveld, W. 107
Van Orden, K. A. 43, 50, 57, 58, 72
Vygotsky, L. S. 89, 92

Wagner, A. D. 90
Webb, T. 91
Weisman, A. 145, 148
Weissman, A. 90
Wenzel, A. 91
Westphal, M. 96, 108
Wetherall, K. 62, 70, 71, 72
Wheeler, G. 112, 123
White, J. 172, 173
White, T. 87, 92
Wieland, J. 107
Williams, C. L. 49
Williams, J. M. G. 58, 63, 65, 72, 91
Williams, L. E. 89, 92
Williamson, W. P. 107
Wills, N. P. 168, 173
Witte, T. K. 48, 50, 72
Wood, A. M. 42, 71

Yakeley, J. 111, 123
Yang, B. 2, 6
Yip, P. 70
Yontef, G. 109, 110, 112, 123
Young, R. A. 173
Yufit, R. I. 122

Zeleskov Djoric, J. 112, 123
Zeppegno, P. 142, 148, 149
Zhang, J. 2, 6
Zoccali, A. R. 42
Zortea, T. C. 61, 62, 72, 170
Zuromski, K. L. 48, 50

Subject Index

acquired capability 43–44, 47–48, 67, 169, 170
ambivalence 13, 47, 101, 115–116, 168, 171
anorexia/anorexic 7, 40, 47, 94, 134, 164, 169
attachment 61–62, 65, 12, 135–136

bioecological 35–36, 41–42, 169
bulimia/bulimic 48, 164

chronosystem 36, 40
connectedness 51, 52, 54–56, 65, 111, 141, 143, 170
consciousness 73, 87, 89, 118
coping 59, 62–63, 78, 83, 93, 96, 98, 106, 134, 142, 158
Cry of Pain model 58, 63, 65

defeat 59, 62, 63, 65–67, 170
depression 28, 37, 40–41, 64, 63, 68, 80, 119, 142–144
diathesis–stress 58, 63

entrapment 59, 62–69, 170
exosystem 36

fearlessness 59, 67–68, 143, 145, 159
fragmentation 119, 138–139

Gestalt therapy 5, 109–116, 121, 170

hallucinations 8, 60
helplessness 20, 106, 113, 155

hopelessness 44, 48, 51–56, 63, 65, 73, 89, 113, 125, 168, 170

ideation-to-action framework 69
impulsivity/impulsiveness 44, 59, 68, 101, 143–145
Integrated Motivational Volitional (IMV) model 38, 57–58, 62–63, 65, 67
Interpersonal-Psychological Theory of Suicide (IPTS) 3, 5, 37, 43–45, 47–49, 57, 65, 67, 169

lack of belonging 37
loneliness 37, 44, 66, 154, 169

macrosystem 36
memory bias 59, 64, 66
microsystems 36

perceived burdensomeness 43–45, 48, 65, 171
pre-motivational 58–60, 62–63, 66, 170
psychache 4, 38

rumination 64, 137, 168

schizophrenia/schizophrenic 7, 48, 94, 126
sexual abuse 40–41, 69, 94

three-step theory 5, 51
thwarted belongingness 43–45, 47–48, 59, 65, 171

worthless/worthlessness 112, 134

Printed in the United States
by Baker & Taylor Publisher Services